Climate Chan;
and Disaster Resil

Climate Change and Disaster Resilience

Challenges, Actions and Innovations in Urban Planning

Edited by
JOAQUIN JAY GONZALEZ III,
ROGER L. KEMP *and* ALAN R. ROPER

McFarland & Company, Inc., Publishers
Jefferson, North Carolina

ISBN (print) 978-1-4766-8243-3
ISBN (ebook) 978-1-4766-4297-0

LIBRARY OF CONGRESS AND BRITISH LIBRARY
CATALOGUING DATA ARE AVAILABLE

Library of Congress Control Number 2021057747

Front cover photograph of fire near
Los Angeles © 2022 Shutterstock / PTZ Pictures

Printed in the United States of America

*McFarland & Company, Inc., Publishers
Box 611, Jefferson, North Carolina 28640
www.mcfarlandpub.com*

Jay dedicates this book to Coral Hong Yi-Jun Gonzalez.

* * *

Roger dedicates this book to his granddaughter,
Kieran, the best and the brightest.

* * *

Alan dedicates this book to Hudson Wade Roper.

Acknowledgments

We are grateful for the support of the Mayor George Christopher Professorship at Golden Gate University and GGU's Pi Alpha Alpha Chapter. We appreciate the encouragement from Dean Amy McLellan and our wonderful colleagues at the Edward S. Ageno School of Business, the Department of Public Administration, and the Executive MPA Program.

Our heartfelt "THANKS!" goes to the contributors listed in the back section and the individuals, organizations, and publishers below for granting permission to reprint the materials in this volume and the research assistance of Elise B. Gonzalez. They all expressed support for practical research and information sharing that benefits our citizens, cities, global community, ecosystems, and the environment.

Alder K. Delloro
American Society for Public Administration
Astrid J. Hsu
Delloro & Saulog Law Offices
Environmental Protection Agency
Evelyn Sagun
Federal Emergency Management Agency
Gabby Moraleda
Golden Gate University Library
International City/County Management
    Association
Jake Rom Cadag
Julie-Ann Ross Deus
Kaiser Health News
Karen Garrett
Kerry Hansen
Maria Fe Villamejor-Mendoza
Melissa A. Diede
Nathan Myers
National Aeronautics and Space
    Administration

National Oceanic and Atmospheric
    Administration
PA Times
Peter Lyn Rene
PM Magazine
ProPublica
San Francisco State University
Sergio Andal, Jr.
theconversation.com
United Nations Environment Programme
University of San Francisco Library
University of the Philippines–National
    College of Public Administration and
    Governance
U.S. Congress
U.S. Department of Agriculture
U.S. Geological Survey
U.S. Global Change Research Program
USAID Strengthening Urban Resilience for
    Growth with Equity (SURGE)

Table of Contents

Part III. Actions and Innovations

• *A. Citizens and Public-Private Partnerships* •

Appendices

Preface

Climate change and natural disasters have always been hot topics of discussion and debate from the living rooms of citizens to United Nations meetings and civil society organizations' candlelight vigils. While we were writing this book, the COVID-19 pandemic and racial protests broke out. We could not help but mention their connections to our work. Some exchanges have shifted to newsfeeds and Zoom meetings on how climate change contributes to natural disasters and consequently habitat destruction and food shortage—increasing likelihoods of cross-species interaction and the transmission of deadly diseases. We also note the fact that climate change and natural disasters have more pronounced effects on marginalized populations across the globe, and America's communities of color, particularly where they live, work, and play. Thus, the need for an increased focus on climate and environmental justice and actions.

Years ago, we saw emerging consensus from the scientific and academic community on the threat of climate change. But during this same time, we also saw a significant lack of consensus from social and political stakeholder groups. Even large percentages of the population questioned the scientific data on climate change. However, in recent years, organizations like the United Nations Intergovernmental Panel on Climate Change (IPCC), NASA, Yale University, the University of California, and the Pontifical Academy for Sciences (to name a few) have produced detailed studies and reports explaining this threat to our planet. Greta Thunberg and the global youth climate movement have global youth climate movement has demonstrated that a new generation of climate champions can sway public opinion and have an important voice in advocating change.

Global climate conferences have brought world leaders together to find resolution on emissions reduction. International agreements to address climate crisis have been evolving over two decades, including the Kyoto Protocol (2005); the European Union Emissions Trading System (2005); the Cancun Agreements (2010); and the Paris Agreement (2015). However, some of the largest contributors to global greenhouse gas emissions are nations who have not entered into these agreements. What can be done if our world or national leaders cannot agree on a strategy to address climate change? As you'll read in this book, many local governments, public private partnerships, innovators in the technology and energy fields, and collaborations that cross national boundaries are discovering innovative solutions.

The United Nation's Intergovernmental Panel on Climate Change sponsored research in 2018 that predicted severe environmental consequences due to increased warming of the planet. This report forecast irreparable conditions if the nations of the world were unable to reduce the amount of warming to 1.5° C above pre-industrial levels in the next 12 years. For those who may still be skeptical about climate change and the impact on global land and ocean surface temperatures, you can look at the average as a whole for March 2020. Surface temperatures are the second highest in a 141-year record, and above the average recorded in the 20th century. Approximately half of sea-level rise since 1900 has been triggered by human-caused global warming. Additionally, these rising temperatures are increasing the destructive force of wildfires, hurricanes, floods, and other natural disasters.

The devastating effects of wildfires in the United States have increased rapidly in recent years due to climate change. Unprecedented wildfires in California, such as the one that wiped out the entire town of Paradise in 2018, call for a new measure in disaster recovery and resilience. Historic super hurricanes (or typhoons) have devastated cities in Florida, Texas, Puerto Rico, and the Philippines. The effects of climate change continue to disrupt weather with droughts, tornados, and heat waves. The ability to provide disaster resilience has become a major concern which requires planning to reduce the impact of these disasters, instead of trying to cope with destruction and loss afterwards.

We have curated the articles and essays in this book to provide a unique perspective on the topics of climate change and disaster resilience to our readers. These readings are not only from scholars and scientists, but from individuals on the front lines who manage international collaborations, who lead local communities, who provide services for people impacted by disasters, and who drive policy change that will lead to a sustainable future. In collecting the studies and stories in this book, we hope to provide ideas that will inspire readers to think as advocates and activists for the future well-being of our homes, our communities, and our planet.

The book is divided into four parts. Part I is a compilation of essays that introduce you to basic terms and discussions on climate change and disaster resilience. Part II explores the challenges, effects, and the threats that directly impact our world. These include an aging infrastructure, carbon emissions, endangered species, hurricanes, and wildfires, among others.

Part III is divided into four sub-sections on what actions and innovations to mitigate climate change and provide for better disaster resilience are being done by citizens, cities, states and federal agencies, international stakeholders, and through public-private partnerships. Collaborative governance and the Philippine climate justice framework is covered in the international section which also includes two articles on Philippine cities that are receiving much needed technical assistance from the generosity of the American people through the U.S. Agency for International Development (USAID)'s Strengthening Urban Resilience for Growth with Equity (SURGE) Project.

In Part IV, we conclude the book with contributions elucidating on the future of climate change and natural disasters. The Appendices include a comprehensive glossary of acronyms, the groundbreaking United Nations Paris Agreement, and FEMA's Climate Change Adaptation Policy Statement.

We hope you have a good read!

PART I

Introduction

1. Climate Change*

U.S. GEOLOGICAL SURVEY

Why Is Climate Change Happening and What Are the Causes?

There are many "natural" and "anthropogenic" (human-induced) factors that contribute to climate change. Climate change has always happened on Earth, which is clearly seen in the geological record; it is the rapid rate and the magnitude of climate change occurring now that is of great concern worldwide. Greenhouse gases in the atmosphere absorb heat radiation. Human activity has increased greenhouse gases in the atmosphere since the Industrial Revolution, leading to more heat retention and an increase in surface temperatures. Atmospheric aerosols alter climate by scattering and absorbing solar and infrared radiation and they may also change the microphysical and chemical properties of clouds. Finally, land-use changes, such as deforestation have led to changes in the amount of sunlight reflected from the ground back into space (the surface albedo).

How Do We Know the Climate Is Changing?

The scientific community is certain that the Earth's climate is changing because of the trends that we see in the instrumented climate record and the changes that have been observed in physical and biological systems. The instrumental record of climate change is derived from thousands of temperature and precipitation recording stations around the world. We have very high confidence in these records as a whole. The evidence of a warming trend over the past century is unequivocal.

Many types of instrumental records point to a climate warming trend. Our streamflow records show an earlier peak in spring runoff; borehole temperature records in Alaskan permafrost as well as water temperature records on land and sea show the warming trend. The physical and biological changes that confirm climate warming include the rate of retreat in glaciers around the world, the intensification of rainfall events, changes in the timing of the leafing out of plants and the arrival of spring migrant birds, and the shifting of the range of some species.

What Are Some of the Signs of Climate Change?

*Public document originally published as U.S. Geological Survey, "Climate Change," https://www.usgs.gov/faqs/why-climate-change-happening-and-what-are-causes-1?qt-news_science_products=0#qt-news_science_products (2020).

- Temperatures are rising world-wide due to greenhouse gases trapping more heat in the atmosphere.
- Droughts are becoming longer and more extreme around the world.
- Tropical storms becoming more severe due to warmer ocean water temperatures.
- As temperatures rise there is less snowpack in mountain ranges and polar areas and the snow melts faster.
- Overall, glaciers are melting at a faster rate.
- Sea ice in the Arctic Ocean around the North Pole is melting faster with the warmer temperatures.
- Permafrost is melting, releasing methane, a powerful greenhouse gas, into the atmosphere.
- Sea levels are rising, threatening coastal communities and estuarine ecosystems.

What Are the Long-Term Effects of Climate Change?

Scientists have predicted that long-term effects of climate change will include a decrease in sea ice and an increase in permafrost thawing, an increase in heat waves and heavy precipitation, and decreased water resources in semi-arid regions.

Below are some of the regional impacts of global change forecast by the Intergovernmental Panel on Climate Change:

- North America: Decreasing snowpack in the western mountains; 5–20 percent increase in yields of rain-fed agriculture in some regions; increased frequency, intensity and duration of heat waves in cities that currently experience them.
- Latin America: Gradual replacement of tropical forest by savannah in eastern Amazonia; risk of significant biodiversity loss through species extinction in many tropical areas; significant changes in water availability for human consumption, agriculture and energy generation.
- Europe: Increased risk of inland flash floods; more frequent coastal flooding and increased erosion from storms and sea level rise; glacial retreat in mountainous areas; reduced snow cover and winter tourism; extensive species losses; reductions of crop productivity in southern Europe.
- Africa: By 2020, between 75 and 250 million people are projected to be exposed to increased water stress; yields from rain-fed agriculture could be reduced by up to 50 percent in some regions by 2020; agricultural production, including access to food, may be severely compromised.
- Asia: Freshwater availability projected to decrease in Central, South, East and Southeast Asia by the 2050s; coastal areas will be at risk due to increased flooding; death rate from disease associated with floods and droughts expected to rise in some regions.

How Can Climate Change Affect Natural Disasters?

With increasing global surface temperatures the possibility of more droughts and increased intensity of storms will likely occur. As more water vapor is evaporated into the atmosphere it becomes fuel for more powerful storms to develop. More heat in the atmosphere and warmer ocean surface temperatures can lead to increased wind speeds in tropical storms. Rising sea levels expose higher locations not usually subjected to the power of the sea and to the erosive forces of waves and currents.

What Is the Difference Between Weather and Climate Change?

Weather refers to short term atmospheric conditions while climate is the weather of a specific region averaged over a long period of time. Climate change refers to long-term changes.

How Do Changes in Climate and Land Use Relate to One Another?

The link between land use and the climate is complex. First, land cover—as shaped by land use practices—affects the global concentration of greenhouse gases. Second, while land use change is an important driver of climate change, a changing climate can lead to changes in land use and land cover. For example, farmers might shift from their customary crops to crops that will have higher economic return under changing climatic conditions. Higher temperatures affect mountain snowpack and vegetation cover as well as water needed for irrigation. The understanding of the interactions between climate and land use change is improving but continued scientific investigation is needed.

How Does Carbon Get into the Atmosphere?

Atmospheric carbon dioxide comes from two primary sources—natural and human activities. Natural sources of carbon dioxide include most animals, which exhale carbon dioxide as a waste product. Human activities that lead to carbon dioxide emissions come primarily from energy production, including burning coal, oil, or natural gas.

How Do We Know Glaciers Are Shrinking?

In addition to qualitative methods like Repeat Photography, USGS scientists collect quantitative measurements of glacier area and mass balance to track how some glaciers are retreating (Glacier Monitoring Studies). For example, ablation stakes show the seasonal gain and loss of snow, snow-pit analyses measure density of snow, and precision GPS measurements document the glacier margin. Also, because on-site GPS measurement of individual glaciers is expensive and labor intensive, aerial photograph analysis is used to determine glacier area through digitization of glacier margins.

Does the USGS Monitor Global Warming?

Not specifically. Our charge is to understand characteristics of the Earth, especially the Earth's surface, that affect our Nation's land, water, and biological resources. That includes quite a bit of environmental monitoring. Other agencies, especially NOAA and NASA, are specifically funded to monitor global temperature and atmospheric phenomena such as ozone concentrations.

The work through programs of our Land Resources mission (Land Change Science, National Land Imaging and Climate Adaptation Science Centers) focus on understanding the likely consequences of climate change, especially by studying how climate has changed in the past.

2. Climate Change

*How Do We Know?**

NATIONAL AERONAUTICS
AND SPACE ADMINISTRATION

The Earth's climate has changed throughout history. Just in the last 650,000 years there have been seven cycles of glacial advance and retreat, with the abrupt end of the last ice age about 11,700 years ago marking the beginning of the modern climate era—and of human civilization. Most of these climate changes are attributed to very small variations in Earth's orbit that change the amount of solar energy our planet receives.

The current warming trend is of particular significance because most of it is extremely likely (greater than 95 percent probability) to be the result of human activity since the mid–20th century and proceeding at a rate that is unprecedented over decades to millennia.[1]

Earth-orbiting satellites and other technological advances have enabled scientists to see the big picture, collecting many different types of information about our planet and its climate on a global scale. This body of data, collected over many years, reveals the signals of a changing climate.

The heat-trapping nature of carbon dioxide and other gases was demonstrated in the mid–19th century.[2] Their ability to affect the transfer of infrared energy through the atmosphere is the scientific basis of many instruments flown by NASA. There is no question that increased levels of greenhouse gases must cause the Earth to warm in response.

Ice cores drawn from Greenland, Antarctica, and tropical mountain glaciers show that the Earth's climate responds to changes in greenhouse gas levels. Ancient evidence can also be found in tree rings, ocean sediments, coral reefs, and layers of sedimentary rocks. This ancient, or paleoclimate, evidence reveals that current warming is occurring roughly ten times faster than the average rate of ice-age-recovery warming.[3]

The evidence for rapid climate change is compelling:

Global Temperature Rise. The planet's average surface temperature has risen about 1.62 degrees Fahrenheit (0.9 degrees Celsius) since the late 19th century, a change driven largely by increased carbon dioxide and other human-made emissions into the atmosphere.[4] Most of the warming occurred in the past 35 years, with the five warmest years on record taking place since 2010. Not only was 2016 the warmest year on record, but eight of the 12 months that make up the year—from January through September, with the exception of June—were the warmest on record for those respective months.[5]

*Public document originally published as National Aeronautics and Space Administration, "Climate Change: How Do We Know?," https://climate.nasa.gov/evidence/ (2020).

Warming Oceans. The oceans have absorbed much of this increased heat, with the top 700 meters (about 2,300 feet) of ocean showing warming of more than 0.4 degrees Fahrenheit since 1969. The oceans have absorbed much of this increased heat, with the top 700 meters (about 2,300 feet) of ocean showing warming of more than 0.4 degrees Fahrenheit since 1969.[6]

Shrinking Ice Sheets. The Greenland and Antarctic ice sheets have decreased in mass. Data from NASA's Gravity Recovery and Climate Experiment show Greenland lost an average of 286 billion tons of ice per year between 1993 and 2016, while Antarctica lost about 127 billion tons of ice per year during the same time period. The rate of Antarctica ice mass loss has tripled in the last decade.[7]

Glacial Retreat. Glaciers are retreating almost everywhere around the world— including in the Alps, Himalayas, Andes, Rockies, Alaska and Africa. Glaciers are retreating almost everywhere around the world—including in the Alps, Himalayas, Andes, Rockies, Alaska and Africa.[8]

Decreased Snow Cover. Satellite observations reveal that the amount of spring snow cover in the Northern Hemisphere has decreased over the past five decades and that the snow is melting earlier. Satellite observations reveal that the amount of spring snow cover in the Northern Hemisphere has decreased over the past five decades and that the snow is melting earlier.[9]

Sea Level Rise. Global sea level rose about 8 inches in the last century. The rate in the last two decades, however, is nearly double that of the last century and is accelerating slightly every year

Global sea level rose about 8 inches in the last century. The rate in the last two decades, however, is nearly double that of the last century and is accelerating slightly every year.[10]

Declining Arctic Sea Ice. Both the extent and thickness of Arctic sea ice has declined rapidly over the last several decades. Both the extent and thickness of Arctic sea ice has declined rapidly over the last several decades.[11]

Extreme Events. Glaciers are retreating almost everywhere around the world— including in the Alps, Himalayas, Andes, Rockies, Alaska and Africa. The number of record high temperature events in the United States has been increasing, while the number of record low temperature events has been decreasing, since 1950. The U.S. has also witnessed increasing numbers of intense rainfall events.[12]

Ocean Acidification. Since the beginning of the Industrial Revolution, the acidity of surface ocean waters has increased by about 30 percent. Since the beginning of the Industrial Revolution, the acidity of surface ocean waters has increased by about 30 percent.[13,14] This increase is the result of humans emitting more carbon dioxide into the atmosphere and hence more being absorbed into the oceans. The amount of carbon dioxide absorbed by the upper layer of the oceans is increasing by about 2 billion tons per year.[15,16]

NOTES

1. IPCC Fifth Assessment Report, Summary for Policymakers. B.D. Santer et.al., "A search for human influences on the thermal structure of the atmosphere," *Nature* vol. 382, 4 July 1996, 39–46. Gabriele C. Hegerl, "Detecting Greenhouse-Gas-Induced Climate Change with an Optimal Fingerprint Method," *Journal of Climate*, v. 9, October 1996, 2281–2306. V. Ramaswamy et.al., "Anthropogenic and Natural Influences in the Evolution of Lower Stratospheric Cooling," *Science* 311 (24 February 2006), 1138–1141 B.D. Santer et.al., "Contributions of Anthropogenic and Natural Forcing to Recent Tropopause Height Changes," *Science* vol. 301 (25 July 2003), 479–483.

2. In the 1860s, physicist John Tyndall recognized the Earth's natural greenhouse effect and suggested that slight changes in the atmospheric composition could bring about climatic variations. In 1896, a seminal paper by Swedish scientist Svante Arrhenius first predicted that changes in the levels of carbon dioxide in the atmosphere could substantially alter the surface temperature through the greenhouse effect.

3. National Research Council (NRC), 2006. *Surface Temperature Reconstructions For the Last 2,000 Years*. National Academy Press, Washington, D.C.

4. http://earthobservatory.nasa.gov/Features/GlobalWarming/page3.php. https://www.ncdc.noaa.gov/monitoring-references/faq/indicators.php. http://www.cru.uea.ac.uk/cru/data/temperature. http://data.giss.nasa.gov/gistemp.

5. https://www.giss.nasa.gov/research/news/20170118/.

6. Levitus, S.; Antonov, J.; Boyer, T.; Baranova, O.; Garcia, H.; Locarnini, R.; Mishonov, A.; Reagan, J.; Seidov, D.; Yarosh, E.; Zweng, M. (2017). NCEI ocean heat content, temperature anomalies, salinity anomalies, thermosteric sea level anomalies, halosteric sea level anomalies, and total steric sea level anomalies from 1955 to present calculated from in situ oceanographic subsurface profile data (NCEI Accession 0164586). Version 4.4. NOAA National Centers for Environmental Information. Dataset. doi:1.7289/V53F4MVP.

7. https://www.jpl.nasa.gov/news/news.php?feature=7159.

8. National Snow and Ice Data Center. World Glacier Monitoring Service.

9. National Snow and Ice Data Center. Robinson, D. A., D.K. Hall, and T.L. Mote. 2014. MEaSUREs Northern Hemisphere Terrestrial Snow Cover Extent Daily 25km EASE-Grid 2.0, Version 1. [Indicate subset used]. Boulder, Colorado USA. NASA National Snow and Ice Data Center Distributed Active Archive Center. doi: https://doi.org/10.5067/MEASURES/CRYOSPHERE/nsidc-0530.001. [Accessed 9/21/18]. http://nsidc.org/cryosphere/sotc/snow_extent.html. Rutgers University Global Snow Lab, Data History Accessed September 21, 2018.

10. R. S. Nerem, B.D. Beckley, J.T. Fasullo, B.D. Hamlington, D. Masters and G.T. Mitchum. Climate-change–driven accelerated sea-level rise detected in the altimeter era. *PNAS*, 2018 DOI: 10.1073/pnas.1717312115.

11. https://nsidc.org/cryosphere/sotc/sea_ice.html.

12. USGCRP, 2017: *Climate Science Special Report: Fourth National Climate Assessment*, Volume I [Wuebbles, D.J., D.W. Fahey, K.A. Hibbard, D.J. Dokken, B.C. Stewart, and T.K. Maycock (eds.)]. U.S. Global Change Research Program, Washington, D.C., USA, 470 pp., doi: 10.7930/J0J964J6.

13. http://www.pmel.noaa.gov/co2/story/What+is+Ocean+Acidification%3F.

14. http://www.pmel.noaa.gov/co2/story/Ocean+Acidification.

15. C. L. Sabine et.al., "The Oceanic Sink for Anthropogenic CO2," *Science* vol. 305 (16 July 2004), 367–371.

16. Copenhagen Diagnosis, p. 36.

3. Scientific Consensus

*Earth's Climate Is Warming**

NATIONAL AERONAUTICS
AND SPACE ADMINISTRATION

Temperature data from four international science institutions. All show rapid warming in the past few decades and that the last decade has been the warmest on record. Temperature data showing rapid warming in the past few decades, the latest data going up to 2019. According to NASA data, 2016 was the warmest year since 1880, continuing a long-term trend of rising global temperatures. The 10 warmest years in the 140-year record all have occurred since 2005, with the six warmest years being the six most recent years.

Multiple studies published in peer-reviewed scientific journals[1] show that 97 percent or more of actively publishing climate scientists agree*: Climate-warming trends over the past century are extremely likely due to human activities. In addition, most of the leading scientific organizations worldwide have issued public statements endorsing this position. The following is a partial list of these organizations, along with links to their published statements and a selection of related resources.

American Scientific Societies

Statement on Climate Change from 18 Scientific Associations
"Observations throughout the world make it clear that climate change is occurring, and rigorous scientific research demonstrates that the greenhouse gases emitted by human activities are the primary driver." (2009)[2]

American Association for the Advancement of Science: "Based on well-established evidence, about 97 percent of climate scientists have concluded that human-caused climate change is happening." (2014)[3]

American Chemical Society: "The Earth's climate is changing in response to increasing concentrations of greenhouse gases (GHGs) and particulate matter in the atmosphere, largely as the result of human activities." (2016–2019)[4]

American Geophysical Union: "Based on extensive scientific evidence, it is extremely likely that human activities, especially emissions of greenhouse gases, are the dominant cause of the observed warming since the mid–20th century. There is no alternative explanation supported by convincing evidence." (2019)[5]

---

*Public document originally published as National Aeronautics and Space Administration, "Scientific Consensus: Earth's Climate Is Warming," https://climate.nasa.gov/scientific-consensus/ (2020).

American Medical Association: "Our AMA … supports the findings of the Inter-governmental Panel on Climate Change's fourth assessment report and concurs with the scientific consensus that the Earth is undergoing adverse global climate change and that anthropogenic contributions are significant." (2019)[6]

American Meteorological Society: "Research has found a human influence on the climate of the past several decades…. The IPCC (2013), USGCRP (2017), and USGCRP (2018) indicate that it is extremely likely that human influence has been the dominant cause of the observed warming since the mid-twentieth century." (2019)[7]

American Physical Society: "Earth's changing climate is a critical issue and poses the risk of significant environmental, social and economic disruptions around the globe. While natural sources of climate variability are significant, multiple lines of evidence indicate that human influences have had an increasingly dominant effect on global climate warming observed since the mid-twentieth century." (2015)[8]

The Geological Society of America: "The Geological Society of America (GSA) concurs with assessments by the National Academies of Science (2005), the National Research Council (2011), the Intergovernmental Panel on Climate Change (IPCC, 2013) and the U.S. Global Change Research Program (Melillo et al., 2014) that global climate has warmed in response to increasing concentrations of carbon dioxide (CO_2) and other greenhouse gases…. Human activities (mainly greenhouse-gas emissions) are the dominant cause of the rapid warming since the middle 1900s (IPCC, 2013)." (2015)[9]

Science Academies

International Academies: Joint Statement: "Climate change is real. There will always be uncertainty in understanding a system as complex as the world's climate. However, there is now strong evidence that significant global warming is occurring. The evidence comes from direct measurements of rising surface air temperatures and subsurface ocean temperatures and from phenomena such as increases in average global sea levels, retreating glaciers, and changes to many physical and biological systems. It is likely that most of the warming in recent decades can be attributed to human activities (IPCC 2001)." (2005, 11 international science academies)[10]

U.S. National Academy of Sciences: "Scientists have known for some time, from multiple lines of evidence, that humans are changing Earth's climate, primarily through greenhouse gas emissions."[11]

U.S. Government Agencies

U.S. Global Change Research Program
"Earth's climate is now changing faster than at any point in the history of modern civilization, primarily as a result of human activities." (2018, 13 U.S. government departments and agencies)[12]

Intergovernmental Bodies

Intergovernmental Panel on Climate Change
"Warming of the climate system is unequivocal, and since the 1950s, many of the

observed changes are unprecedented over decades to millennia. The atmosphere and ocean have warmed, the amounts of snow and ice have diminished, and sea level has risen."[13]

"Human influence on the climate system is clear, and recent anthropogenic emissions of greenhouse gases are the highest in history. Recent climate changes have had widespread impacts on human and natural systems."[14]

Technically, a "consensus" is a general agreement of opinion, but the scientific method steers us away from this to an objective framework. In science, facts or observations are explained by a hypothesis (a statement of a possible explanation for some natural phenomenon), which can then be tested and retested until it is refuted (or disproved).

As scientists gather more observations, they will build off one explanation and add details to complete the picture. Eventually, a group of hypotheses might be integrated and generalized into a scientific theory, a scientifically acceptable general principle or body of principles offered to explain phenomena.

Notes

1. J. Cook, et al, "Consensus on consensus: a synthesis of consensus estimates on human-caused global warming," *Environmental Research Letters* Vol. 11 No. 4, (13 April 2016); DOI:10.1088/1748–9326/11/4/048002. Quotation from page 6: "The number of papers rejecting AGW [Anthropogenic, or human-caused, Global Warming] is a minuscule proportion of the published research, with the percentage slightly decreasing over time. Among papers expressing a position on AGW, an overwhelming percentage (97.2% based on self-ratings, 97.1% based on abstract ratings) endorses the scientific consensus on AGW." J. Cook, et al, "Quantifying the consensus on anthropogenic global warming in the scientific literature," *Environmental Research Letters* Vol. 8 No. 2, (15 May 2013); DOI:10.1088/1748–9326/8/2/024024. Quotation from page 3: "Among abstracts that expressed a position on AGW, 97.1% endorsed the scientific consensus. Among scientists who expressed a position on AGW in their abstract, 98.4% endorsed the consensus." W.R.L. Anderegg, "Expert Credibility in Climate Change," *Proceedings of the National Academy of Sciences* Vol. 107 No. 27, 12107–12109 (21 June 2010); DOI: 10.1073/pnas.1003187107. P.T. Doran & M.K. Zimmerman, "Examining the Scientific Consensus on Climate Change," *Eos Transactions American Geophysical Union* Vol. 90 Issue 3 (2009), 22; DOI: 10.1029/2009EO030002. N. Oreskes, "Beyond the Ivory Tower: The Scientific Consensus on Climate Change," *Science* Vol. 306 no. 5702, p. 1686 (3 December 2004); DOI: 10.1126/science.1103618.
2. Statement on climate change from 18 scientific associations (2009).
3. AAAS Board Statement on Climate Change (2014).
4. ACS Public Policy Statement: Climate Change (2016–2019).
5. Society Must Address the Growing Climate Crisis Now (2019).
6. Global Climate Change and Human Health (2019).
7. Climate Change: An Information Statement of the American Meteorological Society (2019).
8. APS National Policy 07.1 Climate Change (2015).
9. GSA Position Statement on Climate Change (2015).
10. Joint science academies' statement: Global response to climate change (2005).
11. Climate at the National Academies.
12. Fourth National Climate Assessment: Volume II (2018).
13. IPCC Fifth Assessment Report, Summary for Policymakers (2014).
14. IPCC Fifth Assessment Report, Summary for Policymakers (2014).

4. As the Trump Administration Retreats on Climate Change, U.S. Cities Are Moving Forward*

KATHERINE LEVINE EINSTEIN, DAVID GLICK
and MAXWELL PALMER

Despite almost universal scientific consensus that climate change poses a growing threat, President Donald Trump's recent infrastructure plan makes no mention of the need to build resilience to rising global temperatures. Instead, it actually seeks to weaken environmental reviews as a way of speeding up the infrastructure permitting process.

This proposal flies in the face of scientific evidence on climate change. It also contradicts the priorities of many local leaders who view climate change as a growing concern.

During the summer of 2017, we and Boston University's Initiative on Cities asked a nationally representative sample of 115 U.S. mayors about climate change as part of the annual Menino Survey of Mayors. Mayors overwhelmingly believe that climate change is a result of human activities. Only 16 percent of those we polled attributed rising global temperatures to "natural changes in the environment that are not due to human activities."

Perhaps even more strikingly, two-thirds of mayors agreed that cities should play a role in reducing the effects of climate change—even if it means making fiscal sacrifices.

Cleaner, Smarter Cities

In our survey, mayors highlighted a number of environmental initiatives that they were interested in pursuing. Over one-third prioritized reducing the number of vehicles on the road and making city assets, such as buildings and vehicles, more energy-efficient.

Other popular programs included shifting toward green and alternative energy sources; promoting energy efficiency in private buildings; reducing risks of damage from flooding; and installing smart traffic lights that can change their own timing in response to traffic conditions. Many mayors are already implementing these initiatives in their communities.

---

*Originally published as Katherine Levine Einstein, David Glick and Maxwell Palmer, "As the Trump Administration Retreats on Climate Change, U.S. Cities Are Moving Forward," *The Conversation*, https://theconversation.com/as-the-trump-administration-retreats-on-climate-change-us-cities-are-moving-forward-91612 (February 20, 2018). Reprinted with permission of the publisher.

When we asked mayors what would be required for a "serious and sustained effort to make a meaningful impact in my city" in combating climate change, they identified multiple programs. Large majorities agreed that significantly reducing their cities' greenhouse gas emissions would involve steps such as requiring residents to change their driving patterns, increasing residential density, reallocating financial resources and updating building codes and municipal facilities.

Interestingly, mayors largely did not think that such initiatives would require imposing costly new regulations on the private sector. Only 25 percent of mayors said such action was integral to addressing climate change.

Climate Politics Is National and Local

Mirroring national opinion, mayors' views on climate change and environmental policy were sharply divided along partisan lines. While 95 percent of the Democratic mayors we surveyed believed that climate change was a consequence of human activities, only 50 percent of Republican mayors shared that view. And a mere 25 percent of Republican mayors believe that mitigating climate change necessitated fiscal sacrifices, compared with 80 percent of Democrats.

Interestingly, Republican views appear to have become more negative over time. When we surveyed mayors in 2014, just over one-third of Republicans did not believe that their cities should make significant financial expenditures to prepare for and mitigate impacts of climate change. By 2017, that figure had risen to 50 percent. This shift suggests that Republicans are increasingly opposed to major policy initiatives targeting climate change, even at the local level.

However, despite these partisan differences, there was considerable consensus about making sustainability investments in cities, albeit perhaps for different motives. Democrats were more likely to highlight green and alternative energy sources, and Republicans were more inclined towards smart traffic lights, but there was significant support across party lines for these kinds of improvements.

A Missed Opportunity

President Trump's strongest support in the 2016 election came from rural areas, and urban leaders have strongly opposed many of his administration's proposals. We asked mayors about their ability to combat federal initiatives across an array of policies. Mayors identified two areas—policing and climate change—as opportunities where cities could do "a lot" to counteract Trump Administration policies.

Indeed, mayors have already banded together to send a strong political signal nationally, and perhaps even globally, on climate change. After President Trump abandoned the Paris climate agreement, many mayors publicly repudiated Trump and signed local commitments to pursue the accord's goals. A large number of mayors have also more formally allied and joined city-to-city networks and compacts around climate change and other issues. Mayors see political value in these kinds of commitments. As one mayor put it, compacts "increase political voice … [it] give[s] more clout to an issue when mayors unite around common issues."

Almost two-thirds of the U.S. population lives in cities or incorporated places. While mayors and local governments cannot comprehensively tackle climate change alone, their sizeable political and economic clout may make them an important force in national and global sustainability initiatives. In our view, by not proposing substantial investment in infrastructure—including climate resilience in cities—the Trump administration is missing an opportunity to build better relationships with cities through steps that would benefit millions of Americans.

5. A Whole-of-Government Approach

*Embedding Disaster Resilience**

PATRICK HOWELL

As city and county managers across the United States grapple with an unprece-dented public health crisis, the need to build local capacity to withstand, adapt to, and recover from natural and manmade disasters has never been more critical.

However, all too often we find that disaster preparedness is viewed as the sole responsibility of public safety and/or emergency management departments, residing in a silo and rarely receiving the attention or investment from the broader organization, at least until a crisis presents itself. This silo approach is not only precarious, but it misses tremendous opportunity to create collateral benefits within your organization, your staff, and the greater community.

Indeed, focusing your limited time, energy, and resources on a counterfactual effort such as disaster preparedness and mitigation can often times be difficult to jus-tify to both your council and constituents—particularly amid mounting citizen demands for public-facing services and dwindling traditional revenue streams. However, for a moment, consider the past 30 years:

- The average number of billion-dollar disasters per year in the United States has quadrupled, from an average of approximately three per year during the 1980s to a staggering twelve per year in the 2010s.
- The costs associated with these disasters have skyrocketed, from average losses of $13 billion per year in the 1980s to an unprecedented $80 billion per year in the 2010s.[1]

The upward trajectory of both frequency and severity of natural disasters is expected to continue in the United States for the foreseeable future, and the challenges and compli-cations that emerge will put local government preparation to the test. Pervasive issues of social inequity and economic fragility will be exacerbated in this new normal, as will the potential need to address overlapping and/or simultaneous crises (e.g., COVID-19 and the impending hurricane season for coastal communities in the United States). Preparing for such an environment requires a purposeful shift from the silo mentality that so many of us often fall victim to a systems-thinking approach that integrates disaster resilience

---

*Originally published as Patrick Howell, "A Whole-of-Government Approach: Embedding Disaster Resilience," *PM Magazine*, https://icma.org/articles/pm-magazine/whole-government-approach-embedding-disaster-resilience-municipal-operations (May 2020). Reprinted with permission of the publisher.

across the organization and is inclusive of both internal and external stakeholders. Contrary to popular belief, this can be easier than it may seem.

Establish a Resilience Champion

Identify a high-performing, passionate individual in your organization that can galvanize your organization around holistic disaster preparedness. While advantageous to appoint someone with disaster management knowledge and experience, it is not entirely necessary if that expertise is not readily available in your existing roster. The primary responsibility of this person should be the generation and maintenance of momentum among your stakeholder groups.

Muster Your Team

As disasters disrupt nearly every sector of your community, it is imperative that all sectors are represented in each phase of disaster risk reduction: hazard assessment, program planning, and project implementation. Disaster planning requires a whole-of-government approach.

Establish a standing working group that includes municipal officials from across the organization, including (but not limited to) finance, public works, utilities, health and human services, parks, planning/zoning/community development, public safety, and city council. Provide a clear understanding of what each official's role in disaster planning should be and make sure they agree. Give clear action items from one meeting to the next and send reminders so these do not get lost between meetings.

Be Inclusive of External Stakeholders

In addition to department heads and elected officials within your organization, convene a broader stakeholder group that includes representatives from the business community and local nonprofit groups. The interests of these groups typically align with those of the municipality in terms of disaster preparedness, response, and recovery as they advocate for resilient social, economic, and physical infrastructure in their communities. Chambers of commerce can be powerful actors, as issues of resilient infrastructure, economic opportunity, and continuity of operations are of mutual interest between the business they represent and the localities in which they're located.

For example, in one suburban community in the northeast United States, the municipal administrator invited the president of the Chamber of Commerce into a Community Resilience Assessment and Planning Workshop, which identified hazards and vulnerabilities specific to this community, and prescribed practical actions to build disaster capacity. Local officials benefited from the unique insights of the business community related to disaster preparation, and in turn, the chamber became one of the community's strongest advocates for public and private investment in risk mitigation and resilience.

Similarly, the nonprofit sector is often an advocate for the very issues that are fundamental to integrated disaster preparedness, including safe and affordable housing, social equity, and access to services and opportunities. In short, make friends before you need them!

Institute Regular Stakeholder Meetings

Facilitate communication, collaboration, and accountability of all stakeholders through regularly scheduled convenings of all your stakeholder groups. Get your team on the same page with an initial stakeholder workshop to create a common understanding of your community's hazards, vulnerabilities, and assets. Hold subsequent, recurring meetings (perhaps quarterly) to coalesce various interests and identify opportunities for collaboration. Establish well-defined subtopics within disaster preparedness for each meeting to keep the multitude of stakeholders on track, making incremental progress toward integrated disaster management and community resilience. One successful strategy is to rotate meeting hosts between department heads, allowing each meeting to center around a given topic (i.e., planning, finance, economic development, social services, etc.). Assign stakeholder coordination and meeting logistics to your resilience champion.

Integrate Planning Efforts

Each department within your organization likely has a strategic plan unique to the purpose, goals, and initiatives of that department. Without proper collaboration and cross-departmental communication, these plans risk contradiction, potentially reinforcing a silo mentality and creating competition between various service areas. Perform an analysis of the various strategies and initiatives to identify potential collateral benefits of potential projects. Assess how these projects can be leveraged with existing assets across the organization and consider the collateral benefits of cross-departmental project collaboration. The best resilience projects will serve multiple purposes and provide a host of secondary benefits, such as job creation, land reuse, decreased environmental impact, and bankable income. Furthermore, this exercise will also serve as a gap analysis, to see where there may be further opportunities to integrate disaster management into existing departmental plans.

Disaster preparation and resilience planning is a critical component for all local governments but is not something that can be completed all at once—or by one person. To be successful, focus on integrating disaster planning across your organization, engaging others who can help and have a role to play, and maintaining your community's overall progress and commitment to the process.

NOTE

1. NOAA National Centers for Environmental Information (NCEI) U.S. Billion-Dollar Weather and Climate Disasters (2020).

6. Designing Greener Streets Starts with Finding Room for Bicycles and Trees*

Anne Lusk

City streets and sidewalks in the United States have been engineered for decades to keep vehicle occupants and pedestrians safe. If streets include trees at all, they might be planted in small sidewalk pits, where, if constrained and with little water, they live only three to 10 years on average. Until recently, U.S. streets have also lacked cycle tracks—paths exclusively for bicycles between the road and the sidewalk, protected from cars by some type of barrier.

Today there is growing support for bicycling in many U.S. cities for both commuting and recreation. Research is also showing that urban trees provide many benefits, from absorbing air pollutants to cooling neighborhoods. As an academic who has focused on the bicycle for 37 years, I am interested in helping planners integrate cycle tracks and trees into busy streets.

Street design in the United States has been guided for decades by the American Association of State Highway and Transportation Officials, whose guidelines for developing bicycle facilities long excluded cycle tracks. Now the National Association of City Transportation Officials, the Federal Highway Administration and the American Association of State Highway and Transportation Officials have produced guidelines that support cycle tracks. But even these updated references do not specify how and where to plant trees in relation to cycle tracks and sidewalks.

In a study newly published in the journal Cities and spotlighted in a podcast from the Harvard T.H. Chan School of Public Health, I worked with colleagues from the University of Sao Paulo to learn whether pedestrians and bicyclists on five cycle tracks in the Boston area liked having trees, where they preferred the trees to be placed and whether they thought the trees provided any benefits. We found that they liked having trees, preferably between the cycle track and the street. Such additions could greatly improve street environments for all users.

---

*Originally published as Anne Lusk, "Designing Greener Streets Starts with Finding Room for Bicycles and Trees," *The Conversation*, https://theconversation.com/designing-greener-streets-starts-with-finding-room-for-bicycles-and-trees-101064 (September 6, 2018). Reprinted with permission of the publisher.

Separating Pedestrians and Cyclists from Cars

To assess views about cycle tracks and trees, we showed 836 pedestrians and bicyclists on five existing cycle tracks photomontages of the area they were using and asked them to rank whether they liked the images or not. The images included configurations such as a row of trees separating the cycle track from the street or trees in planters extending into the street between parked cars. We also asked how effectively they thought the trees (a) blocked perceptions of traffic; (b) lessened perceptions of pollution exposure; and (c) made pedestrians and bicyclists feel cooler.

Respondents strongly preferred photomontages that included trees. The most popular options were to have trees and bushes, or just trees, between the cycle track and the street. This is different from current U.S. cycle tracks, which typically are separated from moving cars by white plastic delineator posts, low concrete islands or a row of parallel parked cars.

Though perception is not reality, respondents also stated that having trees and bushes between the cycle track and the street was the option that best blocked their view of traffic, lessened their feeling of being exposed to pollution and made them feel cooler.

Factoring in Climate Change

Many city leaders are looking for ways to combat climate change, such as reducing the number of cars on the road. These goals should be factored into cycle track design. For example, highway engineers should ensure that cycle tracks are wide enough for bicyclists to travel with enough width to pass, including wide cargo bikes, bikes carrying children or newer three-wheeled electric bikes used by seniors.

Climate change is increasing stress on street trees, but better street design can help trees flourish. Planting trees in continuous earth strips, instead of isolated wells in the sidewalk, would enable their roots to trade nutrients, improving the trees' chances of reaching maturity and ability to cool the street.

Drought weakens trees and makes them more likely to lose limbs or be uprooted. Street drainage systems could be redesigned to direct water to trees' root systems. Hollow sidewalk benches could store water routed down from rooftops. If these benches had removable caps, public works departments could add antibacterial or anti-mosquito agents to the water. Gray water could also be piped to underground holding tanks to replenish water supplies for trees.

Thinking More Broadly About Street Design

The central argument against adding cycle tracks with trees to urban streets asserts that cities need this space for parallel-parked cars. But cars do not have to be stored on the side of the road. They also can be stored vertically—for example, in garages, or stacked in mechanical racks on urban lots.

Parking garages could increase occupancy by selling deeded parking spaces to residents who live nearby. Those spaces could provide car owners with a benefit the street lacks: outlets for charging electric vehicles, which rarely are available to people who rent apartments.

Bus rapid transit proponents might suggest that the best use of street width is dedicated bus lanes, not cycle tracks or street trees. But all of these options can coexist. For example, a design could feature a sidewalk, then a cycle track, then street trees planted between the cycle track and the bus lane and in island bus stops. The trees would reduce heat island effects from the expansive hardscape of the bus lane, and bus riders would have a better view.

More urban trees could lead to more tree limbs knocking down power lines during storms. The ultimate solution to this problem could be burying power lines to protect them from high winds and ice storms. This costs money, but earlier solutions included only the conduit for the buried power lines. When digging trenches to bury power lines, a parallel trench could be dug to bury pipes that would supply water and nutrients to the trees. The trees would then grow to maturity, cooling the city and reducing the need for air conditioning.

Climate Street Guidelines for U.S. Cities

To steer U.S. cities toward this kind of greener streetscape, urban scholars and planning experts need to develop what I call climate street guidelines. Such standards would offer design guidance that focuses on providing physiological and psychological benefits to all street users.

Developers in the United States have been coaxed into green thinking through tax credits, expedited review and permitting, design/height bonuses, fee reductions and waivers, revolving loan funds and the U.S. Green Building Council's Leadership in Energy and Environmental Design rating system. It is time to put equal effort into designing green streets for bicyclists, pedestrians, bus riders and residents who live on transit routes, as well as for drivers.

7. Climate Change Resilience Could Save Trillions in the Long Run*

DAVID L. LEVY

Is your city prepared for climate change?

The latest National Climate Assessment paints a grim future if U.S. cities and states don't take serious action to reduce greenhouse gas emissions.

The bottom line is that the costs of climate change could reach 10 percent of the entire U.S. economy by the end of the century—or more than US$2 trillion a year—much of it in damage to infrastructure and private property from more intense storms and flooding.

Cities can greatly reduce the damage and costs through adaptation measures such as building seawalls and reinforcing infrastructure. The problem is such projects are expensive, and finding ways to fund the cost of protecting cities against future and uncertain threats is a major financial and political challenge—especially in places where taxpayers have not yet experienced a disaster.

I've been part of a team that has been evaluating options for protecting Boston, one of America's most vulnerable coastal cities. Our analysis offers a few lessons for other cities as they begin planning for tomorrow's climate.

Investing in Adaptation

A team of scientists from 13 federal agencies contributed to the fourth U.S. National Climate Assessment, which recently laid out the stark threats Americans face from sea level rise, more frequent and intense storms, extreme precipitation, and droughts and wildfires.

For example, the report notes that coastal zone counties account for nearly half of the nation's population and economic activity, and that cumulative damage to property in those areas could reach $3.5 trillion by 2060.

The good news is that investing in adaptation can be highly cost effective. The National Climate Assessment estimates that such measures could significantly reduce the cumulative damage to coastal property to about $800 billion instead of $3.5 trillion.

*Originally published as David L. Levy, "Climate Change Resilience Could Save Trillions in the Long Run—But Finding Billions Now to Pay for It Is the Hard Part," *The Conversation*, https://theconversation.com/climate-change-resilience-could-save-trillions-in-the-long-run-but-finding-billions-now-to-pay-for-it-is-the-hard-part-108143 (December 6, 2018). Reprinted with permission of the publisher.

The report does not, however, examine the complex problems of implementing these adaptation solutions.

The Adaptation Devil Is in the Details

The Sustainable Solutions Lab at the University of Massachusetts Boston has been closely involved with its host city and local business and civic leaders in devising such climate adaptation strategies and figuring out how best to implement them, including a study I led on financing investments in climate resilience. Our work identified a series of hurdles that make financing such projects difficult.

One key problem is that while public authorities—and taxpayers—will ultimately bear the cost burden of coastal protection, the benefits mostly accrue to private property owners. Higher property taxes or new "resilience fees" will be on the table—and unlikely to be politically popular.

Another problem is that resilience investments primarily prevent or reduce future damages and costs but don't create much new value, unlike other public investments such as toll roads and bridges. For example, an investment in a sea wall might prevent property prices for coastal homes from falling or insurance premiums from rising, but it won't generate any new cash flows to defray the costs for the city or homeowner.

Beware the Big Fix

In a separate study, we examined the feasibility of building a four-mile barrier across Boston Harbor with massive gates that would close if major storms threatened to flood the city.

We estimated that the project would cost at least $12 billion and could take 30 years to plan, design, finance and build. Ultimately, we concluded it was unlikely to be cost effective and urged city officials to abandon the idea.

One key problem is the uncertainty regarding the extent and pace of sea-level rise, which is forecast to reach anywhere from 2 to 8 feet by the end of the century. But we really don't know. By the time the barrier would become operational mid-century, we might realize that we didn't need it—or worse, that it is woefully inadequate.

As sea levels rise, the gates, which would be the largest of their kind in the world and take many hours to open or close, would need to be activated more frequently and could potentially fail. In addition, the cost of such a barrier would be difficult to finance in an era of growing federal deficits and would choke off capital required for other more urgent adaptation projects.

In other words, it's risky to put all our adaptation eggs in one very expensive basket.

The Incremental Solution

Instead, our group recommends that Boston and other cities pursue more incremental shoreline protection projects focused on the most vulnerable areas.

Examples include constructing seawalls and berms, elevating some roads and parks and creating incentives for property owners to protect their buildings. The key attraction of such an approach is that capital can be targeted in highly cost-effective ways to the most vulnerable areas that need protection in the short term. It also allows for more flexible planning as the science improves and climate impacts come into sharper focus.

Boston is already considering some projects like this that would cost around $2 billion to $2.5 billion over a decade or two. Coming up with that much money is still a big challenge, but it's far more cost effective than the harbor barrier.

Another benefit is that this neighborhood-level approach would facilitate more local economic development and community participation. While making these areas more resilient, such investments would also involve upgrades in housing, transportation and other infrastructure.

This would go a long way toward ensuring that the community and taxpayers are on board when the discussion turns to costs.

Fair and Equitable

Adapting to climate change will be a mammoth challenge for cities and citizens across the country—and world. Finding ways to finance adaptation in a fair and equitable way will be paramount to success.

Miami, for example, last year issued a voter-approved $400 million bond to pay for about half its planned resilience projects. In August—exactly a year after their region was devastated by Hurricane Harvey—most voters in Harris County, Texas, approved a $2.5 billion bond to pay for flood protection. And just last month, citizens in San Francisco approved a $425 million bond to pay a quarter of the costs of fortifying a sea wall.

One problem with these projects is the heavy reliance on bonds. We found that it would be better to spread the costs of protecting cities and towns across multiple levels of government and private sources of capital, and utilize a range of funding mechanisms, including property taxes, carbon-based fees, and district-level charges.

The hope is that voters and cities will approve such projects before disaster strikes—not after.

8. Measuring Up U.S. Infrastructure Against Other Countries*

Hiba Baroud

How does infrastructure in the U.S. compare to that of the rest of the world? It depends on who you ask.

On the last two report cards from the American Society of Civil Engineers, U.S. infrastructure scored a D+. This year's report urged the government and private sector to increase spending by US$2 trillion within the next 10 years, in order to improve not only the physical infrastructure, but the country's economy overall.

Meanwhile, the country's international rank in overall infrastructure quality jumped from 25th to 12th place out of 138 countries, according to the World Economic Forum.

On February 12, the White House revealed its $1.5 trillion plan to rebuild U.S. infrastructure, financed through a combination of federal, local and private sectors. This is a long-awaited plan, as the nation's infrastructure quality continues to suffer.

The quality of infrastructure systems can be measured in different ways—including efficiency, safety and how much money is being invested. As a researcher in risk and resilience of infrastructure systems, I know that infrastructure assessment is far too complex to boil down into one metric. For instance, while the U.S. ranks second in road infrastructure spending, it falls in 60th place for road safety, due to the high rate of deaths from road traffic.

But by many measures, the U.S. falls short of the rest of the world. Two of these characteristics are key to our infrastructure's future: resilience and sustainability. A new class of solutions is emerging that, with the right funding, can help address these deficiencies.

Resilience

Resilient infrastructures are able to effectively respond to and recover from disruptive events. The U.S. is still in the top 25 percent of countries with the most resilient infrastructure systems. But it falls behind many other developed countries because the country's infrastructure is aging and increasingly vulnerable to disruptive events.

For example, the nation's inland waterway infrastructure has not been updated since it was first built in the 1950s. As a result, 70 percent of the 90,580 dams in the U.S. will be over 50 years old by 2025, which is beyond the average lifespan of dams.

*Originally published as Hiba Baroud, "Measuring Up U.S. Infrastructure Against Other Countries," *The Conversation*, https://theconversation.com/measuring-up-us-infrastructure-against-other-countries-78164 (February 13, 2018). Reprinted with permission of the publisher.

In addition, since the 1980s, weather-related power outages in the U.S. have become as much as 10 times more frequent.

Several European countries—such as Switzerland, Germany, Norway and Finland—are ahead of the U.S. in the FM Global Resilience Index, a data-driven indicator of a country's ability to respond to and recover from disruptive events. Though these countries are exposed to natural hazards and cyber risks, their infrastructure's stability and overall high standards allow them to effectively survive disruptive events.

The U.S. infrastructure was built according to high standards 50 years ago, but that's no longer enough to ensure protection from today's extreme weather. Such weather events are becoming more frequent and more extreme. That has a severe impact on our infrastructure, as cascading failures through interdependent systems such as transportation, energy and water will ultimately adversely impact our economy and society.

Take 2016's Hurricane Matthew, which was considered a 1,000-year flood event. The unexpectedly strong rainfalls broke records and caused damages equivalent to $15 billion. A better infrastructure that is modernized and well-maintained based on data-driven predictions of such events would have resulted in less impact and faster recovery, saving the society large damages and losses.

As the country's infrastructure ages, extreme weather events have a greater impact. That means the recovery is slower and less efficient, making the U.S. less resilient than its counterparts.

Sustainability

In terms of sustainability practices designed to reduce impact on human health and the environment, the U.S. does not make it to the top 10, according to RobecoSAM, an investment specialist focused exclusively on sustainability investing.

Average CO_2 emissions per capita in the U.S. are double that of other industrialized countries and more than three times as high as those in France.

The infrastructure in most EU countries facilitates and encourages sustainable practices. For example, railroads are mostly dedicated to commuters, while the bulk of freight moves through waterways, which is considered the most cost-effective and fuel-efficient mode of transportation.

In the U.S., however, 76 percent of commuters drive their own cars, as railroads are mostly reserved for freight and public transit is not efficient compared to other countries. American cities do not show up in the top cities for internal transportation, as do cities such as Madrid, Hong Kong, Seoul and Vienna.

To promote sustainable practices, global initiatives such as the New Climate Economy and the Task Committee on Planning for Sustainable Infrastructure aim to guide governments and businesses toward sustainable decision-making, especially when planning new infrastructure.

Smart Infrastructure as a Solution

To address challenges of resilience and sustainability, future infrastructure systems will have to embrace cyber-physical technologies and data-driven approaches.

A smart city is a city that is efficient in providing services and managing assets using information and communication technology. For example, in Barcelona, a city park uses sensor technology to collect and transmit real-time data that can inform gardeners on plant needs.

While there is no official benchmark to grade countries in this aspect, a number of American cities, such as Houston and Seattle, are considered among the world's "smartest" cities, according to economic and environmental factors.

In order to prioritize dam restoration, the dam safety engineering practice is moving toward a data-driven process that would rank the dams based on how important they are to the rest of the waterway system. And last year, the U.S. Department of Transportation issued a call to action to improve road safety by releasing a large database on road fatalities, which researchers can study to answer important questions.

Similarly, worldwide initiatives are seeking smart solutions that integrate communication and information technology to improve the resilience of cities such as 100 Resilient Cities and Smart Resilience.

It's imperative that we pursue these types of new solutions, so U.S. infrastructure can better and more sustainably withstand future disruptions and deliver better quality of life to citizens, too. Perhaps, by addressing these needs, the U.S. can improve its score on its next report cards.

PART II

Challenges

9. The Causes of Climate Change*

NATIONAL AERONAUTICS
AND SPACE ADMINISTRATION

A layer of greenhouse gases—primarily water vapor, and including much smaller amounts of carbon dioxide, methane and nitrous oxide—acts as a thermal blanket for the Earth, absorbing heat and warming the surface to a life-supporting average of 59 degrees Fahrenheit (15 degrees Celsius).

Scientists attribute the global warming trend observed since the mid–20th century to the human expansion of the "greenhouse effect"[1]—warming that results when the atmosphere traps heat radiating from Earth toward space.

Certain gases in the atmosphere block heat from escaping. Long-lived gases that remain semi-permanently in the atmosphere and do not respond physically or chemically to changes in temperature are described as "forcing" climate change. Gases, such as water vapor, which respond physically or chemically to changes in temperature are seen as "feedbacks."

Gases that contribute to the greenhouse effect include:

Water vapor. The most abundant greenhouse gas, but importantly, it acts as a feedback to the climate. Water vapor increases as the Earth's atmosphere warms, but so does the possibility of clouds and precipitation, making these some of the most important feedback mechanisms to the greenhouse effect.

Carbon dioxide (CO2). A minor but very important component of the atmosphere, carbon dioxide is released through natural processes such as respiration and volcano eruptions and through human activities such as deforestation, land use changes, and burning fossil fuels. Humans have increased atmospheric CO^2 concentration by more than a third since the Industrial Revolution began. This is the most important long-lived "forcing" of climate change.

Methane. A hydrocarbon gas produced both through natural sources and human activities, including the decomposition of wastes in landfills, agriculture, and especially rice cultivation, as well as ruminant digestion and manure management associated with domestic livestock. On a molecule-for-molecule basis, methane is a far more active greenhouse gas than carbon dioxide, but also one which is much less abundant in the atmosphere.

Nitrous oxide. A powerful greenhouse gas produced by soil cultivation practices,

---

*Public document originally published as National Aeronautics and Space Administration, "The Causes of Climate Change," https://climate.nasa.gov/causes/ (2020).

especially the use of commercial and organic fertilizers, fossil fuel combustion, nitric acid production, and biomass burning.

Chlorofluorocarbons (CFCs). Synthetic compounds entirely of industrial origin used in a number of applications, but now largely regulated in production and release to the atmosphere by international agreement for their ability to contribute to destruction of the ozone layer. They are also greenhouse gases.

On Earth, human activities are changing the natural greenhouse. Over the last century the burning of fossil fuels like coal and oil has increased the concentration of atmospheric carbon dioxide (CO_2). This happens because the coal or oil burning process combines carbon with oxygen in the air to make CO.[3] To a lesser extent, the clearing of land for agriculture, industry, and other human activities has increased concentrations of greenhouse gases.

The consequences of changing the natural atmospheric greenhouse are difficult to predict, but certain effects seem likely:

- On average, Earth will become warmer. Some regions may welcome warmer temperatures, but others may not.
- Warmer conditions will probably lead to more evaporation and precipitation overall, but individual regions will vary, some becoming wetter and others dryer.
- A stronger greenhouse effect will warm the oceans and partially melt glaciers and other ice, increasing sea level. Ocean water also will expand if it warms, contributing further to sea level rise.
- Meanwhile, some crops and other plants may respond favorably to increased atmospheric CO,[4] growing more vigorously and using water more efficiently. At the same time, higher temperatures and shifting climate patterns may change the areas where crops grow best and affect the makeup of natural plant communities.

The Role of Human Activity

In its Fifth Assessment Report, the Intergovernmental Panel on Climate Change, a group of 1,300 independent scientific experts from countries all over the world under the auspices of the United Nations, concluded there's a more than 95 percent probability that human activities over the past 50 years have warmed our planet.

The industrial activities that our modern civilization depends upon have raised atmospheric carbon dioxide levels from 280 parts per million to 412 parts per million in the last 150 years. The panel also concluded there's a better than 95 percent probability that human-produced greenhouse gases such as carbon dioxide, methane and nitrous oxide have caused much of the observed increase in Earth's temperatures over the past 50 years.

Solar Irradiance

A compares global surface temperature changes (red line) and the Sun's energy that Earth receives (yellow line) in watts (units of energy) per square meter since 1880. The lighter/thinner lines show the yearly levels while the heavier/thicker lines show the

11-year average trends. Eleven-year averages are used to reduce the year-to-year natural noise in the data, making the underlying trends more obvious.

The amount of solar energy that Earth receives has followed the Sun's natural 11-year cycle of small ups and downs with no net increase since the 1950s. Over the same period, global temperature has risen markedly. It is therefore extremely unlikely that the Sun has caused the observed global temperature warming trend over the past half-century.

It's reasonable to assume that changes in the Sun's energy output would cause the climate to change, since the Sun is the fundamental source of energy that drives our climate system.

Indeed, studies show that solar variability has played a role in past climate changes. For example, a decrease in solar activity coupled with an increase in volcanic activity is thought to have helped trigger the Little Ice Age between approximately 1650 and 1850, when Greenland cooled from 1410 to the 1720s and glaciers advanced in the Alps.

But several lines of evidence show that current global warming cannot be explained by changes in energy from the Sun:

- Since 1750, the average amount of energy coming from the Sun either remained constant or increased slightly.
- If the warming were caused by a more active Sun, then scientists would expect to see warmer temperatures in all layers of the atmosphere. Instead, they have observed a cooling in the upper atmosphere, and a warming at the surface and in the lower parts of the atmosphere. That's because greenhouse gases are trapping heat in the lower atmosphere.
- Climate models that include solar irradiance changes can't reproduce the observed temperature trend over the past century or more without including a rise in greenhouse gases.

NOTES

1. IPCC Fifth Assessment Report, 2014 United States Global Change Research Program, "Global Climate Change Impacts in the United States," Cambridge University Press, 2009.

2. Naomi Oreskes, "The Scientific Consensus on Climate Change," *Science* 3 December 2004: Vol. 306 no. 5702 p. 1686.

3. Mike Lockwood, "Solar Change and Climate: an update in the light of the current exceptional solar minimum," *Proceedings of the Royal Society* A, 2 December 2009.

4. Judith Lean, "Cycles and trends in solar irradiance and climate," *Wiley Interdisciplinary Reviews: Climate Change*, vol. 1, January/February 2010, 111–122.

10. Effects of Climate Change*

NATIONAL AERONAUTICS
AND SPACE ADMINISTRATION

The potential future effects of global climate change include more frequent wildfires, longer periods of drought in some regions and an increase in the number, duration and intensity of tropical storms.

Global climate change has already had observable effects on the environment. Glaciers have shrunk, ice on rivers and lakes is breaking up earlier, plant and animal ranges have shifted and trees are flowering sooner.

Effects that scientists had predicted in the past would result from global climate change are now occurring: loss of sea ice, accelerated sea level rise and longer, more intense heat waves.

Taken as a whole, the range of published evidence indicates that the net damage costs of climate change are likely to be significant and to increase over time.

Intergovernmental Panel on Climate Change

Scientists have high confidence that global temperatures will continue to rise for decades to come, largely due to greenhouse gases produced by human activities. The Intergovernmental Panel on Climate Change (IPCC), which includes more than 1,300 scientists from the United States and other countries, forecasts a temperature rise of 2.5 to 10 degrees Fahrenheit over the next century.

According to the IPCC, the extent of climate change effects on individual regions will vary over time and with the ability of different societal and environmental systems to mitigate or adapt to change.

The IPCC predicts that increases in global mean temperature of less than 1.8 to 5.4 degrees Fahrenheit (1 to 3 degrees Celsius) above 1990 levels will produce beneficial impacts in some regions and harmful ones in others. Net annual costs will increase over time as global temperatures increase.

"Taken as a whole," the IPCC states, "the range of published evidence indicates that the net damage costs of climate change are likely to be significant and to increase over time."[1-2]

---

*Public document originally published as National Aeronautics and Space Administration, "Scientific Consensus: Earth's Climate is Warming," https://climate.nasa.gov/effects/ (2020).

Future Effects

Some of the long-term effects of global climate change in the United States are as follows, according to the Third and Fourth National Climate Assessment Reports:

Change Will Continue Through This Century and Beyond

Global climate is projected to continue to change over this century and beyond. The magnitude of climate change beyond the next few decades depends primarily on the amount of heat-trapping gases emitted globally, and how sensitive the Earth's climate is to those emissions.

Temperatures Will Continue to Rise

Because human-induced warming is superimposed on a naturally varying climate, the temperature rise has not been, and will not be, uniform or smooth across the country or over time.

Frost-free Season (and Growing Season) will Lengthen

The length of the frost-free season (and the corresponding growing season) has been increasing nationally since the 1980s, with the largest increases occurring in the western United States, affecting ecosystems and agriculture. Across the United States, the growing season is projected to continue to lengthen.

In a future in which heat-trapping gas emissions continue to grow, increases of a month or more in the lengths of the frost-free and growing seasons are projected across most of the U.S. by the end of the century, with slightly smaller increases in the northern Great Plains. The largest increases in the frost-free season (more than eight weeks) are projected for the western U.S., particularly in high elevation and coastal areas. The increases will be considerably smaller if heat-trapping gas emissions are reduced.

Changes in Precipitation Patterns

Average U.S. precipitation has increased since 1900, but some areas have had increases greater than the national average, and some areas have had decreases. More winter and spring precipitation is projected for the northern United States, and less for the Southwest, over this century.

Projections of future climate over the U.S. suggest that the recent trend towards increased heavy precipitation events will continue. This trend is projected to occur even in regions where total precipitation is expected to decrease, such as the Southwest.

More Droughts and Heat Waves

Droughts in the Southwest and heat waves (periods of abnormally hot weather lasting days to weeks) everywhere are projected to become more intense, and cold waves less intense everywhere.

Summer temperatures are projected to continue rising, and a reduction of soil moisture, which exacerbates heat waves, is projected for much of the western and central U.S. in summer. By the end of this century, what have been once-in-20-year extreme heat days (one-day events) are projected to occur every two or three years over most of the nation.

Hurricanes Will Become Stronger and More Intense

The intensity, frequency, and duration of North Atlantic hurricanes, as well as the frequency of the strongest (Category 4 and 5) hurricanes, have all increased since the early 1980s

The intensity, frequency, and duration of North Atlantic hurricanes, as well as the frequency of the strongest (Category 4 and 5) hurricanes, have all increased since the early 1980s. The relative contributions of human and natural causes to these increases are still uncertain. Hurricane-associated storm intensity and rainfall rates are projected to increase as the climate continues to warm.

Sea Level Will Rise 1–4 feet by 2100

Global sea level has risen by about 8 inches since reliable record keeping began in 1880. It is projected to rise another 1 to 4 feet by 2100. This is the result of added water from melting land ice and the expansion of seawater as it warms.

In the next several decades, storm surges and high tides could combine with sea level rise and land subsidence to further increase flooding in many regions. Sea level rise will continue past 2100 because the oceans take a very long time to respond to warmer conditions at the Earth's surface. Ocean waters will therefore continue to warm, and sea level will continue to rise for many centuries at rates equal to or higher than those of the current century.

Arctic Likely to Become Ice-Free

The Arctic Ocean is expected to become essentially ice free in summer before mid-century.

U.S. Regional Effects

Below are some of the impacts that are currently visible throughout the U.S. and will continue to affect these regions, according to the Third[3] and Fourth[4] National Climate Assessment Reports, released by the U.S. Global Change Research Program:

- **Northeast**. Heat waves, heavy downpours and sea level rise pose growing challenges to many aspects of life in the Northeast. Infrastructure, agriculture, fisheries, and ecosystems will be increasingly compromised. Many states and cities are beginning to incorporate climate change into their planning.
- **Northwest**. Changes in the timing of streamflow reduce water supplies for competing demands. Sea level rise, erosion, inundation, risks to infrastructure and increasing ocean acidity pose major threats. Increasing wildfire, insect outbreaks and tree diseases are causing widespread tree die-off.

- **Southeast**. Sea level rise poses widespread and continuing threats to the region's economy and environment. Extreme heat will affect health, energy, agriculture and more. Decreased water availability will have economic and environmental impacts.
- **Midwest**. Extreme heat, heavy downpours and flooding will affect infrastructure, health, agriculture, forestry, transportation, air, and water quality, and more. Climate change will also exacerbate a range of risks to the Great Lakes.
- **Southwest**. Increased heat, drought, and insect outbreaks, all linked to climate change, have increased wildfires. Declining water supplies reduced agricultural yields, health impacts in cities due to heat, and flooding and erosion in coastal areas are additional concerns.

NOTES

1. Naomi Oreskes, "The Scientific Consensus on Climate Change," *Science* 3 December 2004: Vol. 306 no. 5702 p. 1686.

2. Mike Lockwood, "Solar Change and Climate: an update in the light of the current exceptional solar minimum," *Proceedings of the Royal Society* A, 2 December 2009.

3. Judith Lean, "Cycles and trends in solar irradiance and climate," *Wiley Interdisciplinary Reviews: Climate Change*, vol. 1, January/February 2010, 111–122.

4. IPCC 2007, Summary for Policymakers, in Climate Change 2007: Impacts, Adaptation and Vulnerability. Contribution of Working Group II to the Fourth Assessment Report of the Intergovernmental Panel on Climate Change, Cambridge University Press, Cambridge, UK, p. 17.

11. Climate Change Threatens Drinking Water Quality Across the Great Lakes*

GABRIEL FILIPPELLI *and* JOSEPH D. ORTIZ

"Do Not Drink/Do Not Boil" is not what anyone wants to hear about their city's tap water. But the combined effects of climate change and degraded water quality could make such warnings more frequent across the Great Lakes region.

A preview occurred on July 31, 2014, when a nasty green slime—properly known as a harmful algal bloom, or HAB—developed in the western basin of Lake Erie. Before long it had overwhelmed the Toledo Water Intake Crib, which provides drinking water to nearly 500,000 people in and around the city.

Tests revealed that the algae were producing microcystin, a sometimes deadly liver toxin and suspected carcinogen. Unlike some other toxins, microcystin can't be rendered harmless by boiling. So, the city issued a "Do Not Drink/Do Not Boil" order that set off a three-day crisis.

Local stores soon ran out of bottled water. Ohio's governor declared a state of emergency, and the National Guard was called in to provide safe drinking water until the system could be flushed and treatment facilities brought back online.

The culprit was a combination of high nutrient pollution—nitrogen and phosphorus, which stimulate the growth of algae—from sewage, agriculture and suburban runoff, and high-water temperatures linked to climate change. This event showed that even in regions with resources as vast as the Great Lakes, water supplies are vulnerable to these kinds of man-made threats.

As Midwesterners working in the fields of urban environmental health and climate and environmental science, we believe more crises like Toledo's could lie ahead if the region doesn't address looming threats to drinking water quality.

Vast and Abused

The Great Lakes together hold 20 percent of the world's surface freshwater—more than enough to provide drinking water to over 48 million people from Duluth to

*Originally published as Gabriel Filippelli and Joseph D. Ortiz, "Climate Change Threatens Drinking Water Quality Across the Great Lakes," *The Conversation,* https://theconversation.com/climate-change-threatens-drinking-water-quality-across-the-great-lakes-131883 (April 29, 2020). Reprinted with permission of the publisher.

Chicago, Detroit, Cleveland and Toronto. But human impacts have severely harmed this precious and vital resource.

In 1970, after a century of urbanization and industrialization around the Great Lakes, water quality was severely degraded. Factories were allowed to dump waste into waterways rather than treating it. Inadequate sewer systems often sent raw sewage into rivers and lakes, fouling the water and causing algal blooms.

Problems like these helped spur two major steps in 1972: passage of the U.S. Clean Water Act, and adoption of the Great Lakes Water Quality Agreement between the United States and Canada. Since then, many industries have been cleaned up or shut down. Sewer systems are being redesigned, albeit slowly and at great cost.

The resulting cuts in nutrient and wastewater pollution have brought a quick decline in HABs—especially in Lake Erie, the Great Lake with the most densely populated shoreline. But new problems have emerged, due partly to shortcomings in those laws and agreements, combined with the growing effects of climate change.

Warmer and Wetter

Climate change is profoundly altering many factors that affect life in the Great Lakes region. The most immediate impacts of recent climate change have been on precipitation, lake levels and water temperatures.

Annual precipitation in the region has increased by about 5 inches over the past century. Changes in the past five years alone—the hottest five years in recorded history—have been particularly dramatic, with a series of extreme rainfall events bringing extremely high and rapidly varying water levels to the Great Lakes.

Record high precipitation in 2019 caused flooding, property damage and beachfront losses in a number of coastal communities. Precipitation in 2020 is projected to be equally high, if not higher. Some of this is due to natural variability, but certainly some is due to climate change.

Another clear impact of climate change is a general warming of all five Great Lakes, particularly in the springtime. The temperature increase is modest and varies from year to year and place to place but is consistent overall with records of warming throughout the region.

More Polluted Runoff

Some of these climate-related changes have converged with more direct human impacts to influence water quality in the Great Lakes.

Cleanup measures adopted back in the 1970s imposed stringent limits on large point sources of nutrient pollution, like wastewater and factories. But smaller "non-point" sources, such as fertilizer and other nutrients washing off farm fields and suburban lawns, were addressed through weaker, voluntary controls. These have since become major pollution sources.

Since the mid–1990s, climate-driven increases in precipitation have carried growing quantities of nutrient runoff into Lake Erie. This rising load has triggered increasingly severe algal blooms, comparable in some ways to the events of the 1970s. Toledo's 2014 crisis was not an anomaly.

These blooms can make lake water smell and taste bad, and sometimes make it dangerous to drink. They also have long-term impacts on the lakes' ecosystems. They deplete oxygen, killing fish and spurring chemical processes that prime the waters of Lake Erie for larger future blooms. Low-oxygen water is more corrosive and can damage water pipes, causing poor taste or foul odors, and helps release trace metals that may also cause health problems.

So despite a half-century of advances, in many ways Great Lakes water quality is back to where it was in 1970, but with the added influence of a rapidly changing climate.

Filtering Runoff

How can the region change course and build resilience into Great Lakes coastal communities? Thanks to a number of recent studies, including an intensive modeling analysis of future climate change in Indiana, which serves as a proxy for most of the region, we have a pretty good picture of what the future could look like.

As one might guess, warming will continue. Summertime water temperatures are projected to rise by about another 5 degrees Fahrenheit by midcentury, even if nations significantly reduce their greenhouse gas emissions. This will cause further declines in water quality and negatively impact coastal ecosystems.

The analysis also projects an increase in extreme precipitation and runoff, particularly in the winter and spring. These shifts will likely bring still more nutrient runoff, sediment contaminants and sewage overflows into coastal zones, even if surrounding states hold the actual quantities of these nutrients steady. More contaminants, coupled with higher temperatures, can trigger algal blooms that threaten water supplies.

But recent success stories point to strategies for tackling these problems, at least at the local and regional levels.

Several large infrastructure projects are currently underway to improve stormwater management and municipal sewer systems, so that they can capture and process sewage and associated nutrients before they are transported to the Great Lakes. These initiatives will help control flooding and increase the supply of "gray water," or used water from bathroom sinks, washing machines, tubs and showers, for uses such as landscaping.

Cities are coupling this "gray infrastructure" with green infrastructure projects, such as green roofs, infiltration gardens and reclaimed wetlands. These systems can filter water to help remove excess nutrients. They also will slow runoff during extreme precipitation events, thus recharging natural reservoirs.

Municipal water managers are also using smart technologies and improved remote sensing methods to create near-real-time warning systems for HABs that might help avert crises. Groups like the Cleveland Water Alliance, an association of industry, government, and academic partners, are working to implement smart lake technologies in Lake Erie and other freshwater environments around the globe. Finally, states including Ohio and Indiana are moving to cut total nutrient inputs into the Great Lakes from all sources and using advanced modeling to pinpoint those sources.

Together these developments could help reduce the size of HABs, and perhaps even reach the roughly 50 percent reduction in nutrient runoff that government studies suggest is needed to bring them back to their minimum extent in the mid–1990s.

Short of curbing global greenhouse gas emissions, keeping communities that rely so heavily on the Great Lakes livable will require all of these actions and more.

12. Long-Term Disaster Recovery*

C.H. "Burt" Mills, Jr., *and* William R. Whitson

In 2017, Hurricane Harvey came ashore in Aransas County near Rockport, Texas, as a Class 4 hurricane. The eyewall crossed over this small jurisdiction, located on the Texas Gulf Coast, packing winds more than 135 mph with torrential rains and an eight-foot storm surge. Harvey raged over 12 hours causing widespread devastation including a 25-percent loss to the local tax base. The courthouse, city hall, local aquarium, hospital, and center for the arts were all destroyed and a main bridge accessing a local island was heavily damaged. Yet in 2019, the area was just beginning to see significant federal and state dollars for rebuilding. Why?

Natural disasters like Hurricane Harvey are becoming ever more common, leaving many communities to recover from environmental catastrophes without adequate, timely support. The federal government, along with state and local partners, are the best in the world at disaster forecasting, event management, and immediate post-event response. When the flood waters recede and life safety is stabilized, and major press conferences with high-ranking officials making promises of support are done, local officials are left alone facing the long and arduous process of long-term recovery. It's the local government leadership at ground zero that must pick-up the pieces and find a way to rebuild the community they know and love. As things currently stand, the overly complex and lengthy federal recovery processes and programs often leave smaller local communities in the lurch at exactly the moment when they most need support.

Knowing That We Will Have More Highly Dangerous Natural Disasters, Why Do We Keep Using the Same Old Processes to Respond?

To be effective, we must seek new ways to simplify and improve the disaster recovery process. After everything we do to respond and stabilize disaster situations, the question remains: why are local governments then left to struggle for years on the pathway to recovery?

Local officials involved in long-term recovery efforts believe that we must work

*Originally published as C.H. "Burt" Mills, Jr., and William R. Whitson, "Long-Term Disaster Recovery: Still a Broken Landscape for Smaller Local Governments," *PM Magazine,* https://icma.org/articles/pm-magazine/long-term-disaster-recovery-still-broken-landscape-smaller-local-governments (May 2020). Reprinted with permission of the publisher.

together to find ways to ensure that federal and state dollars are appropriately spent, while also allowing for flexibility and quicker response times. Speed is critical for communities recovering from natural disasters. Instead of focusing on the missteps leading to federal funding "claw backs," local governments should be focusing on how to rebuild more resilient and sustainable communities. The current process favors extensive documentation and time-consuming methods over agreed-on results. It's time for local governments to work together and ask, "Why can't there be a better way?" It's time to see what can be done to improve the recovery process.

When disasters hit, local governments today turn to programs authorized by the Stafford Act to provide assistance. Under the Stafford Act, the presidential declaration of a state of emergency triggers response by the Federal Emergency Management Agency (FEMA). The National Incident Management System run by FEMA is unrivaled in its ability to handle disaster preparation, storm response, and immediate after-impact phases of an emergency response. The system can rapidly deploy public safety personnel, distribute food and water, clear roads, account for damage, and execute search and rescue operations like clockwork. Yet, when it comes to restoring communities through the long-term recovery process, FEMA, state partners, and local officials seem just as overwhelmed as local officials by the impact of the disaster. This often accompanies inadequate resources to support a sustained, and intense, long road to recovery. It's time for new tools and techniques.

Why Is Our Federal Government Falling Short in Supporting Long-Term Recovery Efforts?

In large part, it's due to the limitations of a cumbersome, top-down system controlled from Washington in which federal dollars are tied to specific appropriations and subjected to lengthy federal procurement processes and rules. Though the Stafford Act was amended following Hurricane Katrina to make the programs more flexible and responsive, the system still functions in much the same way as before.

In Aransas County, we experienced great difficulty in getting water-based debris cleaned up from the community's waterways after Hurricane Harvey. The county is coastal with miles of bays, estuaries, and shores. The economy is based on tourism and fishing. When Harvey came ashore, high winds and storm surge deposited tons of debris into the waters throughout the community. After the disaster, the county worked in concert with FEMA and the state to remove over 3.7 million cubic yards of debris from the land-based right of ways. However, the area's waterways were subject to a never-ending bureaucratic disagreement over jurisdiction. Having debris clogging canals, bays, and waterways was a major barrier to the overall economic recovery of the area. The additional burden of having strings attached to federal funding left FEMA unable to address the conditions threatening the local economy and welfare of citizens. The extra time it took to return the local waters to usable conditions resulted in a direct economic hit to the area, which relies on tourism to sustain them.

Sustainability and Resiliency Are More Than Just Buzzwords

One of the goals of the Stafford Act is to promote hazard mitigation to reduce the risk of loss of life and property from future disasters. However, time and time again,

FEMA's red tape and extensive documentation procedures proved to be a major hindrance to preparing the community for the next disaster. Hazard mitigation dollars had to run through complex cost-benefit analysis formulas, requiring local communities to put time into compiling extensive technical records, historic narratives, and recreate maintenance records. That led to months of delay, especially since many records and documents were destroyed by the storm! Instead of focusing on projects key to the recovery effort that make the area stronger and more resilient to future storms, funds were only approved for projects that met complex and arbitrary cost-benefit ratio formulas. Meeting bureaucratic requirements should not take precedence over developing projects that local and state officials identify as essential to the recovery effort.

Planning for sustainability and resiliency is made more difficult by current federal requirements in other ways as well. Aransas County has many areas with high concentrations of poverty, and over 3,000 low/moderate-income residents lost their homes due to the storm. While Community Development Block Grant—Disaster Recovery (CDBG-DR) funds should be available to help provide relief for these residents, these funds also come with strict limitations. For example, the majority of affordable housing lost in Aransas County was not tied to sewer infrastructure before the storm, relying instead on septic tanks. This is a huge environmental problem for a coastal county with wet soil conditions. Septic tank runoff causes significant environmental harm to water quality in this sensitive coastal environment. Despite the clear benefit of extending sewer infrastructure simultaneous with the development of replacement housing units, CDBG rules prohibited us from doing so. As one state staffer informed us, "If the storm did not break it, then you cannot make it!" This left the community with limited options in the replacement of outdated and environmentally hazardous systems instead of supporting forward-looking improvements simultaneous with recovery. Further, if the goal is to create more stable and storm resilient infrastructure, while saving future disaster dollars and improving the environment, such an investment makes sense. Instead, federal rules—or narrow interpretations of the rules—often prevent help from arriving for many months, and sometimes years after it was promised.

How Can We Better Utilize These Vitally Important Funds to Rebuild Our Communities After Major Disasters?

FEMA and HUD have key roles to play in providing technical assistance in setting upfront goals for long-term disaster recovery. Once those goals are in place, state and local governments supported by federal resources should work toward meeting them. States also need more leeway to direct and approve recovery projects, rather than forcing local governments to deal with the bureaucratic bottleneck of our current system. It takes hundreds of staff hours to research, review, and apply for each separate federal funding stream that are critical to recovery operations. Hundreds more staff hours are essential to meet lengthy, complex administrative reporting processes required by federal procurement rules. Currently, local governments spend months waiting for FEMA or HUD approvals, sending in multiple documents. This leaves cash-strapped local governments to delay the purchases of needed equipment and repairs. For cyclical disasters like hurricanes, these lengthy delays leave communities exposed and even more vulnerable.

Imagine instead state and local partners working together to determine the most pressing needs created by the disaster, meeting them in a matter of weeks, not months. We need to build new recovery strategies with more locally oriented, bottom-up approaches based on the experience and expertise of those with boots on the ground. FEMA and HUD could offer more administrative flexibility in emergency situations, while providing block grant funding support for innovative pilot programs that better support and prepare local officials for long-term recovery. This would allow more administrative discretion in the face of emergency conditions, especially with cleanup efforts for circumstances that threaten the local economy, hinder long-term recovery efforts, or pose a health and safety risk to the public.

Let's Give FEMA and HUD New Tools and Charge Them With Assisting Locals

By having FEMA work with local governments in the development of hazard mitigation and disaster recovery plans, efforts to aid the recovery and resiliency of an impacted community will be strengthened. Local governments under state supervision are best suited to develop plans tailored to fit the unique needs of communities. As such, waivers of some federal rules for grants, system administration, and procurement could be allowed when jurisdictions develop state-approved plans, thereby discontinuing difficult funding applications, stove pipe grant programs, and onerous reporting processes. Furthermore, waivers of rules could be limited to inside the impact zone, and for a specified period, to help expedite the recovery.

In addition, federal, state, and local governments—including the private sector—could apply for block grants, thus helping relieve the delays now happening at the local levels of long-term recovery. This is especially true for housing needs. FEMA could create a new pilot program for smaller jurisdictions, such as those with fewer than 50,000 residents, that would be based on this bottom-up approach. Under one potential model, following a federally declared disaster, local officials would identify needs and together with the state develop a local recovery and response plan, for approval by the governor. At that point, federal, state, and even private sector resources could be allocated in a block grant to fund and execute the local adopted plan. Results would be measured based on outcomes, not compliance with mountains of rules and complex regulations.

FEMA should also encourage the use of technologies aimed at disaster and recovery management. In Aransas County, we asked to pilot "snap-together" modular housing technology to provide housing instead of the traditional manufactured housing units (FEMA trailers). This housing would have been delivered faster and more cost-effectively, giving victims stronger, more resilient permanent housing providing protection in future storm events. FEMA could have authorized pre-bid contracts so that in future natural disaster events, the necessary procurement processes would be fast tracked. Unfortunately, this request was never considered. Local officials identified workforce housing as a top priority for the local recovery effort; however, over 700 units of workforce housing are still in disrepair, have not been redeveloped, and are currently not back online to support the recovery effort.

In closing, long-term recovery needs significant improvement. It's time for federal, state and local partners to come together and authorize new tools and a form of the block-grant model approach to fix the system. It's time for Congress to give the dedicated professionals in FEMA, HUD, and the states new flexibility. With the ever-increasing trend of severe natural disasters hitting the country, surely this is a matter upon which all Americans can agree. We can do better than this. Will our future look like the past? We hope not!

13. Rethinking the "Infrastructure" Discussion Amid a Blitz of Hurricanes*

ANDREW REVKIN

The wonky words infrastructure and resilience have circulated widely of late, particularly since Hurricanes Harvey and Irma struck paralyzing, costly blows in two of America's fastest-growing states.

Resilience is a property traditionally defined as the ability to bounce back. A host of engineers and urban planners have long warned this trait is sorely lacking in America's brittle infrastructure.

Many such experts say the disasters in the sprawling suburban and petro-industrial landscape around Houston and along the crowded coasts of Florida reinforce the urgent idea that resilient infrastructure is needed more than ever, particularly as human-driven climate change helps drive extreme weather.

The challenge in prompting change—broadening the classic definition of "infrastructure," and investing in initiatives aimed at adapting to a turbulent planet—is heightened by partisan divisions over climate policy and development.

Of course, there's also the question of money. The country's infrastructure is ailing already. A national civil engineering group has surveyed the nation's bridges, roads, dams, transit systems and more and awarded a string of D or D+ grades since 1998. The same group has estimated that the country will be several trillion dollars short of what's needed to harden and rebuild and modernize our infrastructure over the next decade.

For fresh or underappreciated ideas, ProPublica reached out to a handful of engineers, economists and policy analysts focused on reducing risk on a fast-changing planet.

Alice Hill, who directed resilience policy for the National Security Council in the Obama administration, said the wider debate over cutting climate-warming emissions may have distracted people from promptly pursuing ways to reduce risks and economic and societal costs from natural disasters.

She and several other experts said a first step is getting past the old definition of resilience as bouncing back from a hit, which presumes a community needs simply to recover.

"I don't think of resilience in the traditional sense, in cutting how long it takes to turn the lights back on," said Brian Bledsoe, the director of the Institute for Resilient

---

*This story was originally published by ProPublica as Andrew Revkin, "Rethinking the 'Infrastructure' Discussion Amid a Blitz of Hurricanes," https://www.propublica.org/article/rethinking-the-infrastructure-discussion-amid-a-blitz-of-hurricanes (Sept. 13, 2017). Reprinted with permission of the publisher.

Infrastructure Systems at the University of Georgia. "Resilience is seizing an opportunity to move into a state of greater adaptability and preparedness—not just going back to the status quo."

In thinking about improving the country's infrastructure, and provoking real action, Bledsoe and others say, language matters.

Bledsoe, for instance, is exploring new ways to communicate flood risk in words and maps. His institute is testing replacements for the tired language of 1-in-100 or 1-in-500-year floods. A 100-year flood has a 1 in 4 chance of occurring in the 30-year span of a typical home mortgage, he said, adding that's the kind of time scale that gets people's attention.

Visual cues matter, too, he said. On conventional maps, simple lines marking a floodplain boundary often are interpreted as separating safe zones and those at risk, Bledsoe said. But existing models of water flows don't provide the full range of possible outcomes: "A 50-year rain can produce a 100-year flood if it falls on a watershed that's already soaked or on snowpack or if it coincides with a storm surge."

"The bright line on a map is an illusion," he said, particularly in flat places like Houston, where a slight change in flood waters can result in far more widespread inundation. Risk maps should reflect that uncertainty, and wider threat.

Nicholas Pinter, a University of California, Davis, geoscientist who studies flood risk and water management, said that Florida is well-situated to build more wisely after this disaster because it already has a statewide post-disaster redevelopment plan and requires coastal communities to have their own.

It's more typical to have short-term recovery plans—for digging out and getting the lights back on, as 20,000 utility workers are scurrying to do right now.

The advantage of having an established protocol for redevelopment, he said, is it trims delays.

"Draw up plans when the skies are blue and pull them off the shelf," he said of how having rebuilding protocols in place can limit repeating mistakes. "That fast response cuts down on the horrible lag time in which people typically rebuild in place."

In a warming climate, scientists see increasing potential for epic deluges like the one that swamped Houston and last year's devastating rains around Baton Rouge, Louisiana. How can the federal government more responsibly manage such environmental threats?

Many people point to the National Flood Insurance Program, which was created to boost financial resilience in flood zones, but has been criticized from just about every political and technical vantage point as too often working to subsidize, instead of mitigate, vulnerability.

As has happened periodically before, pressure is building on Congress to get serious about fixing the program (a reauthorization deadline was just pushed from this month toward the end of the year).

How this debate plays out will have an important impact on infrastructure resilience, said Pinter of the University of California, Davis. If incentives remain skewed in favor of dangerous and sprawling development, he said, that just expands where roads, wires, pipelines and other connecting systems have to be built. "Public infrastructure is there in service of populations," he said.

He also said the lack of federal guidance has led to deeply uneven enforcement of floodplain building at the state level, with enormous disparities around the country resulting in more resilient states subsidizing disaster-prone development in others.

"Why should California, Wyoming or Utah be paying the price for Houston, Mississippi or Alabama failing to enforce the National Flood Insurance Program?" he said.

Bledsoe, at the University of Georgia, said there's no need to wait for big changes in the program to start making progress. He said the National Flood Insurance Program has a longstanding division, the Community Rating System, that could swiftly be expanded, cutting both flood risk and budget-breaking payouts. It's a voluntary program that reduces flood insurance rates for communities that take additional efforts beyond minimum standards to reduce flood damage to insurable property.

Despite the clear benefits, he said, only one municipality, Roseville, California, has achieved the top level of nine rankings and gotten the biggest insurance savings—45 percent. Tulsa, Oklahoma, Fort Collins, Colorado, King County, Washington, and Pierce County, Washington, are at the second ranking and get a 40 percent rate cut. Hundreds of other municipalities are at much lower levels of preparedness.

"Boosting participation is low-hanging fruit," Bledsoe said.

Some see signs that the recent blitz of hurricanes is reshaping strategies in the Trump White House. President Donald Trump's infrastructure agenda, unveiled on August 15, centered on rescinding Obama-era plans to require consideration of flood risk and climate change in any federal spending for infrastructure or housing and the like. The argument was built around limiting perceived red tape.

After the flooding of Houston less than two weeks later, Trump appointees, including Tom Bossert, the president's homeland security adviser, said a new plan was being developed to insure federal money would not increase flood risks.

On Monday, as Irma weakened over Georgia, Bossert used a White House briefing to offer more hints of an emerging climate resilience policy, while notably avoiding accepting climate change science: "What President Trump is committed to is making sure that federal dollars aren't used to rebuild things that will be in harm's way later or that won't be hardened against the future predictable floods that we see. And that has to do with engineering analysis and changing conditions along eroding shorelines but also in inland water and flood-control projects."

Robert R.M. Verchick, a Loyola University law professor who worked on climate change adaptation policy at the Environmental Protection Agency under Obama, said federal leadership is essential.

If Federal Emergency Management Agency flood maps incorporated future climate conditions, that move would send a ripple effect into real estate and insurance markets, forcing people to pay attention, he said. If the federal government required projected climate conditions to be considered when spending on infrastructure in flood-prone areas, construction practices would change, he added, noting the same pressures would drive chemical plants or other industries to have a wider margin of safety.

"None of these things will change without some form of government intervention. That's because those who make decisions on the front end (buying property, building bridges) do not bear all the costs when things go wrong on the back end," he wrote in an email. "And on top of that, human beings tend to discount small but important risks when it seems advantageous in the short-run."

After a terrible storm, he said, most Americans are willing to cheer a government that helps communities recuperate. But people should also embrace the side of government that establishes rules to avoid risk and make us safer. That's harder, he said, because such edicts can be perceived by some as impinging on personal freedom.

"But viewed correctly, sensible safeguards are part of freedom, not a retreat from it," he said. "Freedom is having a home you can return to after the storm. Freedom is having a bridge high enough to get you to the hospital across the river. Freedom is not having your house surrounded by contaminated mud because the berm at the neighboring chemical plant failed overnight."

Thaddeus R. Miller, an Arizona State University scientist who helps lead a national research network focused on "Urban Resilience to Extreme Events," said in an email that boosting the capacity of cities to stay safe and prosperous in a turbulent climate requires a culture shift as much as hardening physical systems:

"Fundamentally, we must abandon the idea that there is a specific standard to which we can control nature and instead understand that we are creating complex and increasingly difficult-to-control systems that are part social, part ecological and part technological. These mean not just redesigning the infrastructure, but redesigning institutions and their knowledge systems."

After the destruction and disruption from Hurricane Sandy, New York City didn't just upgrade its power substations and subway entrances, Miller said in a subsequent phone call. The city also rebooted its agencies' protocols and even job descriptions. "Every time a maintenance crew opens a sewer cover, fixes or installs a pipe, whether new or retrofitting, you're thinking how to enhance its resilience," Miller said.

Miller said another key to progress, particularly when federal action is limited or stalled, is cooperation between cities or regions. Heat was not an issue in Oregon historically, Miller said, but it's becoming one. The light rail system around Portland was designed to work with a few 90-degree days a year, he said. "The last couple of summers have seen 20-plus 90-degree days," he said, causing copper wires carrying power for the trains to sag and steel rails to expand in ways that have disrupted train schedules. Similar rail systems in the Southwest deal with such heat routinely, said Miller, who has worked in both regions. The more crosstalk, the better the outcome, he said.

"At the broadest level, we need to think about risks and how infrastructure is built to withstand them at a landscape level," Miller added. "We can longer commit to evaluating the impacts and risks of a single project in isolation against a retrospective, stationary understanding of risk (e.g., the 100-year flood we've been hearing so much about)."

He said that an emerging alternative, "safe-to-fail" design, is more suited to situations where factors contributing to extreme floods or other storm impacts can't be fully anticipated. "Safe-to-fail infrastructure might allow flooding, but in ways that are designed for," he said.

(With an Arizona State colleague, Mikhail Chester, Miller offered more details in a commentary published last week by The Conversation website, laying out "six rules for rebuilding infrastructure in an era of 'unprecedented' weather events.")

Deborah Brosnan, an environmental and disaster risk consultant, said the challenge in making a shift to integrating changing risks into planning and investments is enormous, even when a community has a devastating shock such as a hurricane or flood or both:

"It requires a radical shift in how we incorporate variability in our planning and regulations," she said. "This can and will be politically difficult. New regulations like California fire and earthquake codes and Florida's building codes are typically enacted after an event, and from a reactive 'make sure this doesn't happen again' perspective. The past event creates a 'standard' against which to regulate. Regulations and codes require a standard that can be upheld, otherwise decisions can be arbitrary and capricious. For climate change, non-stationarity would involve creating regulations that take account of many different factors and where variability has to be included. Variability (uncertainty) is the big challenge for these kinds of approaches."

Stephane Hallegatte, the lead economist at the Word Bank's Global Facility for Disaster Reduction and Recovery, has written or co-written a host of reports on strategies for limiting impacts of climate change and disasters, particularly on the poor. When asked in an email exchange what success would look like, he said the World Bank, in various recent reports, has stressed the importance of managing disaster risks along two tracks: both designing and investing to limit the most frequent hard knocks and then making sure the tools and services are available to help communities recover when a worst-case disaster strikes.

He added: "Facing a problem, people tend to do one thing to manage it, and then forget about it. ('I face floods; I build a dike; I'm safe.') We are trying to work against this, by having risk prevention and contingent planning done together."

14. Cap and Trade Is Supposed to Solve Climate Change, but Oil and Gas Company Emissions Are Up*

Lisa Song

Gov. Jerry Brown took the podium at a July 2017 press conference to lingering applause after a steady stream of politicians praised him for helping to extend California's signature climate policy for another decade. Brown, flanked by the U.S. and California flags, with a backdrop of the gleaming San Francisco Bay, credited the hard work of the VIPs seated in the crowd. "It's people in industry, and they're here!" he said. "Shall we mention them? People representing oil, agriculture, business, Chamber of Commerce, food processing. ... Plus, we have environmentalists...."

Diverse, bipartisan interests working together to pass climate legislation—it was the polar opposite of Washington, where the Trump administration was rolling back environmental protections established under President Barack Obama.

Brown called California's cap-and-trade program an answer to the "existential" crisis of climate change, the most reasonable way to manage the state's massive output of greenhouse gasses while preserving its economy, which is powered by fossil fuels. "You can't just say overnight, 'OK, we're not going to have oil anymore,'" he said.

But there are growing concerns with California's much-admired, much-imitated program, with implications that stretch far beyond the state.

California's cap-and-trade program was one of the first in the world, and it is among the largest. It is premised on the idea that instead of using regulations to force companies to curb their emissions, polluters can be made to pay for every ton of CO_2 they emit, providing them with an incentive to lower emissions on their own. This market-based approach has gained such traction that the Paris climate agreement emphasizes it as the primary way countries can meet their goals to lower worldwide emissions. More than 50 programs have been developed across the world, many inspired by California.

But while the state's program has helped it meet some initial, easily attained benchmarks, experts are increasingly worried that it is allowing California's biggest polluters to conduct business as usual and even increase their emissions.

ProPublica analyzed state data in a way the state doesn't often report to the public,

---

*This story was originally published by ProPublica as Lisa Song, "Cap and Trade Is Supposed to Solve Climate Change, but Oil and Gas Company Emissions Are Up," https://www.propublica.org/article/cap-and-trade-is-supposed-to-solve-climate-change-but-oil-and-gas-company-emissions-are-up (Nov. 15, 2019). Reprinted with permission of the publisher.

isolating how emissions have grown within the oil and gas industry. The analysis shows that carbon emissions from California's oil and gas industry actually rose 3.5 percent since cap and trade began. Refineries, including one owned by Marathon Petroleum and two owned by Chevron, are consistently the largest polluters in the state. Emissions from vehicles, which burn the fuels processed in refineries, are also rising.

Critics attribute these increases, in part, to a bevy of concessions the state has made to the oil and gas industry to keep the program going. They say these compromises have blocked steps that would have mandated real emissions reductions and threaten the state's ability to meet its ambitious goal of slashing its emissions 40 percent by 2030.

"There's no question a well-designed regulation on oil and gas can have an effect," said Danny Cullenward, a Stanford researcher and policy director at Near Zero, a climate policy think tank. "And that was traded away for a weak cap-and-trade program."

Experts say cap and trade is rarely stringent enough when used alone; direct regulations on refineries and cars are crucial to reining in emissions. But oil representatives are engaged in a worldwide effort to make market-based solutions the primary or only way their emissions are regulated.

Officials with the state Air Resources Board, which oversees cap and trade, say those fears are exaggerated, that California's program is doing what it needs to do, and they can tweak it over time as needed. They point to the state's overall drop in emissions since cap and trade began in 2013, even as its economy grew. They tout a host of other, more traditional climate regulations widely considered the best in the country.

But even with all those rules working together, California needs to more than double its yearly emissions cuts to be on track to meet the 2030 target. Meanwhile, the scope of the climate crisis and public pressure for strong regulations on fossil fuel companies have risen exponentially, even in the past year.

ProPublica delved into the mechanics of California's cap-and-trade program, examining 13 years of political horse-trading, regulatory tinkering, and industry lobbying to make sense of rising fears that it will not deliver the emissions reductions it is supposed to.

Five areas of concerns have emerged, some specific to the state's program and some so fundamental that they raise questions about whether market solutions anywhere can do the work that is needed to take meaningful climate action while there is still time.

Cap and Trade Isn't Designed to Hold Any One Company Accountable

It treats every polluting facility as if it were engaged in a giant group project. If enough companies in California reduce their emissions, the entire state gets an A, despite the slackers who didn't pull their weight.

Here's how it works: The state sets a cap, or limit, on CO_2 emissions from major polluters. The emissions under that cap are turned into permits, which each give the owner permission to release 1 metric ton of CO_2. Some are given out for free. Others are sold at auction by the state, and the funds are used for climate programs like electric vehicle rebates. Companies with more permits than they need can sell the extras, enabling other companies to buy the right to emit more, hence the trade.

Supply and demand helps determine how much each permit is worth. The cap gets lowered every year, theoretically applying increasing pressure on polluters to reduce emissions. There were 346 million available permits in 2019.

The program was born of a goal set in an executive order by Gov. Arnold Schwarzenegger in 2005: for the state to lower its CO_2 emissions 25 percent by 2020. The following year, the Legislature put the Air Resources Board in charge of figuring out how to do it. Europe had already put into place a market solution, and a coalition of northeastern American states followed a few years later. In 2013, California launched its cap and trade program.

In 2016, the state hit its climate target four years early. But a government report concluded that the "cap is likely not having much, if any, effect on overall emissions," and that reductions up to that point could be attributed to the 2008 recession, which slowed manufacturing, consumption and travel, as well as climate rules on renewable energy and vehicle standards.

The board predicted cap and trade would account for 30 percent of reductions in 2020—but even after the state met its first benchmark, the board has not calculated how much the program has reduced emissions. This kind of study is hard to do; the only available analysis comes from Chris Busch of Energy Innovation, a climate policy think tank, who estimates that in 2015 and 2016, cap and trade was responsible for only 4 percent to 15 percent of the state's reductions.

Erica Morehouse, a senior attorney at the Environmental Defense Fund, said California's climate policy operates "as a team sport," so it doesn't matter how much of the heavy lifting is being done by cap and trade, as long as the state's overall emissions stay under the cap. She said the other regulations alone can't ensure California will meet the 2030 goal.

Now that cap and trade has been extended, the board predicts it will drive 47 percent of the CO_2 reductions in 2030, but critics wonder how much it will actually deliver. "It's very difficult to have any faith in those projections," given that the board hasn't provided any "quantifiable evidence" of what cap and trade has achieved so far, said Kevin de León, former state Senate president and a candidate running for Los Angeles City Council.

What became most clear about the cap-and-trade program after it hit the first benchmark was how it can mask increases. According to a study from California researchers, almost all the CO_2 savings came from the electricity sector, which cut its use of imported power from out-of-state coal plants. It was low-hanging fruit, cheap savings that will be hard to repeat. The cut was enough to make up for emissions increases even within that sector; pollution from in-state power generation increased.

In fact, most facilities—52 percent—increased average emissions within California during the first three years of cap and trade. These include cement and power plants as well as producers and suppliers of oil and gas.

The way market-based climate change solutions are set up provides loopholes and giveaways.

The success of any cap-and-trade program depends on how it is designed, starting with the cap. Experts warn that California set its early caps too high, allowing companies to buy permits and bank them for the future when the cap gets tougher. A peer-reviewed paper co-authored by Cullenward found that by the end of 2018, companies had banked more than 200 million permits—enough for almost as many tons of CO_2 as the total reductions expected from cap and trade from 2021 to 2030.

Though the purpose of the system is to apply financial pressure to industry, California gave away a bunch of free permits to companies they worried would face a competitive disadvantage compared with those outside the state. Those that couldn't feasibly relocate had to buy permits at market price. A dozen industries, including oil and gas drilling, got most of their permits for free through 2020.

Refineries got the same treatment for the first few years, and the board planned to reduce the free permits in 2018. But when cap and trade was extended in 2017, state officials extended the same level of giveaways through 2030.

Cap and trade offers another way for polluters to avoid reducing emissions at their facilities: Many programs allow companies to cancel out some of their CO_2 by purchasing what are called offsets—paying to protect trees or clean up coal mine emissions in another city, state or country.

Studies raise serious questions about whether offsets in California's program are canceling out the emissions they're meant to. A ProPublica investigation highlighted similar concerns involving international forest offsets, which California supports. The biggest buyers of offsets are the worst polluters in the state, with oil companies at the top of the list.

Although state regulators have reduced the number of future allowable offsets, Barbara Haya, a University of California–Berkeley research fellow who studies carbon markets, said they could account for half of all emissions cuts expected to be achieved by cap and trade from 2021 to 2030, making the environmental integrity of the offsets paramount. Her research found that California regulators have oversold the climate benefit of offsets by underestimating how protecting one patch of forest pushes logging into other forests. The board stands by its calculations, and the two sides have continued to debate the issue.

Cap-and-trade programs usually include offsets, and "offset programs largely don't work," Haya said. At this critical moment, when so many people are developing market solutions, "it really worries me that we are going to implement policies that reduce emissions on paper and not in practice," she said.

Among the most fundamental design elements of cap and trade is the price of carbon, ultimately what is supposed to force businesses to change. Economists have tried to find the lowest cost per ton that will move them. A new paper co-authored by Gernot Wagner, an economist at New York University, found that the accepted wisdom on carbon pricing—which aims for an initial cost of roughly $40 a ton that grows over time—is far from sufficient. His research concluded prices should start much higher, well above $100 a ton, and get lower over time as technologies improve and uncertainties about the extent of climate damage clear up.

California's price is $17 a ton. Regulators can strengthen the program by setting a minimum permit price; in California, it's currently $16. A World Bank report recommends prices of $40 to $80 by 2020 to be on track for the Paris climate goals. Only a handful of the world's market programs meet that standard.

Stanley Young, the board's communications director, said that it can take time for cap and trade to affect industries like oil and gas, and that the mere presence of a carbon price impacts corporate decisions in ways that aren't always visible. Rajinder Sahota, an assistant division chief at the board, points to the fact that permit prices are climbing; state data shows they have increased from about $13 to $17 over the past three years. Sahota says that alone should serve as a warning signal to industry that one day, the cost to pollute will be unaffordable.

California's oil industry has blocked efforts to make cap and trade tougher on them.

The Western States Petroleum Association, the main oil industry group in California, has lobbied on cap and trade every quarter since 2006, spending $88 million on it and other regulations. Records show the industry has advocated on virtually every aspect of its design, including offsets, fees and the allocation of permits.

Its biggest wins happened in 2017, when cap and trade was up for extension. Two bills aimed to make the extension contingent on forcing emissions reductions by restricting offsets and free permits.

One introduced by Sen. Bob Wieckowski tried to force banked permits to expire by 2020 and get rid of offsets. Vox called it "the most important advance in carbon-pricing policy in the U.S. in a decade. Maybe ever." But it needed a two-thirds majority vote to pass the Legislature, thanks to an oil industry-sponsored ballot measure from 2010 that reclassified many state and local fees as taxes. The measure had a huge impact on environmental regulations; the only viable bills now were those that could gain broad political buy-in. Wieckowski's bill was viewed as too radical to support and never got a vote. He said he couldn't even get a meeting with the governor about it.

The other bill, by Assemblywoman Cristina Garcia, proposed using cap and trade to limit the toxic gases that streamed out of smokestacks alongside CO_2. Garcia's district in Los Angeles was among the most polluted in the state. Her bill made companies with rising CO_2 or toxic pollutants ineligible for free permits. In three months in 2017, Chevron spent $6.3 million lobbying against her bill and related regulations, while WSPA lobbied against both Garcia's bill and Wieckowski's. Each effort had a lobbyist who was a former state legislator.

Garcia's bill had initial support from a crucial constituency: labor unions representing construction workers. That changed after Chevron promised the unions a five-year contract to retrofit its refineries—the result of a safety bill inspired by a 2012 fire at its Richmond facility, which sent thousands of people to the hospital with breathing problems. Cesar Diaz, who lobbied for the unions, said his organization supports climate regulation. Its opposition to Garcia's bill had nothing to do with the Chevron deal, he said, but was inspired by fears that it would hurt the economy.

The defeats prompted Brown to step in to save the extension, holding closed-door meetings with moderate legislators and oil interests deep into the night, according to several sources with knowledge of the negotiations.

The industry's influence became clear after articles revealed how draft language in the emerging bill matched a "wish list" from a lobbying firm working for WSPA. The list included tools to slow rising carbon prices and increased free permits for oil and gas among other industries—all things that ended up in the final bill and subsequent amendments. Brown later testified in a state Senate hearing, where he called it the most important vote of the legislators' lives.

Brown, whose term ended in January, declined to be interviewed for this story. In response to ProPublica's inquiries about cap and trade, Brown's spokesman pointed to the broad coalition of environmental, academic and industry interests that supported the bill, and he emphasized that program is just one part of California's extensive climate regulations.

Morehouse, the EDF attorney, said the oil industry may have won a few battles with the bill, but it "lost the war." California has maintained an extremely ambitious 2030 target, she said.

It's no surprise the oil industry advocates for its own interests, Morehouse said.

"First they want no climate policy. Then they want it delayed as long as it can be. Then they want it to be basically meaningless," she said. By the time the industry starts focusing on something like free permits, "you can actually start negotiating."

WSPA, which opposes direct regulations, praised the extension's passage as "the best, most balanced" solution, "the best available path forward for our industry in the toughest regulatory environment in the world."

Dean Florez, an Air Resources Board member critical of the concessions made, said the industry supports the new program because it "figured out how to game the system." The industry got almost everything it wanted, he said, leaving it "offset happy and surplus rich."

More Meaningful Regulations Are Being Sacrificed

One of the industry's biggest victories from the 2017 bill was a provision that prohibits new CO_2 regulations on refineries and oil and gas production. Earlier that year, the Air Resources Board had proposed a regulation to lower refinery emissions 20 percent by 2030. The bill killed that plan.

The bill also prevented local air districts from imposing regional caps on CO_2, heading off a five-year grassroots effort from Bay Area residents. Incensed by the Richmond refinery fire, they packed into hearings held by the Bay Area Air Quality Management District and waited for hours to speak.

The residents lobbied for a cap on CO_2 as a way to force reductions in other pollutants. Their plan was on the verge of approval, with a draft rule that local regulators hailed as an unprecedented "model for the state and nation to follow." Then, the state cap-and-trade bill rendered it moot.

For the oil industry, the strategy of embracing market solutions to avoid more direct regulation extends far beyond California.

At an international climate conference last year, Shell Oil executive David Hone boasted he had written a key part of the United Nations' Paris agreement that makes market solutions the primary way to deal with climate change. "The ideal for a cap-and-trade system is to have no overlapping policies," he told The Intercept.

In Washington state, oil interests led by BP defeated a statewide carbon tax ballot initiative partly because the proposal didn't include provisions to preempt other climate rules. InsideClimate News reported that BP helped derail an earlier attempt to pass the tax through the Legislature after the governor wouldn't make certain concessions, like allowing its refineries to use offsets to lower their tax payments or prohibiting local governments from creating or enforcing their own climate regulations.

On a national level, Exxon Mobil, BP and Shell helped economists, environmentalists and bipartisan former politicians with the Climate Leadership Council design a federal carbon tax of $40 a ton—one that's contingent on eliminating all other federal climate regulations on major polluters such as power plants and refineries. The council cites a report by an energy policy group that says the tax would help the U.S. meet its Paris targets.

"Exceeding the U.S.'s Paris goals is, of course, good and a terrific start. But it's only a start," Wagner, the NYU economist, said. The Paris targets aren't stringent enough to avoid the worst impacts of climate change. Wagner said oil companies support the tax because it's "much too little" for the kind of change that's needed.

"That is a very clear instance where the single-minded push for a carbon tax gets in the way of ambitious climate policy," he said. "Why settle for what Exxon wants?"

We're Dependent on Fossil Fuels

Just 20 fossil fuel companies—including Chevron, BP and Exxon Mobil—are responsible for a third of all global emissions since 1965. There is overwhelming evidence that ensuring a livable planet requires keeping fossil fuels in the ground, unextracted and unburned.

But fossil fuels are so integrated into our lives that phasing them out would require us to change everything about how and where we live, how we get around and how we make money. Fuel prices affect everyone, and while higher carbon prices help the environment, they can be passed on to consumers. The industry is quick to remind everyone of this of any time an environmental regulation comes up.

When California's Air Resources Board held a hearing last year to discuss the maximum allowed permit price, dozens of speakers turned up to testify, including a group of black pastors from Los Angeles who'd advocated against oil and gas drilling in their communities. One by one, the pastors said the board proposal would hurt low-income, minority families.

The group was organized by the Rev. Jonathan Moseley, Sr., who said he heard about the event from a contact at Prime Strategies, a consulting firm that gave him free updates on policy discussions in Sacramento. Moseley said Prime offered to fly the pastors to the hearing, and he believed the money came from a group called Californians for Affordable and Reliable Energy, or CARE.

He said he didn't know CARE was funded by oil interests. CARE's 2017 tax forms, the most recent available, show it raised $9 million that year. Nearly two-thirds of the money came from Chevron and WSPA, according to lobbying records. CARE also gave Prime Strategies $53,000 around the time of the hearing.

Robert Lapsley, the chairman of CARE, said the group represents business interests beyond oil and gas. It is led by the California Business Roundtable, a trade group for the state's biggest companies. Lapsley said CARE advocates for regulators to consider how climate regulations affect consumer costs. CARE helped craft and lobby for the cap-and-trade extension and solicited funds from donors like WSPA who had similar goals, he said.

CARE's public campaigns have used the images of blue-collar workers and people of color to argue against initiatives promoting electric cars and other efforts aimed at reducing fossil fuel consumption. Its homepage features a young man and woman studying a piece of paper. The description, according to a stock images website that sells the photo, is, in part, "African Millennial stressed married couple sitting on sofa at home checking unpaid bills." The page also features a photo and quote from Bishop Lovester Adams, another pastor who testified before the board. Adams and Prime Strategies did not return requests for comment.

At the hearing, the Rev. Oliver Buie said, "I'm here to stand and speak for the community which I represent, which is a brown community, which is deeply injured whenever there's any increase in any cost.... We need to look at the people more than the corporations." But he, too, acknowledged he was unaware that oil interests effectively backed his Sacramento trip. "They didn't tell us they were a wolf," he said. "We thought they were a sheep."

The board seemed puzzled by the resistance at the hearing and voted to maintain the maximum allowable price of nearly $100 a ton by 2030. The effort was mostly symbolic, as regulators assured the crowd they didn't expect prices to get that high. Instead, Sahota, the assistant division chief, predicted it would hover at the minimum price for the next few years, but rise above it by 2030.

Cullenward said the reality of society's reliance on fossil fuels leaves regulators in a bind—stuck between knowing what it will take to manage climate change but adopting a market solution that's too weak by design. Any attempt to seriously strengthen it risks a consumer backlash that makes it "politically toxic," he said.

"Essentially, what we're doing is kicking the can," Cullenward said. "We're saying, keep prices low, let's not do a lot, and later, we'll hope for a miracle."

15. Endangered Species Under GOP?

Climate Change Information on the Web[*]

ANDREW REVKIN

James Rowen, a longtime Wisconsin journalist and environmental blogger, recently discovered a stark remaking of a state Department of Natural Resources webpage on climate change and the Great Lakes.

Until December, the page, dating from the Democratic administration of former Gov. James Doyle, had this headline—"Climate Change and Wisconsin's Great Lakes"—and a clear description of the state of the science, including this line reflecting the latest federal and international research assessments: "Earth's climate is changing. Human activities that increase heat-trapping ('green house') gases are the main cause."

The page described a variety of possible impacts on the lakes and concluded, "The good news is that we can all work to slow climate change and lessen its effects." Nine hyperlinks led readers to other resources.

While the web address still includes /greatlakes/climatechange, the page, managed under agency appointees of Republican Gov. Scott Walker, now has this headline: "The Great Lakes and a changing world." It now says this:

> As it has done throughout the centuries, the earth is going through a change. The reasons for this change at this particular time in the earth's long history are being debated and researched by academic entities outside the Wisconsin Department of Natural Resources. The effects of such a change are also being debated but whatever the causes and effects, the DNR's responsibility is to manage our state's natural resources through whatever event presents itself.

There are now just two hyperlinks, one of which goes to a University of Wisconsin website about the environment and climate in the Yahara River watershed, which is not even connected to the Great Lakes. The other goes to the main page of the Center for Climatic Research at the University of Wisconsin. One has to poke around a while to get back to the issue at hand—the impact of global warming on the Great Lakes.

James Dick, a spokesman for the Department of Natural Resources, sent a response

---

*This story was originally published by ProPublica as Andrew Revkin, "Endangered Species Under GOP? Climate Change Information on the Web," https://www.propublica.org/article/endangered-species-under-gop-climate-change-information-on-the-web (Jan. 4, 2017). Reprinted with permission of the publisher.

explaining the changes on the webpage, asserting that the page "does not say the cause and effects of the change in climate are debatable."

"It says they are being debated. There's a difference," Dick said. "Many scientists may be in agreement but this topic is still the subject of much debate and discussion among the general public."

It's not unusual for elected state or national leaders to filter or shape government sources of information on contentious topics, including climate change, to suit their particular policy goals. Climate scientists decried such efforts through much of the presidency of George W. Bush, particularly when handwritten edits of government climate reports by political appointees were leaked in 2005.

Under President Obama, websites highlight points that supported his carbon-cutting plans, while findings that might point to different policies tended to stay deep in the body of reports.

One example is the treatment of hurricanes in the 2014 National Climate Assessment. The prominent text blurb of the report home page is, "The intensity, frequency, and duration of North Atlantic hurricanes, as well as the frequency of the strongest hurricanes, have all increased since the early 1980s. Hurricane intensity and rainfall are projected to increase as the climate continues to warm."

Buried in the report, there's this line, which seems to qualify the actual threats previously highlighted: "[F]ewer storms have been observed to strike land during warmer years even though overall activity is higher than average, which may help to explain the lack of any clear trend in landfall frequency along the U.S. eastern and Gulf coasts."

And so it's entirely likely that the recent web revisions in Wisconsin portend what's to come in Washington, given how Walker's approach to climate change and industry resonates with that of many people in President-elect Donald Trump's circle of advisers.

In a phone interview, the Wisconsin blogger Rowen said he certainly suspects that his state's experience is a troubling template for what could happen now at the federal level. "If you have one-party control over all units of government and that party has a pro-corporate, anti-environment mindset, everything will be coordinated, whether in law, executive action or judicial review," he said.

Parties on all sides of the climate policy debate are now watching closely to see what happens to a vast array of webpages on climate change created during the Obama administration as Trump's fossil-fuel friendly Cabinet choices and environmental team get to work.

Early signs, including a 74-question survey sent to Department of Energy employees (which the Trump transition team quickly disavowed as unsanctioned), had environmentalists and scientists deeply worried.

Some scurried to set up independent archives for potentially vulnerable climate data, with a repository established by the Technoscience Research Unit at the University of Toronto.

With Republicans in control in most states, and with the incoming White House and Congress committed to undoing President Obama's climate policies, the "uncertainty" theme around climate change appears likely to become popular.

To be sure, enduring uncertainty does surround many of the most consequential aspects of global warming, like the speed of sea-level rise and extent of warming in this century. But for decades risk experts and economists with a varied range of political views have agreed that uncertain, but momentous outcomes are the reason to act—not a reason to delay.

And the data continue to accrue, with 2016 now set to be the warmest on Earth since at least 1880, when thorough temperature record keeping began, and a new study finding that, if anything, warming has been underestimated in recent years because of imperfect analysis of ocean data gathered by ships and buoys.

Lately, the wider climate-skeptic chorus has been dominated by Walker-style references to uncertainty or complexity in climate science, crystallized by phrases like "I'm not a scientist" and "the climate has always changed."

When we wrote to Wisconsin officials seeking an explanation for the changes on the website, Dick, the natural resources department spokesman, sent the following email:

> As we do from time to time with other website pages, we updated a webpage that had not been updated in several years. The update reflects our position on this topic which we have communicated for years—that our agency regularly must respond to a variety of environmental and human stressors from drought, flooding, and wind events to changing demographics.
>
> Our agency must be ready to respond to each of these challenges using the best science available to us. That is our role in this issue. Adaptation has been our position on this topic for some time. The recent update to one single webpage on our website was intended to reflect this perspective and approach to the topic.
>
> The updated page does not deny climate is changing and it does not challenge the dedicated work of the scientists who are working on this issue. In fact, this updated page links to U.W.-Madison programs that include climate change in their research. It also does not say the cause and effects of the change in climate are debatable. It says they are being debated. There's a difference. Many scientists may be in agreement, but this topic is still the subject of much debate and discussion among the general public.

The last line raises a question about the role of government in helping explain to the public what many scientists agree on.

One thing that seems true is that so much information has accrued around climate change science and what it means for policy in recent years that partisans seeking to purge government websites have their work cut out for them.

If you search the Wisconsin Department of Natural Resources website, for instance, for the phrase "climate change" there are still some hits, including an educational resource for kids titled, "Global Warming is Hot Stuff!"

There's still an article posted from the February 2011, issue of the magazine of the natural resources department, in which Jack Sullivan, then the director of the agency's Bureau of Science Services, said, "We need to think about what climate change means for our natural resources and get out ahead of this problem, and we're working hard to do that."

Sullivan, however, retired in 2015, when the agency's science budget was deeply cut under Walker and a Republican-dominated Legislature.

16. California Fires Illuminate Trauma and Resilience*

Anna Maria Barry-Jester

SANTA ROSA, Calif.—Dorothy Hammack had planned to wash her thick, dark hair in the kitchen sink Friday morning. She couldn't yet shower, due to the incision on her breast from a biopsy a few days before. Her doctor had already called to let her know the results: She had breast cancer.

She was supposed to be researching treatment options and organizing doctor appointments. Instead, Hammack, 79, was standing in her pajamas in the parking lot of a makeshift evacuation center in Santa Rosa, the urban center of Sonoma County's celebrated wine country. The Kincade Fire was blazing in the mountains above the home she shared in nearby Windsor with her fiancé, Aldo Lovati, 64. Winds predicted to be fast and furious were expected that evening, and the couple was among the 180,000 people who ultimately would be ordered to evacuate as the fire tore through the rugged terrain of northeastern Sonoma County and bore steadily southwest.

Much to Hammack's dismay, her hair remained wrapped in a gray-and-black nightcap. There had been no time to wash it. She was upbeat, though, laughing at the stream of banter and jokes Lovati told to keep them distracted.

By Saturday, hundreds of others would join them at the shelter set up by the Red Cross at the Santa Rosa Veterans Memorial Building, in the southwestern corner of the city. Across the street, hundreds more evacuees got set up at the Sonoma County Fairgrounds. Like Hammack, many of them came with ongoing health concerns and urgent medical needs made all more challenging by the chaos of evacuation.

Peggy Goebel, a nurse from Windsor, was helping oversee the medical operation, run largely by volunteers who had responded to calls from Goebel or their employers to lend their services. They provided basic care (like making sure Hammack's incision was clean) and helped people fill prescriptions or get medical equipment such as walkers and wheelchairs. There were also licensed therapists trained to counsel people during disasters.

This is Goebel's third year volunteering with the Red Cross, a relationship that began

*Originally published as Anna Maria Barry-Jester, "California Fires Illuminate Trauma and Resilience," *Kaiser Health News*, https://khn.org/news/california-fires-illuminate-trauma-and-resilience-emergency-shelters-health-care/ (October 29, 2019). Kaiser Health News is a nonprofit news service covering health issues. It is an editorially independent program of the Kaiser Family Foundation that is not affiliated with Kaiser Permanente. This story was produced by Kaiser Health News, which publishes California Healthline, an editorially independent service of the California Health Care Foundation. Reprinted with permission of the publisher.

during another fire. Twenty-five hours into a shift with no foreseeable end, she still had enough spunk to organize newly arrived volunteer physicians from the local Sutter Health hospital and nursing students from Santa Rosa Junior College, where she teaches. As she showed them around, a fire blazed across the street from her home in Windsor. She didn't know whether the house would be there when she got back. Her sister's wasn't when she returned after the 2017 Tubbs Fire, a massive wildfire that devastated Santa Rosa, killing 22 people and incinerating thousands of homes.

"It's very traumatic. People just passed the anniversary of the 2017 fires, and they went through this big PTSD," Goebel said. "Lots of people had issues."

Two years ago, the situation was very different. In 2017, people arrived at the shelters in the middle of the night, startled awake by a fire that roared fast and unexpected from the forested hills north of town. They came without shoes, in their nightgowns, without medicines, money or important documents. "That was hard to deal with, trying to provide physical, emotional, medical support," Goebel said.

This time around, people were calmer, because they had time to prepare. The scale of evacuations posed a challenge, but it was nothing like the last time, she said.

That let the medical personnel focus on the extreme needs of some people who ended up at the shelter. There was the frail elderly woman who was near death when she arrived—another volunteer called nearly two dozen convalescent facilities before finding one that could take the woman, ensuring she wouldn't die in the shelter. And there was the elderly man with dementia who had been dropped off alone. Afraid he might wander away or otherwise hurt himself, fellow evacuees volunteered to look after him during the night.

A police officer brought an elderly woman with Parkinson's disease after the people living with her decided they couldn't take her with them during the evacuation. She was taken to a room at the shelter where the elder residents of an assisted living facility in Healdsburg were lined up in hospital beds, many accompanied by their caretakers.

The Red Cross volunteers always ask those caretakers to stay, said Goebel. Not everyone in need came with help, though. Among them were people with Alzheimer's disease and a man with multiple sclerosis.

As she made her way between the veterans' hall and the fairgrounds, Goebel said she was rejuvenated by how quickly people mobilized to help one another, and the resilience of her community after the last set of big fires.

Not only had the community pulled together, but it was much better prepared this time. The winds whipping through the region at 70 to 80 mph were stronger than they had been in 2017. But through mass evacuations and an all-hands-on-deck assault on the fire, authorities and firefighters so far have prevented the worst. As of Tuesday morning, there were no deaths and just a couple of injuries.

Patients in the hospitals across the county that had been evacuated were transferred to other facilities without incident. A doctor described the parade of newborns in their tiny beds, taken from Sutter Santa Rosa Regional Hospital's neonatal intensive care unit and transferred to hospitals farther south. As buses pulled away with patients, two people stood outside clutching a balloon reading, "Congratulations."

On Saturday, the day after his arrival, Aldo Lovati walked across the same parking lot he had stood in the day before, wearing the same green long-sleeve shirt and gray sweatpants. Today, he was much quieter. It had been a rough night of little sleep in close quarters. He was mad at himself for being ungrateful—he desperately wanted to focus on the generosity of strangers, and how lucky they were to have food and shelter. But he was feeling tired, sad and frustrated. "I've lost my dignity in here; I just really feel that I've lost my dignity," he said.

Lovati had struggled through some mental health issues that predate the fire. A breakdown a few years ago had taken a toll on family relationships, and it was all coming to the surface now that he was in need of help. "It's gotten to me. I just want to go home," he said.

Hammack wandered out to find him, her thick, dark hair fluttering in the wind, and the two held hands as they talked. She, too, was feeling more tired than the day before, and the news of her diagnosis was starting to set in. The incision from her biopsy hurt; she was supposed to put hot compresses and pressure on it and made do with unused sanitary pads she'd gotten at the makeshift Red Cross clinic. They began to laugh again, recounting how she'd pulled one out to give him when they couldn't find a napkin at lunch.

Hammack said she was tired and wanted to go back in to lie down on a cot. Lovati agreed she should be lying down and asked why she had come out. "We're a couple, right? We look out for one another," she replied.

17. How to Zero In on Your Final, Forever Home While Skirting Disaster*

JANICE LLOYD

When Martha Powers and Larry Gomberg heard the news about Hurricane Florence bringing horrific winds and catastrophic flooding to Wilmington, N.C., they grimaced.

Then, they felt relieved.

"What if we had decided to build our retirement home there?" they said to each other in September, when the storm was making headlines. "What if our brand-new home had flooded?"

Like many of the 10,000 boomers hitting retirement age each day, Powers and Gomberg are deciding to move now that they've retired. After coming close to putting a deposit on a home in Wilmington this past summer, they found a 55-and-over community just 60 minutes from where they live in Fairfax, Va., outside Washington, D.C. They're building a new home in Lake Frederick, Va., near the Blue Ridge Mountains, and will move there in March.

They examined factors including access to quality medical care, affordability, culture and safety. That includes safety from hurricanes and deadly wildfires, like the ones that gutted the rural town of Paradise, Calif., a popular retirement area filled with senior communities.

During their two-year search, Powers, 63, and Gomberg, 67, kept separate lists. "At first, I thought I wanted to walk on a beach every day," said Powers. "Larry thought he wanted to live in California. I was trying so hard to like California I was making myself sick.

"Then we visited Lake Frederick again and agreed we liked the people, the location and decided we could still use our same doctors if we wanted to. Suddenly, walking on a beach didn't seem as important as all those things."

They visited potential new homes several times and spent the night, research that is invaluable, said Fuller. "Visit the area during every season to make sure the climate suits you," she said.

And when figuring out costs and affordability, be sure to determine the price of flood insurance and other insurance you might need, depending on the location.

---

*Originally published as Janice Lloyd, "How To Zero In On Your Final, Forever Home While Skirting Disaster," *Kaiser Health News*, https://khn.org/news/how-to-zero-in-on-your-final-forever-home-while-skirting-disaster/ (March 13, 2019). Kaiser Health News is a nonprofit news service covering health issues. It is an editorially independent program of the Kaiser Family Foundation that is not affiliated with Kaiser Permanente. Reprinted with permission of the publisher.

Finding an area that has "zero risk is very difficult," Fuller said. Asked if retirees should rule out locations where sea levels are rising or wildfires are becoming more destructive, she said: "It's impossible to answer that with a blanket answer. Many areas of the country have some sort of risk from hurricanes to flooding, to tornadoes, to sinkholes, to wildfires, to scorching heat, to high winds, etc."

Problems with mobility often surface around ages 82 to 85, said Ginny Helms, president of LeadingAge Georgia, making safe surroundings very important.

That dangerous reality surfaced in November during the California Camp Fire blaze. Younger retirees who were still driving were more likely to flee to safety, while some older residents with no means of escape were left behind.

That was almost the case for 93-year-old Margaret Newsum, who was standing outside her home with her walker looking for help as the fire approached, according to CNN. She was whisked to safety by Dane Ray Cummings, a garbageman who had been told to cut short his route. Instead of doing that, he looked for people in trouble. He took Newsum home to care for her rather than take her to a shelter. Since the fire, she's been staying with one of Cummings' close friends.

Older people are resilient, but Helms said seniors should anticipate changes that might accompany aging.

That's a message Rita Parsons understands. Parsons didn't want to have to worry about maintaining a home after her husband passed away two years ago. That's when Parsons, 74, moved to Greenspring Village, a facility in Springfield, Va., with accommodations for independent living, assisted living and nursing home care. Within such communities, residents can move from one level of care to another.

"They take care of everything for me here," she said. "They come and change the filters in the heat pump twice a year. If a lightbulb burns out in the kitchen, I don't have to deal with a ladder to change it. All I have to do is call building services. This makes life easy."

Parsons doesn't have children and feels very secure about having her doctors on campus and optional nursing care if she needs it. When she first moved in, she said, a bad knee made climbing stairs difficult. "But since I've lived here, I walk a couple miles a day, go to the gym and swim several times a week," she said. "Now, my knee is fine, and I try to use the stairs as much as possible to stay in shape."

At Greenspring, home to nearly 2,000 residents, she walks to church services and loves square dancing, line dancing, movies and other classes.

"We say it's a lot like living on a cruise ship, but you don't have to deal with motion sickness," she said.

Plus, it's a tightknit community. "I had lived in a condo at one point in my life and never got to know my neighbors," she said. "One of the best things about living here is everyone looks out for each other.

"I'll be here the rest of my life."

Powers and Gomberg expect to age in place, too. If they can no longer live independently at Lake Frederick, Gomberg said, they will have the financial resources to move to an assisted living facility.

"We've visited several of them, and we know they're not for us yet," he said.

"Then when we toured Lake Frederick—we knew it was right. Many people there are just like us, professionals from the D.C. area, well-educated and liberal. We knew we'd have lots to talk about with them. We also liked the layout of the homes. We have plenty of space, and I found my man cave."

18. Hurricane Maria's Legacy

*Thousands of Puerto Rican Students Show PTSD Symptoms**

Carmen Heredia Rodriguez

Food shortages, damaged homes, fear of death, loved ones leaving. The cumulative stresses of Hurricane Maria contributed to thousands of schoolchildren developing symptoms of post-traumatic stress disorder, or PTSD, in Puerto Rico, according to a study published Friday.

The study in JAMA Network Open found that 7.2 percent of the students reported "clinically significant" symptoms of PTSD. More girls tended to show signs of PTSD than boys.

Researchers surveyed 96,108 public school students five to nine months after the 2017 hurricane. The cohort included youth in third through 12th grades across different regions of the island.

The Puerto Rico Department of Education—which partnered with the Medical University of South Carolina for this study—is using the data to target areas with the greatest need for mental health services, the study said.

Maria, which struck the island as a Category 4 hurricane in September 2017, killed an estimated 2,975 people within the American commonwealth. Residents struggled to access clean water and some remained without electricity nearly a year after the storm.

It had dramatic effects on the students. Nearly 46 percent said their home was damaged. More than 32 percent experienced shortages of food and water. And roughly 58 percent reported they had a friend or family member leave the island. The effects did not vary based on where the students lived or their families' income.

Rosaura Orengo-Aguayo, a clinical psychologist at the Medical University of South Carolina and the study's lead author, said the findings show the breadth and indiscriminate nature of the devastation.

"That just speaks to how big Maria was, how destructive Maria was island-wide," she said. "And it didn't matter what your income was or your location was on the island—you were affected."

---

*Originally published as Carmen Heredia Rodriguez, "Hurricane Maria's Legacy: Thousands of Puerto Rican Students Show PTSD Symptoms," *Kaiser Health News*, https://khn.org/news/hurricane-marias-legacy-thousands-of-puerto-rican-students-show-ptsd-symptoms/ (April 26, 2019). Kaiser Health News is a nonprofit news service covering health issues. It is an editorially independent program of the Kaiser Family Foundation that is not affiliated with Kaiser Permanente. Reprinted with permission of the publisher.

Similar problems have been reported among children in other parts of the Caribbean also affected by hurricanes in 2017.

Congress is at a stalemate in passing an aid bill that would send more resources to Puerto Rico and other areas affected by natural disasters. President Donald Trump has expressed his reluctance to provide more money to the island.

The trauma caused by a natural disaster can manifest itself in a variety of ways, said Frank Zenere, district coordinator of the crisis management program at Miami-Dade County Public Schools, who was not associated with the study. Family units can break down through divorce or domestic violence, he said. Young children can revert to thumb-sucking or wetting the bed. Teens sometimes try to exert control by acting out or turning to drugs to self-medicate.

To be sure, Zenere said, most people who survive a natural disaster do not develop long-term mental health conditions.

"They're distressed by it. It has impact on their life—yes," said Zenere, who helped coordinate mental health efforts in Puerto Rico in Maria's aftermath. "But the great majority are not going to develop psychiatric illness."

Zenere said the differences by gender found among students reporting symptoms of PTSD align with existing literature—boys are more likely to act out, while girls are most likely to show depression and anxiety.

The study's authors said the loss and disruption caused by Maria contributed about 20 percent toward the youth's symptoms of PTSD. While the researchers did not measure what other circumstances played a role, Orengo-Aguayo said, other "protective factors"—like eventually securing basic needs and community support—influence resiliency.

Notably, Orengo-Aguayo said, the level of PTSD symptoms reported in the study is lower than what was expected. Some studies show up to a third of children will develop chronic symptoms after surviving a natural disaster, the authors wrote.

Familial ties or the fact that the study was conducted several months after the storm could have played a role in the children's resilience, she said. Or the children might still be attuned to trying to survive.

"What we might be seeing is that children at that stage were still focused on getting access to basic needs," she said.

Regan Stewart, a clinical psychologist at the Medical University of South Carolina and a study co-author, said the team has secured two grants from the federal Substance Abuse and Mental Health Services Administration to continue work on the island for at least three more years. It plans to use telehealth to expand access to mental health services and train school staff and mental health professionals on trauma-focused interventions.

However, public schools in Puerto Rico are burdened by economic constraints. The island—already facing a budget crisis—closed 300 schools over the past two years due to a lack of enrollment exacerbated by Hurricane Maria.

Zenere said school staff members are among those who need to be cared for first, "because they're going to be the glue that keeps it together for that classroom of 20 children or so."

PART III

Actions and Innovations

• *A. Citizens and Public-Private Partnerships* •

19. Both Conservatives and Liberals Want a Green Energy Future, but for Different Reasons*

Deidra Miniard, Joe Kantenbacher
and Shahzeen Attari

Political divisions are a growing fixture in the United States today, whether the topic is marriage across party lines, responding to climate change or concern about coronavirus exposure. Especially in a presidential election year, the vast divide between conservatives and liberals often feels nearly impossible to bridge.

Our research examines what people know about the energy sources in use today in the United States, and what types of energy they would like to see the nation using in 2050. Energy connects to many important issues, including climate change, jobs and economic growth, equity and social justice, and international relations. It would be easy to assume that America's energy future is a highly polarized topic, especially when the Trump administration is clashing with many states led by Democrats over energy policies.

However, in a nationwide online survey, we recently found that broad support exists across the political spectrum for a future powered mostly by renewable energy sources. Our work highlights a consensus around the idea that the United States needs to move its entire energy system away from fossil fuels to low-carbon energy sources.

Assessing Perceptions

To explore people's views on energy sources, we conducted an online survey of 2,429 adults across the U.S. Our participants represented a range of political ideologies, with 51 percent self-identifying as liberals, 20 percent as moderate and 29 percent as conservative. To investigate patterns in the data, we analyzed responses based on participants' political ideologies.

*Originally published as Deidra Miniard, Joe Kantenbacher, and Shahzeen Attari, "Both Conservatives and Liberals Want a Green Energy Future, but for Different Reasons," *The Conversation*, https://theconversation.com/both-conservatives-and-liberals-want-a-green-energy-future-but-for-different-reasons-134534 (May 5, 2020). Reprinted with permission of the publisher.

Our survey asked people to estimate the shares that various energy sources contributed to all energy use in the United States, including activities like generating electricity, running factories, heating homes and powering vehicles. We asked participants to estimate what percentage of U.S. total energy used came from nine energy sources: coal, oil, natural gas, solar, wind, hydro, biomass, geothermal and nuclear power.

Next, we had participants describe what they viewed as an optimal mix of these nine energy sources that they hoped the U.S. would use in the year 2050. We also asked what kinds of policies they would support to move the nation from its current status to the future that they envisioned. In a follow-on study, we are examining how factors such as cost and environmental impact influence people's preferences for one energy source versus others.

Estimations of Today's Energy Mix

We found that our respondents had some misperceptions about where energy in the U.S. comes from. They tended to underestimate U.S. reliance on oil and natural gas and overestimate coal's contribution. We believe Americans may not realize how dramatically electric utilities have switched from coal to gas for power generation over the past decade and may therefore have dated impressions of coal's prevalence.

Conversely, we found that participants overestimated the contribution of lesser-used energy sources—specifically, renewables like wind and solar power. This pattern may partially be explained by people's general tendency to inflate estimates of small values and probabilities, which has been seen in areas ranging from household energy use and water use to risk of death.

In the case of the U.S. energy system, this bias means that people think our current energy system is greener than it really is, which could reduce the perceived urgency of shifting to lower-carbon sources.

Shared Goals, Divergent Pathways

When we asked participants to indicate the amount of each energy source they hoped the U.S. would use in 2050, the broad consensus favored a future in which the nation primarily relied on renewable energy and used much less fossil fuel. Conservatives, moderates and liberals shared this outlook.

Preferences for a lower-carbon future varied somewhat by political ideology, but on average all groups supported an energy mix in which at least 77 percent of overall energy use came from low-carbon energy sources, including renewable fuels and nuclear power.

This bipartisan consensus wavered, though, when we asked participants whether they supported or opposed 12 energy policies—six that would lead to larger roles for low-carbon energy sources, and six that would increase use of fossil fuels.

Liberal participants showed strong support for policies consistent with increased use of low-carbon energy sources, such as providing government funding for renewable energy and subsidies for purchasing electric vehicles. They strongly opposed actions that would increase reliance on fossil fuels, such as relaxing oil drilling regulations or lowering fuel economy standards.

On average, conservative participants supported several policies that favored low-carbon energy use, though not as strongly as their liberal counterparts. Conservatives tended to be closer to neutral or only slightly opposed to policies that promote fossil fuel use.

The sharpest contrast between the two political groups was over building and completing pipelines to move oil from extraction points to refineries in the U.S. Several proposed pipelines have generated intense controversy in the past years. Conservatives generally supported pipeline development, and liberals generally opposed it.

Achieving a Low-Carbon Future

An important argument for transitioning to low-carbon energy sources is to limit climate change to manageable levels. Recent polls show that climate change remains a politically divisive issue, with far more Democrats than Republicans rating it as extremely important to their vote in the 2020 presidential race.

Recent research has shown that both Democrats and Republicans strongly support renewable energy development but do so for different reasons. Democrats prioritize curbing climate change, while Republicans are more motivated by reducing energy costs. We see these motivations playing out in the real world, where conservative oil-producing states like Texas are experiencing huge booms in renewable energy generation, driven primarily by the improving economics of renewable energy.

Realizing the shared vision of an energy system dominated by renewable energy will mean reconciling partisan differences over how to achieve that future. While there is no single rationale that will convince all Americans to support a transition to low-carbon energy sources, our results are encouraging because we find consensus on the U.S. energy future—everyone agrees that it should be green.

20. Volunteering During a Disaster*

BENJAMIN PALEY

If you are anything like me, then spending time volunteering with your local government is a great way to utilize the skills you learned in your public administration classes. Local governments thrive on volunteers, who have been a hallmark of American society since the founding of this nation.

In the wake of major disasters that have struck at the hearts of people around the world, local government organizations, non-governmental organizations (NGOs) and not-for profits have taken the helm to assist. Thus far, my columns for PA Times have focused on ways those with degrees in public administration can utilize their knowledge for the benefit of all. This time, I want to focus on an area of volunteerism that is often featured center fold in the news: volunteering at a disaster site in the days and weeks after disaster has struck. There are individuals in the local vicinity and outside it that want to step up to the plate to help their fellow human beings recover from a disaster.

As a Floridian, and specifically a south Floridian, I appreciate the hard work and dedication of the countless individuals who dedicate their time to those affected by disasters. For example, after Hurricane Irma struck south Florida in 2017, many Floridians were left without power, city streets were badly damaged, and local grocers were at a need for supplies. Within days of Irma's strike, volunteers were on the ground across the state of Florida to assist.

In order to present this information in the best way possible, I am going to split this piece into two parts: In part 1, I will discuss the history of volunteerism in the wake of disasters as well as some theory. In part two, I will discuss ways you can get involved in post-disaster volunteerism.

American's desire to volunteer post-disaster goes back to the very founding of this nation. Motoko Imai, a lecturer at Tokiwa University in Japan, while comparing United States volunteers to volunteers in Japan, wrote that the idea of, "The people," preceded the idea of, "The government." This instilled in Americans at that time a sense of community and brotherhood/sisterhood. And Teresa R. Johnson, an intern for the International Institute of Global Resilience, in a paper titled "Disaster Volunteerism," wrote that, "[T]he founding fathers were disappointed with their former countries and did not want an all-powerful government, so they formed their own voluntary associations."

Johnson continues by writing about how in disaster situations, there is a concept called convergence. Specifically, there are two types of convergence: external and internal

*Originally published as Benjamin Paley, "Volunteering During A Disaster," *PA Times,* https://patimes.org/volunteering-during-a-disaster/(August 24, 2019). Reprinted with permission of the publisher.

convergence. Charles E. Fritz and J.H. Mathewson in a 1957 book titled *Convergence Behavior in Disasters; a Problem in Social Control*, defines convergence as, "Movement or inclination and approach towards a particular point." They define external convergence as, "Movement towards the disaster-struck area from the outside," and internal convergence as, "Movement towards specific points within a given disaster-related area or zone." Both types of convergence provide benefits and consequences for law enforcement and emergency personnel, as well as the volunteers involved; The safety of the volunteers could be compromised when going into a disaster zone if the area has not been deemed safe or free of hazards.

Now that you understand some of the history and theory behind disaster volunteerism, how can you get involved? There are a variety of ways for volunteers to help out after a disaster has hit. One organization that has chapters not only across the United States but also around the world is the American Red Cross. According to their website, "Volunteers constitute about 90 percent of the American Red Cross workforce. Volunteers make it possible to respond to an average of more than 62,000 disasters every year, most of them home and apartment fires. Find out about the needs in your area by searching for current volunteer opportunities." Volunteers can help out in the following ways:

- Volunteer management
- Disaster services
- Disaster Action Team
- Disaster Preparedness Presenter

Public Affairs

One final great way for locals to get involved in disaster relief in their communities is through joining a Certified Emergency Response Team (more commonly known as CERT). An article on Ready.gov describes CERTs as programs that educate, "Volunteers about disaster preparedness for hazards that may impact their area and trains them in basic disaster response skills, such as fire safety, light search and rescue, team organization and disaster medical operations. CERT offers a consistent, nationwide approach to volunteer training and organization that professional responders can rely on during disaster situations, which allows them to focus on more complex tasks. Through CERT, the capabilities to prepare for, respond to and recover from disasters is built and enhanced." In total, "There are over 2,700 local CERT programs nationwide, with more than 600,000 individuals trained since CERT became a national program."

Disaster volunteerism is a very special way for locals to assist their communities during a time of great strife and vulnerability. The need for calm and civility, as well as efficient service delivery post-disaster, creates an environment that, when used right, could be of great benefit not only to the recipients, but also to those who are volunteering their time to help out.

21. From Pledges to Action

Cities Need to Show Their Climate Progress with Hard Data*

CONOR K. GATELY *and* LUCY HUTYRA

As world leaders negotiate rules for cutting greenhouse gas emissions at the COP24 meeting in Poland, U.S. cities have a vested interest in the outcome. About 85 percent of Americans live in cities, and urban areas produce some 80 percent of our nation's greenhouse gas emissions. Many cities are highly vulnerable to climate change impacts such as flooding and heat waves.

Cities are central to shaping effective solutions, too. After President Donald Trump announced in 2017 that he planned to withdraw the United States from the Paris climate accord, more than 400 U.S. mayors—representing 69 million people—pledged to fulfill it. Some cities are going further and aiming for net carbon neutrality by 2050. Their efforts are sorely needed: According to a Dec. 5 report from the Global Carbon Project, global carbon dioxide emissions grew 2.7 percent in 2018, the largest rise in seven years.

Mayors believe they can make a climate impact while making their communities greener and cleaner. To succeed, they will have to take bold policy actions and demonstrate that emissions are declining. However, tracking greenhouse gas emissions requires models, forecasting tools and lots of data. Today most of that information is organized at the national or state level, not at city scales.

Now, though, this is changing. Over the last decade, our work on urban greenhouse gas emissions has shown that with the right combination of instruments, data and modeling techniques, it is possible to independently quantify carbon dioxide and methane emissions from urban areas. Just as researchers measure local smog concentrations for public health, they now can measure local greenhouse gases for climate action.

Move Fast and Measure Carefully

Many steps cities need to take to hit their 2050 targets must be undertaken within the next decade. Investments in energy systems, transportation infrastructure and new housing stock can lock in consumption and emissions patterns for decades to come.

---

*Originally published as Conor K. Gately and Lucy Hutyra, "From Pledges to Action: Cities Need to Show Their Climate Progress with Hard Data," *The Conversation,* https://theconversation.com/from-pledges-to-action-cities-need-to-show-their-climate-progress-with-hard-data-99200 (December 6, 2018). Reprinted with permission of the publisher.

As an example, by reducing urban and suburban vehicle travel, making electric vehicles more affordable, and expanding use of public transit, cities can cut carbon emissions and also reduce local air pollution. But such actions require very long lead times. The much-anticipated Westside subway extension project in Los Angeles has a construction timeline of 14 years but was preceded by decades of planning and negotiation.

To track actual progress over time, urban agencies also need to generate and share local-scale information. Nongovernment organizations like the Carbon Disclosure Project and ICLEI have produced tools that make this kind of data more accessible and transparent, but it is still challenging to accurately quantify city-scale emissions. Resource constraints, data gaps and shifting local priorities make it difficult for many cities to regularly report emissions in a consistent way.

We work with a growing network of U.S. cities where researchers are quantifying greenhouse gas emissions across urban regions. For example, in Boston we are analyzing how trees within the city influence greenhouse gas levels, and how local traffic congestion increases emissions of carbon dioxide as well as air pollutants. And in Salt Lake City, researchers have outfitted train lines with sensors to measure greenhouse gases and air quality in real time.

Remote sensing is another promising data source. Several greenhouse gas observing satellites are already in orbit, with more to follow. The Orbiting Carbon Observatory 3 (OCO-3), soon to be installed on the International Space Station, will focus on observing cities and urban areas across the globe. It will provide scientists and city governments regularly with vital data on local carbon dioxide concentrations.

Avoiding Surprises

Regular air measurements aren't just valuable for measuring progress. They also can help researchers identify unknown emissions sources through "atmospheric detective work," spotting sources that aren't well controlled or illicit "dumping" of pollutants into the atmosphere.

This happened in 2014, when scientists using satellite instruments to monitor atmospheric methane concentrations detected a giant methane hotspot in northwestern New Mexico that did not appear in any existing emissions inventories. A targeted field campaign using aircraft and ground-based sensors narrowed down the source to leaks associated with oil and gas development in the San Juan Basin.

More recently, atmospheric measurements published in May 2018 detected a rapid increase in concentrations of a chemical known as CFC-11 that had been targeted for phase-out under the 1987 Montreal Protocol on Substances That Deplete the Ozone Layer. Using atmospheric models, researchers narrowed down the source region of these emissions to somewhere in East Asia. Investigations subsequently identified over 18 companies in China illicitly producing and selling CFC-11.

The Problem with Offsets

Cities are unlikely to cheat on their own pledges in this way, but they may use strategies that are hard to measure or verify. A key example is buying energy and carbon credits instead of directly reducing emissions. In these transactions, buyers receive credit for investing in renewable energy or other green initiatives, such as planting trees, to "offset" their own carbon-intensive activities.

Buying offsets is a popular way to show support for the environment. For example, the ride sharing company Lyft has pledged to buy enough carbon offsets that "every ride will now contribute to fighting climate change." And cities may meet clean energy commitments by buying renewable energy credits from power providers outside their limits.

Offset projects can be very cost-effective and important for reducing overall U.S. emissions, but they may not do anything for improving local air quality in cities. Those Lyft drivers will still be generating air pollution. So will the urban power plants that keep running while local governments buy green power credits from sources elsewhere. As these examples show, the more cities rely on offsets to meet their climate targets, the harder it will be to assess whether they are actually reducing their contributions to climate change.

You Can't Manage What You Can't Measure

To sustain momentum and achieve their climate goals, we believe U.S. cities should embrace the transparency and validation that direct measurements can provide to show that progress is real and not just on paper. In our view, it also is time for a major push to connect local climate action plans across cities with observations and data. Ambitious climate targets are a key first step, but now cities need to show their residents—and each other—that they are making verifiable progress.

22. Becoming Crisis Ready*

Melissa Agnes

From the impact of climate change, to acts of terror, to cyberattacks, and the list goes on, there's no denying that we live in uncertain times and that with these uncertainties come increased risk and exposure.

It is true that we can never be entirely sure of when a catastrophic incident will strike. Will the impending hurricane pass around your community, or will its eye drive straight through? Will your district's school or your city's nightclub be the next to experience a devastating tragedy, or will your community remain safe from such horror? What if, however, I tell you that many of the uncertainties that leave you increasingly exposed can be anticipated and foreseen in ways that can give you, your team, and your organization a strategic advantage in trying times?

It Begins With Understanding the "Why"

When you take the time to understand the why behind today's uncertainties, not only will the risks associated with them significantly decrease, but you also gain the advantage of preparing yourself to respond to any rising threat in ways that:

- Help you quickly get ahead of the narrative of the story and position your organization as the voice of trust, credibility, and leadership, which is the voice that your community will look to you to have in times of crisis.
- Foster increased trust and credibility in your team and organization, rather than suffering a potentially irreversible depreciation of those attributes.
- Ultimately, put you in a position to successfully work with your community's emergency managers and, together, save more lives when the crisis is of a catastrophic nature.

Achieving this level of readiness requires more than the typical, stagnant crisis-management plan. Why? Because a plan is an extremely linear and siloed approach to a non-linear, cross-organizational situation.

With all the added exposure that things like social media, mobile technology, and the 24/7 news cycle bring to today's crisis and issue management, that plan does little to truly serve in times of heightened risk.

---

*Originally published as Melissa Agnes, "Becoming Crisis Ready," *PM Magazine*, https://icma.org/articles/pm-magazine/becoming-crisis-ready (May 2019). Reprinted with permission of the publisher.

Instead, today's organizations gain the most strategic advantage when they approach their crisis readiness as the development of a program that is then embedded into the culture of the organization. Being crisis ready means managers have an entire organization of people who are trained and empowered to:

- Identify rising risk in real time, no matter what that risk may be, or how it may strike.
- Properly assess its material impact on community and the brand—is it an issue or is it a crisis?
- Respond in a way that both effectively manages the incident and fosters increased trust and credibility in the organization.

How to Gain a Strategic Advantage

If risk can strike from anywhere and we live in a world of uncertainty, then having a team that is equipped to instinctively identify, assess, and respond to any negative event in ways that foster increased trust and credibility in your organization, will put you at a strategic advantage to be the leader that your community needs you to be when it matters most.

The good news is that achieving this level of readiness is easier than most initially believe. In fact, there are four steps you can take today that will put your team at a strategic advantage in dire times.

Step 1: Identify and understand your risks.

This includes everything from your high-risk scenarios—the most-likely, high-impact issue and crisis scenarios that pertain to your organization and community—to the risks within those risks, including the risk of emotional relatability and the impact it threatens to have on an incident's escalation.

To identify and understand your risk, you first need to begin by defining the difference between an "issue" and a "crisis" for your organization, and determine the thresholds where the crossover from one type of incident to the other lies.

Defining issue and crisis. As a baseline, a crisis is a negative event or situation that stops business as usual to some extent as it requires escalation straight to the top of leadership. It requires this escalation because the incident threatens long-term material impact on one to all these five things:

1. Stakeholders (people).
2. The environment.
3. Business operations.
4. Your reputation.
5. Your bottom line.

An issue, on the other hand, is a negative event or situation that does not stop business as usual because it does not require escalation straight to leadership. I refer to issue management as a form of business as usual on hyperdrive. Why? Because it does not threaten long-term material impact on any of those five attributes listed above.

An emergency, for example, is a negative event that requires real-time management. Depending, however, on the specifics of the emergency and the long-term material impact it threatens to have, any given emergency situation can be either an issue or a crisis.

Being able to quickly and accurately evaluate the long-term material impact of a given situation puts you and your team in a position to respond effectively in a way that can protect both the people of your community and the long-term reputation of your local government's brand.

Action Item: Now that you have these definitions, your first task is to use them as a baseline to identify the most-likely, high-impact issues and crises to which your organization is most prone or vulnerable.

From there, define the thresholds and factors that would escalate each of your identified issues into crises, as well as de-escalate any given crisis down to an issue level.

This is a crisis-ready action that you are entirely in a position to take now. The simple act of doing this will help you gain better clarity and understanding about the risks of those uncertainties that are probably plaguing your leadership team.

Step 2: Develop strong emotional intelligence.

We can never be entirely sure when a negative event will go viral against our organization, increasing the real-time challenges, exposures, and impacts of the situation on the brand.

If you want to understand both sides of emotional relatability, however, you can then train your team to be able to quickly detect the probability of virality and get ahead of it in a way that de-escalates the situation and the long-term negative impact it threatens to have on your organization.

This Crisis Ready™ formula was designed to help your team quickly identify the potential of negative virality: Emotion + Relatability + Shareability = Heightened Risk of Virality. If a negative event has high emotional impact and if, by sharing it the sharer knows that emotion will relate to those within his or her network, it is likely to be shared, consumed, related to … shared, consumed, related to … and so forth, increasing its probability for virality.

Action Item: Teach your team to be able to quickly assess and evaluate the emotional relatability of a given situation, and then design an escalation protocol for team members to follow once strong emotional relatability is identified.

There's also another element to developing strong emotional intelligence, which is to understand one of my Crisis Ready™ rules: Logic will never overpower emotion.

If strong emotional relatability is detected, it doesn't matter whether that emotion is rational or irrational, logical or illogical. It is real, it is powerful, and it will be impactful.

To reason with and overcome negative emotional relatability, your response to the incident needs to adhere to this Crisis Ready™ formula: Heightened Risk of Virality = Logic (Validation + Relatability + Proof).

A common mistake I see is when leaders attempt to speak rationally in emotionally charged situations. To resonate logically in such instances, you have to first get into the hearts of those you are trying to reach.

This is done by taking your logical explanations, statistics, and commitments, and wrapping them in emotional relatability that matches, if not surpasses, that of the capacity of the negative sentiment.

Action Item: Teaching your team to detect emotional relatability and then to be able to act and communicate with emotional intelligence is one of the secrets to being crisis ready.

Step 3: Proactively find opportunities to consistently build trust.

Building up trust now, which means proactively finding ways to strengthen the relationships you share with your community, will give you powerful advantages in the midst of a crisis or a viral issue. Here are two major crisis-ready benefits of this approach:

- Truly knowing the members of your community and other stakeholder groups. This knowledge leads to your team instinctively understanding what is expected of it and how to meet those expectations in real time, during a breaking crisis or viral issue.
- Gaining the benefit of the doubt at the onset of an incident. In a world where controlling the narrative is next to impossible, gaining the benefit of the doubt at the start of a breaking incident means those who matter most to your organization will have the instinctive reflex to say, "We will wait to hear from the organization because we trust that it will do what's right and be forthcoming with the information."

This offers a powerful advantage that only comes with earned trust.

Action Item: What does your team do each day to strengthen the trust it shares with your stakeholders? Trust is earned over time and it takes a cultural mindset of proactively seeking small opportunities to, as Captain Chris Hsiung of the Mountain View, California, Police Department says, "Make daily deposits in your bank of community trust."

Step 4: Choose to embed a crisis-ready culture.

While I've shared some powerful, actionable strategies with you here, there are five distinct phases to becoming crisis ready and truly building out a culture of crisis readiness.

Having a true culture of readiness takes commitment and dedication, and the rewards are immense and far exceed the sole acts of issue and crisis management.

The current status quo of developing a linear and siloed crisis management plan that sits on a shelf collecting dust does not suffice in today's uncertain world of increased risk and exposure. In fact, this approach puts today's organizations at a disadvantage.

Instead, the objective is to embed a culture of readiness whereby the entire team is empowered to detect, assess, and respond to any negative incident in a way that does right by stakeholders and increases the trust and credibility in the organization.

My Crisis Ready™ model, outlined in my book, takes you through the process of designing your Crisis Ready™ program and embedding a culture that will help you mitigate the risks of uncertainty and strengthen your team's leadership for your community.

I wish you and your community all the invincibility you are committed to earning.

23. Top Five Tips for Planning, Preparing and Adapting to Climate Change*

Niles Anderegg

If you've already listened to the Local Gov Life podcast Fighting the Threat of Climate Change and Rising Sea Levels, you are familiar with why climate change is happening and how it's impacting communities.

But how, as a local leader, can you make effective choices supporting resilience to the impacts of climate change in your community? During the 2018 ICMA Annual Conference session "Planning, Preparing, and Adapting to Climate Change," three session leaders shared their ideas on how local government leaders can shape decisions that enhance the safety and welfare of their residents. Here are five tips for planning, preparing, and adapting to climate change in your community.

1. Consider a Semi-Centralized Organizational Structure

Florida State University Professor Richard Feiock conducted a report on how local governments organize themselves around sustainability. He found that communities that tended to have the most sustainability policies in place organized themselves around a semi-centralized structure, where local government agencies or departments operated on their own.

This type of organizational structure includes a "headquarters agency" that coordinates a community's sustainability efforts. Feiock's research found that communities with a headquarters agency were often the best performing and were often led by an organization's environmental department.

By considering a semi-centralized organizational structure, you can eliminate the silo issues that local governments often face, as well as eliminate the tension between those focused on sustainability and those focused on resilience.

2. Be Open to Partnerships

Local governments who participate in partnerships with nonprofits and universities can take advantage of the knowledge and expertise that these entities possess to

*Originally published as Niles Anderegg, "Top 5 Tips for Planning, Preparing and Adapting to Climate Change," https://icma.org/blog-posts/top-5-tips-planning-preparing-and-adapting-climate-change (Oct. 15, 2018). Reprinted with permission of the publisher.

complement the work they are doing on climate change. Another advantage of partnerships is with budgeting, namely that partnerships can help absorb some of the financial costs of addressing climate change. Partnerships can also be used to help communities with their work of adapting to climate change, which might be too small for local governments to spend a lot of staff time or community resources on. By giving a little bit of help to local nonprofits, individual neighborhoods can meet their environmental challenges.

In Ann Arbor, Michigan, for example, an important partner in this area is the University of Michigan. This partnership is important for two reasons. First, the university has the skill and expertise to partner with the city on ways to adapt to climate change and second, the university accounts for some 25 percent of the city's emissions. This partnership has helped Ann Arbor deal with such issues as aging in place. Aging in place involves planning for future changes in an environment and for the people who currently live in a community. In the case of Ann Arbor, this involves helping community members modify their homes to adapt to such changing weather conditions as an increase in large rain events.

Another partnership that Ann Arbor is pursuing is with a nonprofit organization that is helping neighborhoods better use their composting resources. Increasing the use of composting benefits Ann Arbor, as it reduces the amount of waste going to landfills and reduces the community's greenhouse gas emissions. These examples demonstrate how partnerships can help local governments leverage community resources to combat climate change.

3. Educate Your Residents on Climate Change Issues

An important part of adapting and planning for the impacts of climate change is educating residents. In Dubuque, Iowa, educating residents about climate change meant having a conversation about resiliency. Local government staff and residents focused on the characteristics of what makes a person or a family resilient. Participants were able to set resiliency goals and priorities, and the city was able to take one step forward on combating climate change issues related to stormwater management and disaster preparedness with the help of its residents.

4. Improve Equity While Addressing Climate Change

One of the best ways communities can look at climate change is through an equity lens. While climate change will affect everyone, it will disproportionately affect poor and older populations in a community.

Planning and preparing for the effects of climate change involve trying to find ways to identify the communities that will be impacted the most. In Ann Arbor, mapping technology was used to identify vulnerable neighborhoods. Another example of an equitable climate change policy is in housing. Ann Arbor has been working on a program that will create new affordable housing that has net-zero energy use. The goal here is to use sustainable practices along with renewable sources of energy to create housing that generates as much energy as it uses. This type of housing project allows lower-income residents to reduce their energy costs while making their homes more environmentally friendly.

Dubuque, Iowa, has a similar focus on equity, making it one of the values that defines the city's sustainable framework. One particular climate change equity issue is food security and safety. As climate change occurs, the type and quantity of food available will also change. It is important, therefore, for communities to find ways to conserve and use their food resources wisely. Dubuque has instituted a food recovery program to connect local businesses and farmers with food banks and other resources that allow the most vulnerable populations access to food that otherwise would have been thrown away. This not only improves the food resources of lower-income populations but also allows better management of the community's food system.

5. Add Climate Change to Your Regular Planning Processes

Identifying the areas your community needs to address in terms of climate change is part of the planning process. Dubuque followed the standards set by STAR Communities and used its new resilience guide to help the city frame climate change in its planning process.

Once your community has identified the areas of concern, there are ways to incorporate climate change into your regular budgeting and planning processes. In Dubuque, the public works director had to budget for changes in how often a big snowfall will occur in the future, especially regarding overtime budgeting.

The Parks and Recreation Department, on the other hand, had to change the type of vegetation it needed to plant in public parks because as the temperatures vary, the variety of plants that will survive the new environmental conditions will also change.

24. Seven Strategies for Managing Uncertainty*

Nicole Lance

"I don't know where I'm going, but I know exactly how to get there."
—Boyd Varty, *A Lion Tracker's Guide to Life*

I first read this quote in Boyd Varty's book in early fall 2019. It stuck with me, and in recent weeks I find myself continually coming back to it. One of the greatest challenges in our current time is the vast amount of uncertainty that exists on a global, local, organizational, and even individual scale. Every day I talk to community leaders and public servants who all echo the same refrain, "We just wish we could predict where this is headed so we can put some plans in place." Energy is waning, employees are asking for information, furloughs are being extended, citizens are getting restless, businesses are frustrated, and budgeting continues to be a massive exercise in conjecture.

Managing uncertainty is difficult at best and sometimes seemingly impossible. I recommend using these strategies to help manage your own uncertainty.

1. Create Predictability in Small Doses

You can't have the future predictability you might desire or that your team is asking for, but is there a daily or weekly practice you can commit to that will help you routinize your way of managing through this time? Identifying small "anchor points" throughout the day or week can orient you and your team and provide some of that desired continuity.

2. Reframe

Develop the cadence of asking, "What am I learning from this? What are we learning from this as a team?" Applying curiosity and inquiry to the situations you are navigating will help you reframe challenges as an opportunity to practice skills or learn new ways of managing. You will also keep track of lessons learned and positive developments you want to continue to incorporate into how you do business.

---

*Originally published as Nicole Lance, "Seven Strategies for Managing Uncertainty," *PM Magazine*, https://icma.org/blog-posts/seven-strategies-managing-uncertainty (May 11, 2020). Reprinted with permission of the publisher.

3. Pinpoint Your Power Phrase

I like to think of a Power Phrase as a guidepost that helps me remember how I want to operate during a challenging time and how I want to feel about my work after. Select a word or phrase that can keep you focused not just on the what of your work, but on the how. Some phrases to try out:

- Frantic is not my framework.
- Calm, capable, caring.
- Peaceful and present.
- Reduce friction and accelerate.
- People first.
- Be intentional.

4. Make Plans, but Be Willing to Change Them!

Uncertainty does not prevent you from planning. The trick is to make plans while being completely willing to change them. Fluid and flexible become your two favorite words when it comes to planning. Focus your planning on a shorter timeframe and break tasks and necessary steps down into the smallest increments possible.

5. Intentionally Involve Others

Do not go it alone. Fear and uncertainty often make us retract like turtles pulling into their own shells. This cuts you off from valuable support and information networks and increases feelings of isolation. If you are uncertain about a way forward, challenge yourself to get as many data points of input from other people as possible. Consider it all research for making your best decision. I also assign many of my coaching clients the "ask for help challenge" where, for an entire week, they must find one thing a day to ask for help with. The exercise teaches two valuable lessons. First, that asking for help is okay and even a good thing. Second, asking for help bolsters our capacity. There is much more support available than we often allow ourselves to comprehend, let alone leverage.

6. Use Your Imagination for Good Instead of Evil

The human brain is powerful. Unfortunately, many of us primarily use this power for imagining worst-case scenarios and exploring ways everything can go wrong. It is like poking at a sore tooth over and over until your gums are throbbing and you have given yourself a headache. While leaders should always keep an eye out for managing through the next disaster or challenge, it is also beneficial to consider all the things that are going right. Celebrate the wins where you can and ensure your mental exercises in scenario-planning have an appropriate cut-off point. Ask yourself, "Is this line of thinking still productive and helpful?"

7. Find a Foothold

If you are isolating with children in the house, the phrase "Do the next right thing" might immediately conjure up images from the movie *Frozen II*. In the context of managing uncertainty, this is a powerful approach to take! Like the Boyd Varty quote at the beginning of this post, you may not know exactly where you are going, but you know exactly how to get there. Lean on experience to simply inform your next step. You do not need to solve for every variable or plan for every contingency all at once. Take one action, evaluate, and then do the next right thing.

25. The Role of Education in Environmental Activism

ALAN R. ROPER

In June of 2018, Pennsylvania Republican gubernatorial candidate Scott Wagner held a town hall meeting where 18-year-old environmental activist and student at the University of California Rose Strauss publicly confronted him about donations from the fossil fuel industry. Wagner responded to Ms. Strauss by saying "You're 18 years old. You know, you're a little young and naive." Unfortunately for candidate Wagner, a video of this public exchange was taken by Sunrise Pennsylvania, a local branch of the Sunrise Movement, and quickly went viral on social media, and the hashtag #YoungandNaive initiated a social movement. Following this the *New York Times* interviewed Rose Strauss about her commitment to asking these tough questions of politicians on the campaign trail. Obviously, Ms. Strauss was not nearly as "young and naïve" as gubernatorial candidate Wagner thought she was. She represents a growing youth movement for climate activism, who are fluent in environmental science, informed on policy, and have the technological wherewithal to make a difference.

Rose Strauss is an undergraduate student at the University of California, Santa Barbara. In the spring quarter (prior to the exchange with Scott Wagner), she had taken a new course on her campus, Bending the Curve: Climate Change Solutions. This course was developed as a collaborative effort by 23 University of California professors who are experts in their fields, representing 9 campuses. Being a freshmen student, she had to petition her advisor to allow her to take this upper division course.

Bending the Curve: Climate Change Solutions is a multifaceted education project representing the vision of Distinguished Professor of Atmospheric and Climate Sciences, Veerabhadran "Ram" Ramanathan. Professor Ramanathan distinguished himself in this field in 1975 when he discovered the greenhouse effect of CFCs (chlorofluorocarbons; belongs to family of halocarbons) and showed that a ton each of CFC-11 and CFC-12 has more global warming effect than 10000 tons of CO_2. He was honored as the science advisor to Pope Francis' holy see delegation to the historic 2015 Paris climate summit and in addition advises California Governors Jerry Brown and Gavin Newsom. He was named the UN Climate Champion in 2013; has been elected to the U.S. National Academy and the Royal Swedish Academy which awards the Nobel prizes.

Professor Ramanathan envisioned the power of young people as a strong resource to address the impacts of climate disruption. His vision in creating this course was to empower a million climate champions across the world to solve the climate change problem. The project to develop this course was initiated by the University of California and facilitated collaboration from the Berkeley, Davis, Irvine, Los Angeles, Merced, Riverside, Santa Barbara, San Diego, Santa Cruz, San Francisco campuses. The course draws inspiration from the report Bending the Curve: 10 Scalable Solutions; written by 50 University of California (UC) academics in natural sciences including engineering and technology, social sciences, and humanities. The course has been offered on 7 University of California campuses, and now is being licensed at Stockholm University, Stockholm, Sweden; San Diego State University, San Diego, CA; National Taiwan University, Taipei, Taiwan; and MiraCosta College, San Diego, CA.

The Bending the Curve: Climate Change Solutions course is an upper division undergraduate course that also provides a unique opportunity for students. Students taking this course have an opportunity to have class projects published through the California Digital Library. Opportunities for undergraduate students to publish their work are rare, and thus far several student group projects are published and publicly accessible. This solutions-based course has also produced an open-source digital textbook, available to anyone for free. Professor Ramanathan believes that the solutions to climate change may come from young students like Rose Strauss who are empowered by their learning and are ready to take action.

International Youth Movement for Climate Activism

The Swedish climate activist Greta Thunberg is probably the most well-known teenage climate activist. At age 15, Thunberg brought her activism to widespread public attention in August 2018 when she organized a movement outside the Swedish parliament calling for a school strike for the climate. Since this time, she has gone from a lone schoolgirl striking outside the Swedish parliament to an international figurehead for a youth movement for climate activism.

In 2019 Thunberg led worldwide international climate strikes where large numbers of students walked out of their classrooms across the United States, Africa, Asia, Australia, Europe, and South America (the largest climate demonstration in human history). In New York City, San Francisco, and other major cities, school districts allowed and encouraged students to take part without penalizing them for missing school. Schools are currently adopting textbooks and reading materials on climate change in unprecedented numbers. Named *Time Magazine*'s Person of the Year, Thunberg addressed heads of state at the U.N., met with the Pope, and even debated with the President of the United States. Isra Hirsi, a co-founder of Youth Climate Strike, spoke about her climate activism and her experience as an African American teenager in the environmental movement. She called for more inclusivity and asked more privileged activists and groups to share resources (Mercado, 2019). The fact that climate disruption is disproportionately impacting developing countries, the poor, and communities of color has motivated a new generation of activists who are more diverse than their predecessors.

Young people have been active in environmental issues going back to the 1960s. However, the new generation of protestors is louder and more coordinated than its predecessors, says Dana Fisher, a sociologist at the University of Maryland in College Park who studies activism. The movement's visibility on social media and in the press has created a powerful feedback loop. "Young people are getting so much attention that it draws more young people into the movement," she says, (Marris, 2019). The coordination of the world-wide climate strike which involved 1.4 million activists is an example of the sophisticated level of coordination which is enhanced by the generation's use of technology.

The Youth Climate Movement (YouNGO) or International Youth Climate Movement (IYCM) refers to an international network of youth organizations that collectively aims to inspire, empower and mobilize a generational movement of young people to take positive action on climate change, (International Youth Climate Movement, 2019).

Despite the impressive efforts of youth climate activists, federal support for climate action in the United States has been slow to respond. Lack of commitment at the federal level remains a major obstacle for the young climate advocates, but there are opportunities at the state and even local level. "In 2018 the Utah Youth Environmental Solutions, a teen council which aims to advance pro-environmental solutions statewide, saw the fruits of their lobbying events when the state passed House Concurrent Resolution 7 entitled 'Economic and Environmental Stewardship,' which recognized climate change and called for the use of science when making environmental decisions," (Ramadan, 2019). The youth climate movement also played a role in the state of Colorado, where the Air Quality Control Commission adopted the Low Emission Vehicle Program after 7,600 Coloradoans actively called for it in 2018, (Ramadan, 2019).

The Role of Education in Addressing the Impact of Climate Change

Youth of today have a significant stake in the future. The education they receive today will influence the ways in which they participate in society, as well as how they, as future leaders, will help form and guide climate and sustainability policies and practices in both public and private sectors. "We should work hard to ensure that we're teaching about all the ways we can take action to mitigate the effects of climate change," says modified language arts educator Jennifer Hall, the Earth Club advisor for West Seattle High School, (Long, 2019). Educating young students in the effects of climate change and subsequent disaster preparedness will have far-reaching value. Researchers Raya Muttarak and Wolfgang Lutz, (2014) found that "[h]ighly educated individuals and societies are reported to have better preparedness and response to the disasters, suffered lower negative impacts, and are able to recover faster." Education's role in propelling climate action goes beyond providing activists with the information needed to initiate a social movement. Our investment in the future through education will prepare a new generation to seek scientific and technological solutions, to mitigate natural disasters, to plan sustainable urban development, and to establish governance and policy.

The State of California has invested significantly in developing curriculum for public education on the topic of climate change. The California Education and the Environment Initiative (EEI) Curriculum highlight the deep relationship between humans and the natural world and are the foundation of the environmental content taught in the model curriculum available to students at any level. Climate education and environmental science was once focused on post-secondary learning. That focus has changed in the past few years to develop programs and resources for K-12 education in California schools. The following list identifies some examples where California public education has partnered with environmental agencies to develop curriculum and resources:

Classroom Curriculum (California)

- The Education and the Environment Initiative (EEI) is led by the California Environmental Protection Agency and CalRecycle. The resulting standards-based curriculum for grades K-12 spans a variety of environmental education topics, including climate change.
- The National Science Foundation and NBC Learn have partnered to create Changing Planet, a series of 13 videos and associated lesson plans about our planet's changing climate. These materials are especially useful for high school or college Earth Science classes.
- The Bay Area Air Quality Management District has climate change and clean air resources for youth outreach and education.
- The Lawrence Hall of Science has developed Global Systems Science, an earth science course for high-school students that includes climate change.
- The U.S. Environmental Protection Agency and other federal agencies have developed a Climate Change, Wildlife, and Wildlands Toolkit for Educators to help educators inside and outside the classroom teach middle school students about climate change and its impact on the environment and wildlife.
- The U.S. Geological Survey provides Science Education Materials including resources that are matched to California content standards.
- The U.S. Department of Energy has a portal for educators with a wealth of energy resources including curriculum.
- The California Regional Environmental Education Community (CREEC) network has an extensive database of environmental education resources (including curriculum and other classroom resources), as well as updates on the latest environmental education initiatives in the state.
- The California Department of Education provides Environmental Education Resources, including grant information, curriculum, events, and information about state planning for environmental education.

Programs for Classrooms and Schools

- The Alliance for Climate Education provides classroom and assembly presentations to high school students on climate change and recognizes students and schools that are taking action on climate change through scholarships and grants.

Additional Resources

- The California Air Resources Board provides climate change resources for kids, including fun climate activities and green tips, and a variety of curriculum resources sorted by grade level.
- GlobalWarmingKids.net and ClimateChangeEducation.org feature additional resources for students and teachers interested in learning and teaching about climate change.

- The U.S. EPA's Teaching Center provides climate change and other resources for teachers and students.
- The Climate Generation holds teacher training Summer Institutes that help teachers from around the country teach climate change curriculum to their students.

Earth's complex climate system can be explained in somewhat simple terms. When energy from the sun is reflected off the earth and back into space (mostly by clouds and ice), or when the earth's atmosphere releases energy, the planet cools. When the earth absorbs the sun's energy, or when atmospheric gases prevent heat released by the earth from radiating into space (the greenhouse effect), the planet warms, (NRDC, 2019). There are many factors which can influence the earth's climate system, and some of them can be controlled by humans. Since the effects of climate action and policy today will have an impact on the world over a span of many years, this is an issue young people are significantly invested in. Education in climate change, solutions, and sustainability may be one of the best investments for the future today's society can make.

Conclusion

Scott Wagner did not win the gubernatorial election in Pennsylvania in 2018, being defeated by incumbent Democrat Tom Wolf. His public criticism of 18-year old climate activist Rose Strauss, and the social movement that followed did not help his unsuccessful campaign. The movement did not end there. After the election, the Clean Air Council on behalf of 7000 contributors and 35,000 activists across Pennsylvania launched a campaign to get their governor to take the lead on climate policy. In October 2019, Governor Tom Wolf took executive action instructing the Pennsylvania Department of Environmental Protection (DEP) to join the Regional Greenhouse Gas Initiative (RGGI), a market-based collaboration among nine Northeast and Mid–Atlantic states to reduce greenhouse gas emissions and combat climate change while generating economic growth.

Steven Cohen, director of the Earth Institute's Research Program on Sustainability Policy and Management at Columbia University, was recently interviewed by the Harvard Political Review. Cohen stated "having young people say, 'Hey, you older people messed it up. You didn't do what you're supposed to, and you're leaving me a planet that is damaged' … is a really tough argument to refute," (Ramadan, 2019).

Public leaders at every level of government should be aware of the youth movement for climate activism. The rising movement represented in youth-led organizations like Zero Hour, the U.S. Youth Climate Strike, and Sunrise Movement, demonstrate how a new generation of climate activists are demanding change, and greater climate accountability on the part of elected officials. Technology plays a key role in the impact of these movements, (climate activists Haven Coleman and Isra Hirsi met over Instagram to form the U.S. Youth Climate Strike). The youth climate movement should not be mistaken for a passing fad, it is building momentum and engaging new champions every day. These young people from every corner of the globe have demonstrated commitment and capability. One of the most effective investments we can make in the future is in promoting education that will empower the next generation for the vital role they will play in addressing climate change.

REFERENCES

International Youth Climate Movement. (2019). Retrieved from https://youthclimatemovement.wordpress.com/.

Long, C. (2019). The "Greta Effect" On Student Activism and Climate Change, NeaToday, National Education Association, Retrieved from http://neatoday.org/2019/09/19/the-greta-effect-student-activism-climate-change/.

Marris, E. (2019). Why young climate activists have captured the world's attention. As the movement prepares for a massive global protest, researchers break down why its message is gaining ground. *NatureResearch*, ISSN 1476-4687 (online).

Mercado, A. (2019). The Youth Climate Movement Is Just Getting Started; The nascent activist movement has continued to expand across the world, and politicians are taking notice, *The Nation*, Retrieved from https://www.thenation.com/article/the-youth-climate-movement-is-just-getting-started-global-warming-fridays-for-future/.

Muttarak, R. & Lutz, W. (2014). Is Education a Key to Reducing Vulnerability to Natural Disasters and hence Unavoidable Climate Change? *Ecology and Society*, 19 (1). pp. 1–8. ISSN 1708-3087.

Ramadan, J. (2019). The Rise of U.S. Youth Climate Activism, *Harvard Political Review*, Retrieved from https://harvardpolitics.com/united-states/youth-climate-activism/.

Rolen, E. (2018). Gubernatorial candidate Scott Wagner called this 18-year-old "young and naïve" when she asked him about climate change, Philly Voice, Retrieved from https://www.phillyvoice.com/young-naive-scott-wagner-rose-strauss-climate-change/.

Scripps Institute of Oceanography, University of California San Diego. (2019). Bending The Curve: Climate Change Solutions, Retrieved from https://bendingthecurve.ucsd.edu/.

26. The University of California's Carbon Neutrality Initiative

ALAN R. ROPER

The global issue of climate disruption has brought together thousands of leaders representing international governance, science, social movements & climate justice, and sustainable growth. The United Nation's Intergovernmental Panel on Climate Change (IPCC) established by the World Meteorological Society and the United Nations Environment Programme in 1988, has been operating for the past 30+ years on a mandate to provide the world with a clear scientific view on the current state of knowledge in climate change and its potential environmental and socio-economic impacts (United Nations Foundation, 2019). Despite the dedication and Herculean efforts of world leaders in their respective fields, a collective response to climate disruption may progress at a slower rate than the significant factors which threaten the warming of the climate system.

Finding local solutions to address the issues of climate disruption represents an important step toward preparing for a sustainable future. We may no longer have the luxury of simply waiting for our Federal government(s) to take care of this problem for us. Local solutions may be more attainable soon. From looking at large universities, which in a way are social systems or cities unto themselves, achievable solutions for sustainability may be tested and recommended for local communities. Throughout the world, universities have historically played a significant role in teaching and learning, in education, as well as in research and technological innovation. These academic institutions support new research and provide new knowledge and understanding which contribute to society in its ongoing development in meeting new challenges. In this important role, universities can also demonstrate internal policies and practices which explore carbon sequestration solutions aimed at reducing greenhouse gas emissions.

The most important asset any university has are their students. In the same way universities expect academic performance and achievement from students, students have collective power to demand accountability from the schools they choose to attend. The reason institutions of higher learning have played such an important role in societies going back hundreds of years is the fact that the university is an environment in which young learners can question society's status quo. Most of the significant social changes which have evolved modern societies have originated on college campuses. This relationship between institutions of higher learning, their students, and the societies in which they exist can provide new ideas and innovation in the way cities develop and manage solutions to climate disruption.

The University of California's Carbon Neutrality Initiative

The University of California (UC) is one of the world's leading public institutions of higher education. Currently the UC operates 10 California campuses, 5 medical centers, and 3 national laboratories. The 280,380 students attending the UC can select from 160 academic disciplines and 800 degree programs. The UC system also has 227,700 employees and contributes $46.3 billion to California economy. In November 2013, University of California President Janet Napolitano announced an innovative Carbon Neutrality Initiative, "which commits UC to emitting net zero greenhouse gases from its buildings and vehicle fleet by 2025, something no other major university system has done," (Carbon Neutrality Initiative, 2019).

Part of the initiative was to use the UC and campus operations as a *living laboratory* where new technologies and strategies can be tested and evaluated. This provides an opportunity to model real-world solutions which can be applied to cities, or at a national level. Part of the University of California's efforts in this regard involved development of the *Bending the Curve: Ten scalable solutions for carbon neutrality and climate stability* study conducted by 50 leading experts representing multiple disciplines. From that report, authors Matt St. Clair and Lifang Chiang (2016) identified the model of the *living laboratory* as a way to evaluate sustainability solutions to meet the University of California's institutional goal of de-carbonization by 2025. "For a university system pursuing carbon neutrality, this means that the physical operations of each campus can be a test-bed for clean energy, efficiency, and sustainability technologies. The campus itself is used for student study, research projects, and experiential learning," (St. Clair & Chiang, 2016). This concept involves the entire campus community, including students, staff, faculty and post-doctoral researchers. "The initiative builds on UC's pioneering work on climate research and furthers its leadership on sustainable business practices. UC is improving its energy efficiency, developing new sources of renewable energy, and enacting a range of related strategies to cut carbon emissions," (Carbon Neutrality Initiative, 2019).

The Role Students Played in Getting The University of California to Commit to Sustainability at an Institutional Level

Students have a strong voice, and that collective voice has impact at the University of California. The students who organized to get the UC to commit to a sustainability policy formed what they call the California Student Sustainability Coalition (CSSC). "The CSSC in turn was an inspiration and model for a national student coalition called the Energy Action Coalition. The Energy Action Coalition organized two national summits, the largest gathering of students anywhere in the world, to address the climate crisis. They managed to get 6,000 students to come to Washington DC in 2007," (St. Clair, 2017). A year later, the United States Congress Select Committee on Climate Change organized a special hearing and invited student leaders of the Energy Action Coalition to address the United States Congress. This provided an opportunity for these student activists to express what students thought the country should be doing about the climate crisis. In 2009, they organized an even bigger summit of student activists, with 10,000 students coming from all over the country to Washington, D.C. That time, President

Obama invited the student leaders to the White House to discuss with them what the students thought that he and the nation should be doing to address the climate crisis (St. Clair, 2017).

University of California students have let their advocacy for green programs and policies be known at the UC long before the term *sustainability* became associated with environmentalism. Some early efforts led by students included an organic farm created at UC Santa Cruz in 1967 and a student-run public bus system started in 1968 at UC Davis, (Mok, 2011). Students have been involved in the numerous sustainability initiatives on University of California campuses dating back to the 1960s. Student advocacy for sustainability has guided the redevelopment of classrooms, student centers, school common areas, and transportation thoroughfares at UC campuses.

UC Berkeley Involves Students in New High-Performance Buildings on Campus

UC Berkeley's master plan to revitalize student life by Sproul Plaza involved valuable input from students themselves. "This project is innovative in its design approach with a high level of student involvement. While many involved will not be here to enjoy the fruits of their labor, they have created a legacy to benefit future students," said Senior Project Manager Teri Mathers (Agnew, 2015). The project includes four buildings and two outdoor spaces that define Upper and Lower Sproul Plaza and together constitute the Student Center at UC Berkeley. Aligning with the UC Carbon Neutrality Initiative, the buildings in lower Sproul have been designed with innovative sustainability features. Martin Luther King Jr. (MLK) Student Union is on track for LEED™ Silver certification, and Eshleman Hall is on track for LEED™ Gold certification—going above and beyond the campus-wide requirement that major construction projects achieve LEED™ Silver certification at a minimum, (St. Clair, 2017). New solar panels on the MLK Student Union and Eshleman Hall produce 153,901 KWH per year, and the panels on Eshleman Hall are estimated to produce 16,103 KWH per year. These panels are on movable frames which are automated to tilt in the direction of the sunlight.

Other sustainability features in the new Lower Sproul include:

- A bicycle repair station in the plaza
- 108 added bicycle racks
- Improved pedestrian and transit access on Bancroft
- Low emitting materials
- Low flush toilets flushed with the possibility for gray water or captured rainwater
- White roofs (to reduce the heat island effect)
- Cesar Chavez Student Center has increased energy efficiency with HVAC and reduced solar gain on South Side
- Smart Systems and enhanced commissioning (HVAC, windows, lighting controls)
- Recycling and compost centers
- Green housekeeping program
- Vendors have LEED requirements in their contracts

Innovative waste reduction efforts were implemented throughout the construction process. Of the 8,810,067 lbs. of waste generated in the entire construction process, 8,269,201 lbs., resulting in 94 percent of waste diverted. This has been achieved through measures such as reusing materials whenever possible and contracting with a waste disposal company that recycles waste from the site (Agnew, 2015).

The context of the UC Berkeley student center as a hub of campus life began as early as the 1964/65 academic year when the Free Speech Movement made national headlines from Sproul Plaza in the heart of the Berkeley campus. The student advocates in that movement challenged the existing restrictions on political speech and action on campus, (the traditional restrictions were based on the theory that students attending a state funded school should not use those facilities to criticize their government). Issues of the day like the Civil Rights Movement and escalation of the military involvement in Viet Nam were some of the topics students spoke out about. As a result, the new acting chancellor at the time, Martin Meyerson (who had replaced the previous resigned Edward Strong), established provisional rules for political activity on the Berkeley campus on January 3, 1965. Moving forward to this decade, the collective student voice is still powerful at UC Berkeley. The sustainable design and construction approach to the new Lower Sproul is also the result of a student movement in which environmental stewardship is something students see as a significant priority.

The Campus as a Model for Sustainability: UC Irvine

UC Irvine (UCI) stands out as a sample of the university campus as a living laboratory for carbon neutrality. The campus has been selected for The Princeton Review's Green College Honor Roll five times, earning a perfect score of 99 in The Princeton Review's sustainability rating system. An example of the campus' commitment to sustainability can be seen with the new Mesa Court Towers, a mid-rise residential complex which features sustainable building design and zero-waste food service operations. The design was centered around healthy biophilic design principles, including daylight harvesting, captured views to landscape, and opportunities for indoor-outdoor connections. The towers include a mix of triple and quad rooms, with spaces for meeting and places to study on every floor: two-story lounges, group study rooms, a computer lab, and quiet study areas.

Dr. Jacob Brouwer is Associate Professor of Mechanical and Aerospace Engineering and Associate Director of the National Fuel Cell Research Center and Advanced Power and Energy Program at UCI. He recently discussed some of the achievements at his campus in a lecture to undergraduate students. "We happen to be the first campus to dramatically introduce energy efficiency measures which have resulted in saving over 5.5 kilowatt hours per square foot. This was accomplished using smart lab facilities, interior and exterior lighting that includes LED lighting for the most part but also very efficient fluorescent lighting thereafter" (Brouwer, 2017). Other energy saving measures have included heating, ventilation, and air conditioning (HVAC) systems which utilize occupancy sensors. With the warm climate in Irvine, California, air conditioning systems represent one of the biggest consumers of energy on campus. Brouwer (2017) explains: "We monitor the individual circuits of our campus, and so we can tell where the big energy losses, big energy demands are. And then we also have automated programs for turning down fans and responding to demands instead of continuously operating these at high energy consuming levels."

Another area where UCI is taking the lead in sustainability is in measuring their performance. "Throughout all of this, we are making sure that we actually have metrics against which we can compare our measured performance characteristics so that we can take corrective action. If we design a building and we want it to actually operate with these kinds of energy demands, we need to monitor those and then establish the metrics for when we need to go in and fix something" (Brouwer, 2017). This strategy is used for all energy demands on campus buildings. "Regarding lighting loads, we're measuring them and making sure that the watts per square foot and all of the metrics that we've established are actually achieved by our energy efficiency measures" (Brouwer, 2017). Other UC campuses are developing innovative measures to meet the carbon neutrality goals. The UC Santa Barbara campus has also demonstrated leadership in energy efficiency by installing lot of the new LED technologies. Many of these technologies have been developed right on their own campus, at the center that's led by Shuji Nakamura, who won the Nobel Prize for developing the blue LED light.

What We Can Learn from the University of California's Carbon Neutrality Initiative

The operations of the 10 University of California campuses create a large carbon footprint. The measure of the total greenhouse gas (GHG) emissions generated by the university's medical research facilities, laboratories, student housing, recreational and health facilities, transportation, and thousands of classrooms is significant. But the impact the students have is also significant in bringing about more environmentally responsible practices. Student-led movements that begin on college campuses have historically been the model for large scale social change. Just like the Free Speech Movement which started at UC Berkeley's Sproul Plaza, the numerous student campaigns for sustainability have helped the University of California's Carbon Neutrality Initiative become a reality. As the UC students leading these campaigns enter the workforce, their environmental advocacy will come with them. The sustainability model set by the University of California can extend to public and private organizations, with a new generation of climate champions leading the way.

References

Agnew, L. (2015). Berkeley Sustainability: Lower Sproul Will Soon be Back and Greener than Ever, Retrieved from https://sustainability.berkeley.edu/news/lower-sproul-will-soon-be-back-and-greener-ever.

Brouwer, J. (2017). Energy Efficiency Management, lecture for online course Bending the Curve: Climate Change Solutions.

Carbon Neutrality Initiative, University of California. (2019). retrieved from https://www.universityofcalifornia.edu/initiative/carbon-neutrality-initiative.

Mok, H. (2011). Students inspire UC sustainability policies, UC Newsroom, Retrieved from https://www.universityofcalifornia.edu/news/students-inspire-uc-sustainability-policies.

St. Clair, M. and Chiang, L. (2016). Chapter 2. The University as a Living Laboratory for Climate Solutions. Collabra, 2(1): 16, pp. 1–19, DOI: http://dx.doi.org/10.1525/collabra.61.

St. Clair, M. (2017). Carbon Neutrality Initiative of UC, lecture for online course Bending the Curve: Climate Change Solutions.

UC Irvine Mesa Court Towers. (2017). Best Practices, 2017, Retrieved from http://greenbuildings.berkeley.edu/bestpractices/2017/uci-mesa-court-towers.html.

United Nations Foundation. (2019). The Intergovernmental Panel on Climate Change: 30 Years Informing Global Climate Action, retrieved from http://www.ipcc.ch.

27. Role of Mobile Apps in Public Administration of Disaster Relief*

PETER LYN RENÉ

Mobile apps are now taken for granted in our society, not because they are unimportant but because they are plentiful and readily available. When we download apps from the Android's Play Store or Apple's App Store, it is a relative mundane task. We search for free apps or pay for an app to help us remain organized, stay in shape, meet our deadlines, check our bank balance or remind us, remind us, remind us. Thanks to this wonderful era of mobile technology, there is an app for practically everything needed to make our lives an absolute joy.

But apps are not just relegated to bring laughs, joy or structure to our lives. They can also be practical, necessary and life-saving. In the last five years, we have witnessed a paradigm shift in emergency management by which the reliance of "brick and mortar" procedures—such as telephones, computers, ships, planes and vehicles used to assist in disaster relief—are now nicely complemented with mobile apps specifically designed for disaster relief. One technological marvel should not be left out of the conversation: the use of unmanned automated vehicles (UAVs), better known as drones.

When discussing emergency management, it can be divided into two parts: disaster preparedness and the actual disaster. Nowhere more than the Caribbean region is disaster preparedness an essential practice. Natural disasters, such as hurricanes and tropical storms, will batter nations.

Mobile Apps and Disaster Relief (1) One of the best apps according to CNN is Hurricane Tracker. This app includes live video briefings on hurricanes, real time condition updates, push alerts, dozens of maps and minute-by-minute updates. This app also has access to the NOAA weather radio, complete with high resolution animation. Another app that focuses specifically on the Atlantic, Caribbean and Gulf of Mexico region is Hurricane Express. Like Hurricane Tracker, it provides forecasts, video updates and satellite imagery with information from The National Hurricane Center.

In a study by Paul Cerrato and Iltifat Husain, M.D., the Red Cross Apps were identified as the group with the most useful applications for natural disasters. Dr. Husain indicated that with the advancements in social media and a surge in the prevalence of smartphones, we are now seeing live Twitter and Facebook updates and

*Originally published as Peter Lyn René, "Role of Mobile Apps in Public Administration of Disaster Relief," *PA Times*, https://patimes.org/role-mobile-apps-public-administration-disaster-relief/ (April 15, 2016). Reprinted with permission of the publisher and author.

emergency-related applications being used in disaster response efforts. Perhaps one of the best apps to assist in emergency management is the FEMA app. It includes an interactive emergency kit list, emergency meeting locations that can be stored and a map of open shelters. This free app provides a feature that lets users create Global Positioning System photo reports that can be inserted in a map for others to see.

At the ninth Caribbean Conference on Comprehensive Disaster Management, hosted by the Caribbean Disaster Emergency Management Agency (CDEMA) and the Bahamas' National Emergency Management Agency (NEMA) in November 2015, the Red Cross Apps were the leading instrument discussed, promoted and supported. The Bahamas Red Cross, through their Resilience in The Americas (RITA) program, has a multihazard smartphone app which features information on natural hazards, basic first aid procedures and emergency messaging, including location, emergency lights and sound. This app was well-received and viewed as useful to the natural disaster-prone Caribbean.

Not to be outdone by mobile apps, responding to and executing disaster relief just got easier thanks to drones that are patiently waiting their turn to be officially called up to assist first responders. CNN's Heather Kelly indicated as far back as 2013 that these portable, affordable aircraft can launch quickly in dangerous situations, locate survivors and send data about their whereabouts to responders on the ground. The UAV industry and emergency responders are preparing for the day when they can launch drones after tornadoes, earthquakes, hurricanes, floods and any other disaster.

Challenges to emergency management and public policy have changed and continue to change to stay in step with technological advances. Gone are the days when disaster relief meant supply ships and military assessments and where areas devastated by natural disasters remained technologically cut off from the rest of the world. The smartphone, in its many forms, has proven itself to be a powerful tool in emergency management and the use of drones continues to grow.

Emergency management agencies and other companies have now developed hundreds of apps to assist individuals to be better prepared for impending storms and hurricanes. These apps not only keep emergency managers informed but also connected to efforts on the ground. DeeDee Bennett exclaimed this is a wonderful time to be in emergency management. The progression of technology will forever change our vulnerability, preparedness, response, recovery and resilience. The new use of drones, robots, smartphones and even wearables during disasters will certainly spark more growth in the practice of emergency management.

• B. Cities •

28. Meeting Climate and Energy Action Plan Goals in Ashland, Oregon*

Talia Shea *and* Alan R. Roper

The city of Ashland, Oregon, is at risk of devastation from the effects of climate change. As a community surrounded by forests, Ashland is already at fire risk and prone to poor, smoky air quality. The small city's livelihood is dependent on tourism from its renowned Shakespeare Festival, rafting, skiing and hiking the Pacific Crest Trail.

Ashland has been a forward-thinking community on the cutting-edge of the environmentalist and renewable energy movements since the 1960s. Now, in the face of climate change, the city of 21,000 has the opportunity to serve as a model for other small cities, utilities and communities (U.S. Census Bureau, Ashland, Oregon, 2019). With a unanimous vote by the City Council, Ashland adopted a Climate and Energy Action Plan (CEAP) in March 2017 (City of Ashland, 2017). CEAP's long-term benchmarks include (1) a community goal of reducing greenhouse gas emissions by eight percent on average every year through 2050 and (2) a City of Ashland operations goal to achieve "carbon neutrality in City operations by 2030, and (3) to reduce fossil fuel consumption by 50 percent by 2030 and 100 percent by 2050" (City of Ashland, 2019).

CEAP is modeled after larger Pacific Northwest climate action plans, "including the State of Oregon, which established a statewide target to reduce emissions by 75 percent below 1990 levels by 2050" (City of Ashland, 2017). However, the city does not yet have an effective regulatory framework for promoting the plan and needs to create a feasible strategy in order to meet these goals. Ashland is not alone in this endeavor. Other communities, states and even countries are implementing climate action plans with the idea of mitigating greenhouse gas emissions associated with climate change. It appears likely that Ashland's climate action plan can be achieved.

The small neighboring community of Talent, Oregon, to Ashland's north is home to 6,500 residents (U.S. Census Bureau, Talent, Oregon, 2019). In 2015, Talent was recognized by the Environmental Protection Agency (EPA) as an EPA Green Power Community, which is a community that "collectively use(s) green power that meets or exceeds five percent of the community's electricity use" (U.S. Environmental Protection Agency, 2019a). This recognition is a result of customer and city engagement in the Pacific Power Blue Sky renewable energy program (Boom, 2015). Over 20 percent of Talent community members voluntarily opt to pay more on their electric bill for renewable energy, which makes Talent among the top four cities enrolled in Blue Sky in Oregon per capita (Boom,

---

*Published with permission of the authors.

2015; City of Talent, 2018; U.S. Environmental Protection Agency, 2019a). This therefore reduces customer's personal carbon footprint for electricity. The renewable energy purchase is facilitated through renewable energy certificates (RECs) that guarantee one megawatt-hour of renewable energy is purchased for every one megawatt-hour of electricity used (U.S. Environmental Protection Agency, 2019a; U.S. Environmental Protection Agency, 2019b). The RECs are audited and guarantee that this purchase is accounted. The purchase equates to roughly 7,015,700 kilowatt-hours of renewable energy that the residents of Talent are responsible for matching with their home electric use with RECs and bringing online (U.S. Environmental Protection Agency, 2019b). Based on the free carbon emissions calculator provided by the Carbon Fund, this means that Talent has reduced the city's carbon footprint overall by 3,852 metric tons of CO_2 per year ("How We Calculate," 2019). This is huge. In 2017 Talent was the recipient of a Blue Sky grant that provided funding for a solar array that was installed on the Talent Community Center's roof (City of Talent, 2018). In addition to the Blue Sky program, Talent has its own Clean Energy Action Plan, adopted in 2017 (City of Talent, 2017). The success of Talent's carbon reduction provides the impetus to review the feasibility of applying this model to meet Ashland's CEAP goals.

In 2016, Ashland conducted a greenhouse gas (GHG) inventory based on 2011–2015 emissions from the city's buildings, transportation sector, goods and food production, and city government operations (City of Ashland, 2017). The breakdown of emissions is as follows:

- Residential and commercial energy: 24 percent
- Transportation: 23 percent
- Production of residential goods: 22 percent
- Production of food: 15 percent (City of Ashland, 2017).

Total emissions from Ashland were estimated to be 300,000 metric tons of carbon dioxide or 0.5 percent of Oregon's total greenhouse gas emissions (City of Ashland, 2017). The largest sector was residential and commercial energy use, hence the focus on energy use in the feasibility study. The GHG inventory found reductions to be "the result of decreases in electricity and natural gas use in the residential sector, decreases in natural gas use in the commercial sector, and increased hydro electricity generation on the regional electricity grid" (City of Ashland, 2017). The findings from the GHG inventory were used to compose CEAP.

The City of Ashland has an independent, publicly-owned electric utility that is supplied by the Bonneville Power Administration (BPA) (City of Ashland, 2019b). Much of the electricity generated is already renewable or zero-emission from hydroelectric and nuclear power (City of Ashland, 2019b). Despite this purchase of low-emission electricity, Ashland does not appear on the EPA Green Power Community list and is not currently reaching CEAP goals.

It is assumed that the eco-minded community of Ashland, which is similarly-minded to Talent residents, would like to be an EPA Green Power Community and be enrolled in a green power program like Blue Sky. In fact, Ashland has a green power option that offers wind RECs, similar to Blue Sky's REC program, yet many Ashlanders do not know about the program. Additionally, Ashland has a net-metering program. Since Ashland's power supply is low-carbon, matching total energy consumption (including both electric and gas) in homes and businesses via a REC and offset program could be a strong option for the city and its residents to tackle emissions generated in homes and businesses. The feasibility study investigates why (1) Ashland is not currently fulfilling CEAP, (2) workable options for Ashland to meet CEAP, (3) an implementation roadmap for communities choosing to implement climate action plans successfully.

Research Process and Results

The following research is focused on informing the process of partnering with a private organization that would further the development of CEAP implementation. Specialty companies exist to support agencies in strategic planning and implementation via public-private partnership (P3). A case study was conducted to further explore partnering with 3Degrees Inc., a renewable energy and climate solutions company that partners with utilities including Pacific Power and private companies who want to reduce carbon emissions and "take urgent action on climate change" (3Degrees, 2019). It is a B Corporation with built-in accountability measures, so it is an industry leader in accountability, social equity and environmental stewardship.

The feasibility study involved collecting and analyzing data via in-person structured interviews with representatives of the City of Ashland, the City of Talent, Benton County, Oregon, 3Degrees Inc., and a renewable energy consultant. Thirty-nine Ashland residents participated in a survey to provide a community perspective.

An interview was conducted with research participant Mayor John Stromberg of Ashland, Oregon. He explained how the story of Ashland's progress on climate action has the potential to be popularized and could inspire the fulfillment of community climate action plans worldwide. Ashland is already an iconic destination community, therefore Stromberg suggested promoting and capitalizing on its reputation, connections, and the story of how Ashland became carbon-neutral. This would not only be advantageous to Ashland but could benefit the world.

In a second interview, Stu Green, Ashland's Climate and Energy Analyst, suggested the city move away from natural gas. Green identified some challenges with implementing a program that forces homeowners to switch from gas to electric: they would have to get new appliances, and likely retrofit their homes for greater efficiency. Green observed that the biggest barrier to CEAP and home retrofits and investment in renewable energy was funding.

A representative from a renewable energy consulting company, who chose to remain anonymous, was included in the research. They described how Ashland is already low-emission for electricity, since the city purchases 98 percent hydroelectric power from the Bonneville Power Authority (BPA) and two percent nuclear. Based on this, they saw some difficulty for the feasibility of Ashland becoming carbon-neutral through a green power program. Since Ashland's electricity is already low-emission, they felt that the electric sector may not be the best approach to reduce home and business emissions in Ashland. The interview exposed problems that could potentially arise if Ashland goes forward with a green power program.

Councilor Emily Berlant of Talent, Oregon, participated in the research. She suggested eliminating natural gas in homes and businesses as an excellent way to reduce fossil fuel consumption. She, like Green, agreed that Ashland and other cities can move away from on-site gas heating, stoves, and other appliances. Green offered the City of Berkeley,

California's 2018 example, the Fossil Free Berkeley ordinance, that banned natural gas in new construction (City of Berkeley, 2018). Additionally, Berlant suggested that, "Ashland can do the right thing and adopt renewable energy as the default energy mix. Then the city can consider a 100 percent renewable option REC-based program so customers can go above and beyond." Since Santa Clara's basic mix is already low emission like Ashland, Berlant saw similarities in a potential green power option for Ashland.

Ryan Pawling, Senior Business Manager, 3Degrees Inc., stated that "The answer to the common client question 'What can I do?' is actually a lot broader than meets the eye." Budget is a major hurdle for climate action plans. Identifying who has *pain* around the issue of climate change is important for a climate plan to receive funding, he said. For example, if there is pain around acute issues, like homelessness and fire, these will take priority. The Mayor Stromberg interview reinforced this sentiment. Yet, long-term climate plan funding is often overlooked, Pawling continued. As increasingly more people have pain around climate change issues, from flooding to fire associated with climate change, more people will look to leaders who address climate change in their campaigns. Pawling suggested that voters experiencing these acute pains will elect a mayor who is running on a climate action plan platform. He explained that emission reductions could be tackled through a "universe of options." For example, the city can identify whether it has land to build a renewable energy project, like a solar array or whether it should purchase RECs. By identifying these options, the city can build a roadmap to establish plan phases and what type of emissions to tackle during a given phase.

Kali Lamont, former Benton County, Oregon Climate Action Intern, cited funding as the biggest obstacle to cities and counties becoming carbon neutral now. In her experience, climate action planning (phase one) can be strong but implementation (phase two) is often at a standstill. She elaborated that only a handful of residents is usually on-board to pay more and money needs to be spent thoughtfully. Despite lack of funding for climate action plans today, Lamont is hopeful for creative solutions and a clean energy future.

Survey findings from Ashland residents confirmed that Ashlanders want to do more to fight climate change. Sixty-six percent wanted to do more to reduce their own carbon footprint. Others explained that they were already doing their part by purchasing solar panels and electric vehicles. Forty-four percent of those polled would even pay ten percent more on their utility bill to ensure that their home's energy usage is matched with carbon offsets or RECs. This is key because it only takes five percent of residents to sign up for a voluntary REC program to be eligible for EPA Green Power Community status (U.S. Environmental Protection Agency, 2019a). Sixty-seven percent of Ashlanders agreed that a community solar program like a community choice aggregation (CCA) would be a good option for Ashland.

Summary of Interview and Survey Findings

The information gathered from the interviews and survey is valuable for Ashland and other communities. If implementation is challenging, Ashland can reach beyond city limits and create public-private partnerships with industry experts, like 3Degrees. Nearly all the results of the interviews concurred that climate action plans need funding. Several representatives wanted to phase out natural gas to reduce emissions and electrify homes and vehicles. Nearly half of Ashlanders surveyed are willing to pay more on their bill to reduce carbon emissions. The following four implementation recommendations are offered for Ashland and other organizations.

Recommendation 1: Acquire funding

Funding for a climate action plan may come externally from large donors, internally from each resident, or both. Without funding, CEAP is stuck in place. Considering the success of Blue Sky in Talent, in which residents pay up to ten percent more for renewable energy on their electric bill, Ashland residents too are likely to participate in a green power program. A public-private partnership (P3) between a city and an expert service can be costly, however costs can be negotiated into the price of a green power program upon plan construction. This may be less expensive in the long run than implementing a plan from within the organization.

Recommendation 2: Hire an expert and use a REC and/or offset program to transition to a community renewable generation project

Before climate action planning, the community must understand its carbon emissions. First, the community must do a greenhouse gas inventory either on its own or with a private partner. Then, as Ashland has done, the agency can explore its options like RECs, offsets, or renewable energy generation projects.

It is possible to create a program that reduces carbon emissions now via RECs or offsets and fundraises for a future community-based renewable energy project, like a city-owned solar farm. This is a solution for communities that are championing climate action plans and want to generate their own renewable energy but may not like the idea of purchasing RECs from other communities or states to reach their carbon reduction goals. Through RECs and offsets Ashland can reduce its carbon footprint by the eight percent per year needed to meet CEAP goals while investing in future renewable energy independence.

Some REC programs, like Blue Sky, provide local communities with renewable energy projects at schools, airports, and municipal buildings. REC programs not only quantifiably reduce emissions but can fundraise for community renewable energy projects like solar farms that residents really desire. Building in this type of fundraising rate structure is recommended for the success of the REC program. A similar offset program could be created for gas emissions. For a city such as Ashland, which is struggling to implement its climate action plan, it could be beneficial to partner with an outside adviser who specializes in helping organizations move from planning to implementation of their renewable energy and climate plans.

Recommendation 3: Electrify!

Offsets and RECs are a great place to start, but they still allow for the city or agency to produce fossil fuel emissions. Eliminating those emissions or reducing and offsetting the remainder of emissions are better solutions than just paying to emit elsewhere. For example, many cities, including Ashland, are reducing emissions by electrifying their auto fleets. There are even grant programs funding new electric vehicle (EV) charging stations across Oregon (Pacific Power, 2019). Reducing and eliminating residential natural gas was important to the interviewed representatives. As the national electric grid becomes more renewable, electricity will become cleaner.

Recommendation 4: Make Ashland the model for small-town climate action plans

Ashland can become the go-to model for those aspiring to fulfill climate action plans. People already come to the idyllic community for inspiration, why not make it a carbon-neutral climate change success story? Legislation can be inspired by CEAP. Branding and marketing are part of telling this story effectively. Ashland has a unique quality that invites monetary expenditure, grant funding and private donations. By telling its tale, Ashland can not only raise project funds but can influence local and state legislation and be a national and international inspiration.

Summary

Many cities worldwide are struggling to achieve their climate action goals. This research is intended to benefit government agencies that are also struggling to meet climate plan goals. Case study analysis followed a public-private partnership with a B Corporation that manages climate action plans on behalf of their clients and partners. Primary data was collected via interviews and a residential survey. Secondary data was collected and analyzed to further support primary data. The research is impactful because it offers a roadmap for communities to gauge if their climate action goals are attainable and therefore, communities can take further action locally on climate change.

The study gives evidence that it is feasible for Ashland to fulfill CEAP, however, feasibility is only part one of a longer path to implementation success. Part two involves Ashland deciding if that path to carbon neutrality is still its goal. Are CEAP's goals and benchmarks still applicable three years later? If not, they need to be reworked. Ashland and communities worldwide are ready to execute their climate action plans and reduce their carbon emissions.

References

2017 Green-e Verification Report. (2019 June 04). Retrieved June 2019 from https://resource-solutions.org/g2017/.

2019 Champions Retreat. (2019). Retrieved June 2019 from https://bcorporation.net/about-b-lab.

3Degrees Inc. (2019) Renewable Energy Projects—Sustainability Programs. Retrieved June 2019 from https://3degreesinc.com/supply/.

A year after Trump announced his intent to pull out of the Paris agreement, climate action rises from the bottom-up. (2018, May 31). *Targeted News Service*. Retrieved June 2019 from https://search.proquest.com/docview/2047897040?accountid=25283.

The B Economy: How benefit corporations benefit society, not just the bottom line. (2018). *Directors and Boards*, 42(5), 13. Retrieved June 2019 from https://search.proquest.com/docview/2132686025?accountid=25283.

Banerjee, S.B. (2012). A climate for change? Critical reflections on the Durban united nations climate change conference. *Organization Studies*, 33(12), 1761–1786. doi:http://dx.doi.org/10.1177/0170840612464609.

Bezozi, H. (2019). Public benefit corporations 101. *Wealth Management,* Retrieved June 2019 from https://search.proquest.com/docview/2166314734?accountid=25283.

Blue Sky Renewable Energy. (2019). Retrieved June 2019 from https://www.pacificpower.net/bluesky.

Boom, T. (2015 December 28). Talent joins ranks of green-power cities. Retrieved July 1, 2019, from https://mailtribune.com/news/top-stories/talent-joins-ranks-of-green-power-cities.

Bulkeley, H. 2010. Cities and the governing of climate change. Annual Review of Environment and Resources 35:229–53.

California Energy Commission. (2019). Renewable Energy. Retrieved from https://www.energy.ca.gov/programs-and-topics/topics/renewable-energy.

City of Ashland. (2017). Climate and Energy Action Plan. Retrieved June 2019 from: https://www.ashland.or.us/Page.asp?NavID=17626.

City of Ashland. (2019a). Chamber of Commerce: Electric Department. Retrieved June 2019 from http://www.ashlandchamber.com/ChamberDirectoryDetail.asp?MemberID=1108.

City of Ashland (2019b). Hydroelectric Power–Conservation Division–Administration–City of Ashland, Oregon. Retrieved June 2019 from http://www.ashland.or.us/Page.asp?NavID=14046.

City of Berkeley. (2018). "Fossil Free Berkeley" Executive Summary . Retrieved September 7, 2019, from https://www.cityofberkeley.info/uploadedFiles/Planning_and_Development/Level_3_-_Commissions/Commission_for_Energy/EC2018-12-05_Item 7.pdf.

City of Talent. (2017). Talent Clean Energy Action Plan Retrieved July 2019 from http://www.cityoftalent.org/SIB/files/Planning/Conservation/2017–2018 Talent Clean Energy Action Plan.pdf.

City of Talent. (2018). Harvesting Talent's Energy. Retrieved July 2019 from http://www.cityoftalent.org/Page.asp?NavID=171.

Dillon, L. (2018 September 10). California to rely on 100% clean electricity by 2045 under bill signed by Gov. Jerry Brown. Retrieved June 2019 from https://www.latimes.com/politics/la-pol-ca-renewable-energy-law-signed-20180910-story.html.

Exec. Order No. SB100, 3 C.F.R. 99 (2018).

Featherly, K. (2014, Apr 23). Can corporations benefit everyone? Minnesotan Jeff Ochs wants to create the "Public Benefit Corporation." *Saint Paul Legal Ledger.* Retrieved June 2019 from https://search.proquest.com/docview/1519439973?accountid=25283.

Franco, G., Cayan, D., Luers, A., Hanemann, M., & Croes, B. (2008). Linking climate change science with policy in California. *Climatic Change, 87*(s1), S7–S20. https://doi.org/10.1007/s10584-007-9359-8.

Garrett, T.M. (2019). Kickstarting Creativity. *America, 220*(7), 26–31. Retrieved June 2019 from http://search.ebscohost.com/login.aspx?direct=true&AuthType=sso&db=a9h&AN=135542668&site=ehost-live&scope=site.

Gillenwater, M., Lu, X., & Fischlein, M. (2014). Additionality of wind energy investments in the U.S. voluntary green power market. *Renewable Energy: An International Journal, 63*, 452–457. https://doi.org/10.1016/j.renene.2013.10.003.

Greenhouse Gas Inventory Community and City Operations Results, Analysis and Recommendations. (2016). (pp. 1–36) (United States, City of Ashland Oregon). Ashland, OR.

How We Calculate. (2019). Retrieved June 2019 from https://carbonfund.org/how-we-calculate/.

Jabareen, Y. (2013). Planning for Countering Climate Change: Lessons from the Recent Plan of New York City—PlaNYC 2030. *International Planning Studies, 18*(2), 221–242. https://doi.org/10.1080/13563475.2013.774149.

Kousky, C., and S.H. Schneider. (2003). Global climate policy: Will cities lead the way? Climate Policy 3:359–72.

Leedy, P. D., Ormrod, J. E., & Johnson, L.R. (2019). *Practical research: Planning and design.* New York: Pearson.

McGee, M., Dr. (2019 July 07). *Lecture Slides.* Lecture presented at EMPA 396 in CA, San Francisco, CA.

Oregon passes one of most significant U.S. legislative actions on climate since Paris agreement. (2016, Mar 02). *Targeted News Service* Retrieved June 2019 from https://search.proquest.com/docview/1769987938?accountid=25283.

Pacific Power. (2019). Electric vehicle charging station projects across Oregon receive funding from Pacific Power grant program. (2019 July 31). Retrieved December 15, 2019, from https://www.pacificpower.net/about/newsroom/news-releases/oregon-electric-vehicle-grants.html.

Prophet, T. (2007, Jan 05). Utility goes green: Victorville switches gears to take advantage of new law. *McClatchy–Tribune Business News* Retrieved June 2019 from https://search.proquest.com/docview/46295 3171?accountid=25283.

Shea, T. (April 2019). *The P3 B Corp Model: How to Renew Public Faith in Public Private Partnerships.* Golden Gate University EMPA 304.

Stephenson, S. R., Oculi, N., Bauer, A., & Carhuayano, S. (2019). Convergence and Divergence of UNFCCC Nationally Determined Contributions. *Annals of the American Association of Geographers, 109*(4), 1240–1261. https://doi.org/10.1080/24694452.2018.1536533.

Sukdeo, V.H. (2015). What is the benefit of a "benefit corporation"? examining the advantages and detriment. *Banking & Finance Law Review, 31*(1), 89–111. Retrieved June 2019 from https://search.proquest.com/docview/1736460238?accountid=25283.

U.S. Census Bureau QuickFacts: Ashland city, Oregon. (2019). Retrieved July 7, 2017, from https://www.census.gov/quickfacts/ashlandcityoregon.

U.S. Census Bureau QuickFacts: Talent city, Oregon. (2019). Retrieved July 1, 2019, from https://www.census.gov/quickfacts/talentcityoregon.

U.S. Environmental Protection Agency. (2019a). Green Power Partner List. Retrieved July 2019 from https://www.epa.gov/greenpower/green-power-partner-list-0.

U.S. Environmental Protection Agency. (2019b). Green Power Partnerships: Renewable Energy Certificates (RECs). Retrieved June 2019, from https://www.epa.gov/greenpower/renewable-energy-certificates-recs.

Updated California climate action plan builds on successful programs, economic growth. (2014, May 16). *Targeted News Service* Retrieved June 2019 from https://search.proquest.com/docview/1525233077?accountid=25283.

Wang, R. (2013). Adopting Local Climate Policies: What Have California Cities Done and Why? *Urban Affairs Review*, *49*(4), 593–613. https://doi.org/10.1177/1078087412469348.

Webb, T. (2003 Oct 12). Emissions trading will cost electricity customers dear. *Sunday Business* Retrieved from https://search.proquest.com/docview/333228231?accountid=25283.

Acknowledgments

Thank you to Dr. Alan Roper, Dr. Mick McGee and Dr. Jay Gonzalez for your dedication and assistance with this project. Thank you to Scott for your support and sacrifice throughout my research. The best is yet to come!

29. The Future of Napa County Environmental Impact Decisions*

Melissa Diede

The rolling hills of vineyards are pleasing to the eyes of many tourists in the Napa Valley. For those who come to visit the arcadian valley, the colors of the vines and the distinct smell of freshly crushed wine grapes, one can think there is never too much of a good thing. Be that as it may, the residents have a different perspective of the Napa Valley. The Napa river, once a playground for the residents was deemed impaired in 1987 by the California Water Quality Control Board and since that time residents have been advised not to swim in it. Battles such as planting more lush vineyards and protecting the Napa County's steelhead and salmon with canopy coverage, are still conversations. With great soil, comes great consequences.

Residents today face new challenges. Those who are looking to buy a home in this region are having difficulty insuring their property. What does this have to do with climate change? The undeniable concern for this prestigious valley is the risk of fire. Just a mere decade ago wildfires were manageable and rarely occurred in the Napa Valley. Today, fire risk is prevalent enough to change the way insurance companies set boundaries on eligibility requirements. In October of 2017, The Atlas Fire burned Napa County (north of the city of Napa), near Napa Soda Springs. Combined with other wildfires (Tubbs fire and Nuns fire) the total area destroyed was at least 245,000 acres, with 8,900 buildings destroyed, (Artemis, 2018).

Climate change efforts cannot suffice in a one-size-fits-all policy. The west coast is burdened with wildfires that most states never have to experience. Therefore, climate change efforts must be diligently studied and tailored to each region. These efforts will involve the participation of the public, local and federal organizations to come up with a plan to minimize future risk which are specific to where the regional challenges may exist.

Background

On average, there are 18,857 visitors per day in the Napa Valley and both the wine industry demand and the need for housing have increased significantly. Areas where there were once apple and walnut orchards have now been replaced with residential housing and new vineyards. The valley's agricultural, tourism, and real estate businesses

---

*Published with permission of the author.

are changing their strategy to keep the City of Napa thriving. In 2018, Napa pulled in $2.2 Billion in visitor spending. In that same year, Napa hit a record with $1.038 billion in wine grape revenue. All of that with only about 9 percent of the valley producing wine related agriculture, according to the agricultural crop report of 2018.

Global warming and the increasing need for climate change solutions have been at the top of many Napa community topics. 2018 sparked a controversial debate about the future of removing the Napa Oak Woodlands in order to build more housing or increase agricultural acreage. This acreage is what brings in a good majority of revenue that supports the Napa Valley lifestyle. This topic morphed into a measure on the County's ballot referred to as Measure C, also known as the Napa County Watershed And Oak Woodland Protection Initiative of 2018.

The Napa County Watershed And Oak Woodland Protection Initiative of 2018 was designed "to protect the water quality, biological productivity, and economic and environmental value of Napa County's streams, watersheds, wetlands and forests, and to safeguard the public health, safety and welfare of the County's residents" (Napa County Watershed And Oak Woodland Protection Initiative of 2018, 2018). Local policies include the Napa County Green Certification for wineries that seek to reduce energy, water and waste resources. *The causes of climate change* by the Intergovernmental Science-Policy Platform on Biodiversity and Ecosystem Services (IPBES) report (2019) discusses global climate change about the earth warming from heat blocking gases such as carbon dioxide; the same carbon dioxide that would be increasing if the Napa oak woodlands are removed due to overdevelopment of the land. Supporters of the initiative were asking if anything was being done to protect these watersheds from being overrun with vineyards and the consequences of maintaining them?

Statement of the Problem

Any change in climate significantly affects the Napa Valley region as this determines the rate of harvest, wine production per ton, quality of the wine, and ultimately … tourism. The question is how to proceed with protecting the land and water resources of the Napa Valley while maintaining its historic agricultural status that brings in $1 billion in revenue. How does the Napa County grow and still protect the land that is valued so high for its rich soil?

With climate change discussions elevating, the Napa County election in 2018 was focused on the Napa County Watershed and Oak Woodland Protection Initiative suggesting stricter limitations on removing oak trees in agricultural zones, typically where the soil provides rich nutrients for vineyards. The issue affected not only the residents of the Napa Valley but major wineries for continued economic growth. This initiative did not pass. However, the reasons why were not because it's not important, but because the opposition party (which included the wineries) had spent more advertising dollars at a 4:1 ratio than the group supporting the measure. If trees cannot be removed, how were wineries supposed to expand the land? The margin of difference in votes was only about 451, a close call.

Purpose and Significance of This Study

This study was to examine, identify and provide recommendations on how a public policy which integrates ecologically sustainable development with smart projected growth in Napa County. It was to describe what County residents can expect to see in land and water policies that stem around decisions such as the Napa Oaks Watershed Protection Initiative of 2018. The IPBES agency released a report in early 2019 about global climate change, primarily on what is assessed and studied, how it contributes to global warming and consequences, and what measures should be taken by each state to prevent future and any unforeseen crisis. The report suggests a policy called the "Global Deal for Nature: Guiding principles, milestones, and target."

Measure C, (also known as the Napa County Watershed and Oak Woodland Protection Initiative of 2018), was part of the 2018 Napa County general election. This measure was created in hopes of addressing global warming concerns and proposing specific guidelines that would help protect this prestigious valley. The measure included putting restrictions on removing the Napa oak trees that reside in the lands agricultural watershed zones, as well as, creating setbacks for preventing tree removal within 150 feet of any wetland (*Napa County Watershed and Oak Woodland Protection Initiative of 2018*); furthermore, these setback would start one parcels larger than 1 acre. Research into this included the recent release of the IPBES report that stressed the significance of protecting 30 percent–50 percent of both land and water resources to offset the future of a declining climate using the Global Deal for Nature agreement (2018).

Upon investigation, it was noted that Napa County did not have an established Climate Action Plan as of today. However, Napa County officials were requiring new permit application to include an environmental impact report that followed the rules established by the California Environmental Quality Act. Although, this report was self-executing and has no weight on whether the city approves the application or not, there was a small standard to prevent over-development of the land.

The significance of this study was to identify any real threats to the Napa County watersheds using the expert knowledge in the field and comparing it to the analysis of the IPBES report for smart growth. Interviews and a public survey were completed a year after Measure C was defeated to determine if Napa County voters would respond to environmental policy changes with more awareness. This can be used for future policy making decisions by the Napa County voters and/or officials as necessary. During the research it was noted that the Americas are the second largest carbon producers and second largest per capita in the world (Union of Concerned Scientists referencing the International Energy Agency Report, 2018). Napa had established a baseline of carbon dioxide in 2014 and was set at 484,283 tons according to Napa's revised draft of the Climate Action Report (2018), to which agriculture was 10 percent of the total.

Results and Findings

The findings of this research include agriculture in the Napa County accounts for about 9 percent of available land yet is responsible for about 10 percent of all carbon dioxide in 2015. However, there is a lack of data and mapping to identify which areas are protected, which areas are selected for future development, and what circumstances include as not being an obstacle for the Napa County general plan. Current surveys of the rate of Oak tree degradation is inconclusive.

This invokes a question of not being able to complete one goal without the compromise of another opportunity cost. Napa County has a Climate Action Plan proposal and currently reviews projects with environmental impact reports but does not have requirements as to what would cause a project to be denied. California Environmental Quality Act (CEQA) guidelines are only self-executing, when the concern prompts that another party might be more helpful in accountability. Current literature review does not address this yet.

The results of the survey showed that there is a concern for protecting Napa County's land and water resources. There was also a need for public awareness since there was little familiarity with organizations such as the IPBES and CEQA organizations. Overall, there was some level of importance to also plan for the proposed increase in population. Unfortunately, there may be an unavoidable consequence as communities grow and develop beyond capacity.

The research demonstrates that Napa County voters will likely respond with more awareness when making environmental impact decisions. Although, when addressed with multiple priorities, it is difficult to evaluate actual decision-making outcomes. There were quantitative responses that suggests a positive outcome for Napa County voters to respond with more awareness when given the information about the IPBES report. Contrarily, there was also qualitative responses that suggest there may be political resistance or avoidance to fully address the issue of preserving the earths land and water resources while planning for growth.

Recommendations Include:

- Napa County Board of Supervisors works with the current residents and expert agencies like the IPBES organization regarding environmental policy changes for Napa County starting fiscal year 2020.
- Implement a climate action plan for Napa County that works with the current residents and expert agencies like the IPBES organization by the fiscal year 2025.
- Put the zoning maps on public websites to show actual growth dedication, agricultural planning, and current zoning for Napa County by the fiscal year 2025.
- Create public awareness programs such as seminars on local or global environmental impact reports, create local blogs that the residents can share information, expert knowledge, and voice concerns by fiscal year 2020.
- From the survey results in this study it is apparent the Napa County voters may have been inadequately informed about all considerations of Measure C. In addition to public awareness programs, accurate voter information is critical.
- Make CEQA a requirement for every project started and track progress (or loss of) environmental factors such as Greenhouse Gases and Oak tree removal or planting starting Jan 1, 2020.
- Provide the public with a map or actual fact sheet of currently protected lands. This may give the voter a sense that Napa County is already meeting the needs of the IPBES report.

The accentuation is that Napa County take this information and make it local and relevant to their needs. For example, Measure C put restrictions on removing oak trees, however, another action item that was equally important during the interviews that were conducted was not building homes in agricultural watershed areas to begin with. These are areas that experience a higher fire risk. Regardless, population growth is inevitable and figuring out sustainability is a reoccurring inevitable challenge.

There is a need for Napa County to act with responsible growth. Some issues may involve public initiatives, such as the Napa County Watershed and Oak Woodland Protection Initiative of 2018. The Napa County needs to adopt a climate action plan so that these issues can be addressed appropriately and involve the public's awareness. It is critical to plan for the county's current and future growth that reflects the values of its residents.

REFERENCES

Artemis. (2018). California wildfire industry losses put at $13.2bn by Aon Benfield, January 25, 2018. Retrieved from https://www.artemis.bm/news/california-wildfire-industry-losses-put-at-13–2bn-by-aon-benfield/.
IPBES Global Assessment Chapter 2. (2019). Chapter 2. Status and trends; indirect and direct drivers of change. IPBES Global Assessment on Biodiversity and Ecosystem Services Draft Version. https://www.ipbes.net/system/tdf/ipbes_global_assessment_chapter_2_1_drivers_unedited_31may.pdf?file=1&type=node&id=35278.
Napa County Watershed And Oak Woodland Protection Initiative of 2018. (2018). Watershed and Oak Woodland Protection. https://protectnapawatersheds.org/read-the-full-initiative.
Revised Draft Climate Action Plan. (2018). Planning, Building, and Environmental Services. Napa County California. https://www.countyofnapa.org/DocumentCenter/View/9247/Revised-Draft-Climate-Action-Plan.
Union of Concerned Scientists. (2019). Each Country's Share of CO2 Emissions. https://www.ucsusa.org/global-warming/science-and-impacts/science/each-countrys-share-of-co2.html.

30. San Rafael Climate Change Action Plan

*An Excerpt**

CITY OF SAN RAFAEL

What's a Climate Action Plan?

A Climate Action Plan (CAP) is a tool that any organization can use to develop the programs and actions needed to reduce greenhouse gas emissions (GHGs), which are the pollutants that cause climate change. Generally, these CAPs are focused on this "mitigation" aspect of climate change, but some also lay out a strategy for "adaptation," or how the organization will plan to deal with the effects of climate change such as sea level rise, or increased flooding, heat waves, and wildfires. San Rafael's CAP is called the Climate Change Action Plan and mainly deals with mitigation.

Background

San Rafael has a rich history of climate action and environmental protection. Mayor Al Boro signed on to the Mayor's Climate Protection Agreement in 2006. The first Climate Change Action Plan was adopted in 2009. San Rafael received the first state-wide Beacon Award for Sustainability by the Institute for Local Government in 2013. Several hundred citizens volunteer on behalf of the environment each year, totaling thousands of hours of volunteer work worth hundreds of thousands of dollars in in-kind contributions. San Rafael has thousands of acres of open space and parks and is a Tree City USA community. These are just a few of the actions and programs San Rafael has undertaken over the years.

In 2017 the City Council identified updating the Climate Change Action Plan as a high priority in the annual Sustainability Priorities. A 20-member Green Ribbon Working Group was identified by Councilmember Kate Colin, the City Manager's Office, and the President of Sustainable San Rafael. This Working Group included people from various neighborhoods, businesses, high schools, and organizations in order to get a diverse

*Public document originally published as City of San Rafael, "San Rafael Climate Change Action Plan: An Excerpt," https://www.cityofsanrafael.org/documents/climate-change-action-plan-2030/ (June 2019).

set of voices and perspectives. Throughout the year they participated in a series of meetings with subject matter experts to develop measures for each section of the Plan. Throughout the summer of 2018, the City solicited input from a variety of community members through meetings, pop-up events at community gathering spots, online surveys, a business mixer, and in-person surveys at organizations and activities. This has all been synthesized into the following Plan.

There is broad scientific agreement that to stave off the worst effects of climate change, communities will need to reduce their greenhouse gas emissions by 80 percent below 1990 levels by the year 2050. But time is of the essence. We are already seeing the effects of climate change locally and throughout the world with hotter temperatures, more severe storms, and more volatile and unpredictable weather. San Rafael has met the State GHG reduction target for 2020 and is on track to meet its more stringent local target by 2020. These emissions come from residents, businesses, and visitors, with only less than 1 percent coming from government operations and facilities. Recently, the State of California set interim reduction targets of 40 percent below 1990 levels by 2030 to stay on track. This updated Plan, coming from broad community input, sets out a road map to do just that. We're all in this together; we can do this.

What's Been Done So Far: San Rafael Actions

San Rafael businesses, agencies, and residents have been at the forefront of mitigation efforts such as renewable energy, low-carbon transportation, composting, and water conservation. In 2010 Marin Clean Energy was adopted by the City of San Rafael and most electricity users went immediately to purchasing 50 percent carbon-free electricity for their homes and businesses. San Rafael was one of the first communities to participate in curbside recycling thanks to Marin Sanitary Service's (MSS) forward-thinking owners. In 2014 MSS and Central Marin Sanitation Agency began converting food scraps into energy through their innovative Food to Energy project. By the end of the 2011–2017 drought, San Rafael water users reduced their water consumption by an average of approximately 17 percent. And in 2017, Marin Municipal Water District began purchasing 100 percent renewable Deep Green electricity from MCE Clean Energy, which reduced San Rafael resident and businesses' water-related greenhouse gas emissions dramatically.

The City of San Rafael has implemented 40 of the 48 measures in the original Climate Change Action Plan, completing the majority of those that could be completed and moving most of the rest into an ongoing implementation status. Most measures will need to be continued in order to continue to get emissions reductions!

Where We Are At: Emissions Trend and Status

The City prepares an annual community-wide greenhouse gas inventory to track emissions in seven sectors: residential energy, commercial energy, transportation, off-road vehicles and equipment, waste, water and wastewater. The majority of emissions come from vehicle trips generated by San Rafael residents and businesses. Community emissions totaled 473,440 metric tons of carbon dioxide equivalents (MTCO2e) in 2005. By 2016, emissions had dropped to 389,035 MTCO2e, an 18 percent reduction. This is well below the State target for San Rafael, which is 15 percent below baseline (2005) emissions by 2020, and the trendline shows that emissions are on track to meet the City's local reduction target of 25 percent below 2005 levels by 2020. While emissions declined in almost all sectors, the largest reductions were due to energy conservation and efficiency, a reduction in the carbon intensity of electricity, and improvements to vehicle fuel efficiency. Emissions from City operations, which make up less than 1 percent of community-wide emissions, fell 16 percent by 2016. For more details, see the City's latest Greenhouse Gas Emissions Inventory.

Emissions Forecast and Reduction Targets

The Climate Change Action Plan includes a "business-as-usual" (BAU) forecast in which emissions are projected in the absence of any policies or actions that would occur beyond the base year to reduce emissions. The forecasts are derived by "growing" (increasing) 2016 emissions using forecasted changes in population, number of households, and jobs according to projections developed by the Association of Bay Area Governments. Transportation emissions are projected utilizing data provided by the Metropolitan Transportation Commission, which incorporate the vehicle miles traveled (VMT) reductions expected from the implementation of Plan Bay Area 2020 and the Regional Transportation Plan adopted in 2017. Emissions are expected to rise about 2.4 percent by 2030 and 3.3 percent by 2040. Although the regional agencies have not made official projections for 2050, continuing the trendline suggests emissions would reach approximately 405,530 MTCO2e by 2050 under the BAU forecast.

The Climate Change Action Plan establishes targets like the State's goals to reduce emissions to 40 percent below 1990 levels by 2030 and 80 percent below 1990 levels by 2050. In San Rafael, that means emissions would need to drop to 241,455 MTCO2e by 2030 and 80,485 MTCO2e by 2050. The Plan lays out measures that will exceed the 2030 target and put the City on a trajectory to meet the 2050 goal.

Our Carbon Footprint

The Bay Area Air Quality Management District (BAAQMD) and U.C. Berkeley developed a Consumption-Based Inventory to better understand how our purchasing habits contribute to global climate change. A consumption-based inventory includes emission sources that don't get counted in the typical "in-boundary" GHG inventory, as well as other items that are difficult to quantify like airplane travel and upstream emissions from the production, transport and distribution of food and household goods.

According to this inventory, the average San Rafael household generates 44 MTCO2e per year. As a comparison, the City's community-wide emissions of 389,035 MTCO2e works out to about 17 MTCO2e per household. Our consumption drives climate change more than anything and although San Rafael is meeting its state targets for strict "in-boundary" emissions reductions, we as a community have a long way to go. For more information on this and to see carbon footprints by census tract, visit the SF Bay Area Carbon Footprint Map. To learn how to measure and reduce your household carbon footprint, check out our local Resilient Neighborhoods program.

San Rafael doesn't exist in a vacuum. While we are leveraging or trying to combat regional, state-wide, national and even international actions and trends, we also have the ability and responsibility to collaborate with other efforts and campaigns. San Rafael is known for collaborating and it's our collective imagination and cooperative efforts that make San Rafael such a successful and wonderful place to be. If you've ever been to a San Rafael City Council meeting or Climate Change Action Plan quarterly forum you will know this first-hand.

The State of California established the Six Pillars framework in 2015 when Governor Jerry Brown was inaugurated for his second term as governor. These include (1) reducing today's petroleum use in cars and trucks by up to 50 percent; (2) increasing from one-third to 50 percent our electricity derived from renewable sources; (3) doubling the energy efficiency savings achieved at existing buildings and making heating fuels cleaner; (4) reducing the release of methane, black carbon, and other short-lived climate pollutants; (5) managing farm and rangelands, forests and wetlands so they can store carbon; and (6) periodically updating the state's climate adaptation strategy: Safeguarding California. The measures contained in this Climate Change Action Plan are designed to support and implement the Six Pillars and the goals of California's 2017 Climate Change Scoping Plan on a local level.

The County of Marin, noting the need for all residents and businesses to actively reduce emissions and plan for climate adaptation has created an engagement framework based on the research and book by local author, entrepreneur, and environmentalist Paul Hawken called DRAWDOWN: Marin. DRAWDOWN: Marin is a comprehensive, science-based, community-wide campaign to do our part to slow the impacts of climate change. It is an effort to recognize our need to reduce our "carbon footprint" and to provide a road map to doing so. Like the State's Six Pillars, there are six areas of focus: (1) 100 percent Renewable Energy, (2) Low-Carbon Transportation, (3) Energy Efficiency in Buildings and Infrastructure, (4) Local Food and Food Waste, (5) Carbon Sequestration, and (6) Climate Resilient Communities.

Actions to Reduce Greenhouse Gas Emissions

The Climate Change Action Plan includes a variety of regulatory, incentive-based and voluntary strategies that are expected to reduce emissions from both existing and new development in San Rafael. Several of the strategies build on existing programs while others provide new opportunities to address climate change. State actions will have a substantial impact on future emissions. Local strategies will supplement these State actions and achieve additional GHG emissions reductions. Successful implementation will rely on the combined participation of City staff along with San Rafael residents, businesses, and community leaders.

The Action Plan identify the State and local strategies included in the Climate Change Action Plan to reduce emissions in community and government operations. Emissions reductions are estimated for each strategy; combined, they show that the City could reduce emissions 19 percent below 1990 levels by 2020 (equivalent to 31 percent below 2005 levels), and 42 percent below 1990 levels by 2030, which is enough to surpass the City and State goals for those years. Community emissions are projected to be 233,920 MTCO2e in 2030 with all State and local actions implemented, while the reduction target is 241,455 MTCO2e. State actions represent about 40 percent of the reduction expected through implementation of the Climate Change Action Plan while local actions represent about 60 percent.

31. Building Climate Resilience in Cities

*Lessons from New York**

Cynthia Rosenzweig *and* William Solecki

We live in an urbanizing world. Up to two-thirds of the world's population—some six billion people—may live in cities by 2050.

Cities have emerged as first responders to climate change because they experience the impacts of natural disasters firsthand and because they produce up to 70 percent of greenhouse gas emissions.

To protect urban dwellers from climate change impacts, such as more frequent and more intense heat waves, heavy downpours and coastal flooding, cities need to make themselves more resilient.

That's why cities figured so prominently at the Paris climate conference last month, where hundreds of mayors pledged to reduce emissions and improve city resilience. As of today, 447 cities have signed on to the Compact of Mayors, a coalition of city leaders who have pledged to reduce greenhouse gas emissions, track progress and prepare for climate change impacts.

We codirect the Urban Climate Change Research Network (UCCRN), a group of over 600 experts who provide climate science information on adaptation and mitigation to urban leaders and practitioners from governments, the private sector, nongovernmental organizations, and the community. At the Paris conference, the UCCRN released the Summary for City Leaders of its Second Assessment Report on Climate Change and Cities.

Based on our work with UCCRN, we believe that cities have great potential to lead on climate change solutions but must be transformed in order to do so.

We also believe that New York City's experience in rebuilding after 2012's Hurricane Sandy offers useful lessons for other cities.

Adaptable Plans

UCCRN has identified transformative strategies that cities can pursue to become climate leaders.

*Originally published as Cynthia Rosenzweig and William Solecki, "Building Climate Resilience in Cities: Lessons from New York," *The Conversation*, https://theconversation.com/building-climate-resilience-in-cities-lessons-from-new-york-52363 (January 22, 2016). Reprinted with permission of the publisher.

They should link preparations for near-term disasters and long-term climate change; meld activities that reduce greenhouse gas emissions and build resilience; involve multiple stakeholder groups and scientists in the planning process; focus on protecting the most vulnerable; enhance local credit worthiness and management skills; and look outward by joining city networks.

New York City is already pursuing these objectives, motivated largely by the damages it has already suffered from extreme weather.

On October 29, 2012, Hurricane Sandy hurtled ashore in the New York metropolitan region, killing 44 people and causing US$19 billion in damages in New York City alone. The flood inundation zone in New York City encompassed approximately 88,700 buildings, which contained 300,000 homes and 23,000 businesses, and left two million people without electricity.

Sandy was a wake-up call that showed how vulnerable New York City was to extreme climate events. In its wake, city leaders resolved to take steps that would make New York stronger and more resilient in the face of climate change.

New York's experience in rebuilding after Hurricane Sandy highlights three main messages that are transferable to other cities.

First, there is enough information to act on climate change today based on the best-available science. Cities can update their climate projections and urban climate change action plans as scientific understanding improves and city leaders learn more about resiliency, but there is no reason to delay climate action planning.

In New York City, the New York Panel on Climate Change (NPCC), a body of experts first convened by Mayor Bloomberg in 2008, developed a concept of Flexible Adaptation Pathways that the city adopted in its long-term planning. Originally conceived in London, this approach calls for agencies to start adopting resiliency measures immediately, monitor how well they work, and continually update their understanding of climate risk information and responses as the climate system and resilience actions evolve.

If cities do not start acting now, many of the world's vulnerable cities and populations will endure significant impacts from heat waves, heavy downpours and coastal flooding due to sea level rise.

The second important priority is to plan across entire metropolitan regions. In preparing for climate change, the city of New York is taking an approach that encompasses the entire "infrastructure-shed" of the city.

For example, the New York City climate action task force includes regional transportation providers who manage the subways, buses, and railroads that run within and around the city into the extended metropolitan region. Plans must also consider how extreme droughts and inland floods can affect the watershed that supplies New York City's drinking water.

Disasters and extreme events do not respect political boundaries, so steps to make cities more resilient cannot stop at city limits. Instead, they need to encompass the interconnected energy, water, transportation, telecommunications, sanitation, health, food and public safety systems that extend beyond municipal borders to the wider metropolitan region and beyond, including national and international supply chains.

New York City's third key step is bringing together city decision-makers, infrastructure managers, citizens groups and other key actors with researchers to develop shared understanding of New York's specific climate change vulnerabilities and climate science needs.

That's because climate change will not impact every city in the same way. For example, some cities will be exposed to repeated and worsening droughts, while others may be more exposed to flooding or extreme heat events. Scientists and stakeholders need to work together to understand the risks that are relevant for each city so that they can find effective ways to prepare for climate change.

Critical Vulnerabilities

The most critical vulnerability in New York City that Hurricane Sandy spotlighted is coastal flooding. Currently, an estimated 400,000 New York residents, 71,500 buildings and much of the city's critical infrastructure are located within the 100-year flood zone—that is, the area that has a one percent chance of flooding in any given year. Sea levels in New York City are rising at almost twice the global average rate, and the NPCC projects that sea levels will continue to rise in the coming decades, which will put more residents, buildings and infrastructure at risk.

Coastal cities across the world are vulnerable to sea level rise and more intense coastal storms. And cities everywhere face risks including more frequent and more extreme heat waves and increasing heavy downpours.

Critical infrastructure systems in cities exposed to these changing hazards include energy, transportation, telecommunications, water and waste. These systems are interdependent, so impacts on one of them can cause cascading effects onto other infrastructure systems during an extreme event.

For example, Hurricane Sandy caused gas shortages in the New York metropolitan region: loading docks on the water were physically damaged, refineries and terminals lost power and pipelines shut down, making it impossible to receive or ship fuel.

This caused major failures in the gasoline supply chain, forcing drivers to wait in line at gas stations and limiting New Yorkers' mobility. Fuel shortages also made it more challenging for ambulances to respond to emergencies, for utility workers to restore electricity and for relief workers to reach the hardest-hit areas of the city.

Certain groups of people in cities are disproportionately vulnerable. For example, more intense and longer-lasting heat waves threaten people with underlying health problems, the young and the elderly, and low-income residents.

Investing in Resilience

The UCCRN recommends that cities should take a portfolio approach to investing in resilience measures that spreads resources across multiple categories. They include implementing citywide policies, such as upgrading building codes; hardening critical protective structures; investing in green infrastructure, such as green roofs and bioswales; and strengthening social safety nets.

To develop specific, localized climate action plans, stakeholders and scientists need to work together to learn about climate risks, brainstorm strategies and prioritize implementation. This process should include groups that represent a cross-section of the city's population, including the most disadvantaged citizens, as well as the private sector.

The Paris Agreement signals a new era for climate change, and cities are generating positive energy for this new phase. Early-adopter cities such as New York need to continue to strengthen and share their actions and lessons learned.

Cities that have not yet started need to begin planning and preparing for climate change. The good news is that many urban leaders are committed to meeting these challenges, and there is a great deal of knowledge that researchers can share on how to proceed. By starting to plan and invest now, cities can lead the effort to avoid dangerous climate change and adapt to a warming world.

32. Eye on Climate Change*

INTERNATIONAL CITY/COUNTY
MANAGEMENT ASSOCIATION

The nature of climate change impacts is highly localized. To be successful, adaptation or mitigation interventions need to be tailored to fit the geographic region, community demographics, and resources available. Therefore local governments are especially important and well-positioned to take action.

During the past two years, the United States has seen landmark shifts in its efforts to combat climate change. In 2015, both the U.S. Department of Defense and the Council on Foreign Relations declared climate change a threat to national security.

The Federal Emergency Management Agency (FEMA) now will only grant disaster preparedness funds for states whose hazard mitigation plans address climate change. (To find out if your state has taken this step, visit www.fema.gov/hazard-mitigation-plan-status.)

And, in 2016, the Department of Housing and Urban Development awarded $48 million to the first American climate refugees: Members of a tribal community in Louisiana need to relocate from the Isle de Jean Charles, which has experienced a 98 percent loss of land since 1955.[1]

The Isle de Jean Charles residents won't be alone for long; nearly 5 million people in the U.S. live within four feet of the local high-tide level in their communities.[2] The National Oceanic and Atmospheric Administration (www.noaa.gov) reports that more than 2 billion people around the world live within 60 miles of a coastal boundary. In the coming years, climate projections show that sea-level rise and land subsidence combined with storm surges at high tide will increase flooding in many of these regions.

Yet, coastal communities are not the only ones at risk. Rising temperatures, changes in seasonal variation, and increases in extreme weather events will impact communities all over the world.

The United Nations Development Programme estimates that more than 70 percent of climate change reduction measures and up to 90 percent of climate change adaptation measures are undertaken by local governments.

According to the Local Government Sustainability Practices survey conducted by ICMA in 2015, less than a third (32 percent) of local governments in the U.S. have adopted a sustainability plan even though almost half (47 percent) identified environmental

---

*Originally published as International City/County Management Association, "Eye on Climate Change," https://icma.org/articles/article/eye-climate-change (Sep 20, 2016). Reprinted with permission of the publisher.

protection as an overall community priority, and only 19 percent have dedicated budget resources specifically to sustainability or environmental protection.

Why is this? According to the same survey, lack of staff capacity and support (59 percent), lack of information on how to proceed (51 percent), and lack of community and resident support (49 percent) are among the most significant factors hindering local sustainability efforts.

Addressing the Challenge

Here are steps that local governments can take to address climate change challenges:

Identify Key Vulnerabilities

The first step in designing effective adaptation and mitigation strategies is to identify the likely impacts on the community and how the changing climate will affect a local government's ability to deliver services. A variety of tools are available for completing a climate risk assessment (see https://climatescreeningtools.worldbank.org/content/complementary-risk-analysis-tools).

Women, children, seniors, disabled, and impoverished residents are all more vulnerable to such climate change impacts as urban heat island effect and increased instances of flooding and drought. Climate change also will impact storm and wastewater management, delivery of clean drinking water, waste and chemical management, and air quality.

Make Sata Available

Access to and dissemination of climate data is critical to a local government's ability to make informed decisions and identify key vulnerabilities. Coordinating data and projections beyond single teams and areas of service delivery allows for consistent and comprehensive planning across multiple sectors.

Unfortunately, information sharing between departments, agencies, and local research institutions is often overly bureaucratic or nonexistent. Finding ways to liaise between or partner with these entities will help you direct resources toward analyzing existing data and filling gaps rather than duplicating work. Data transparency is important for both local governments and the residents they serve.

Lead by Example

Just because data is available, it doesn't mean local government staff members understand or know what to do with it. In 2015, Fort Lauderdale, Florida, piloted a citywide staff climate training for all full-time employees. The mandatory two-and-a-half-hour training focused on climate science and impacts, along with the city's sustainability projects (http://gis.fortlauderdale.gov/GreenYourRoutine).

The city held 32 sessions, including evening options, with 85 employees per class for two months. Sixty-nine percent of attendees felt they could use the information learned during their everyday activities at work. Fort Lauderdale also trained the assistant city manager and the department heads to serve as climate ambassadors for the community.

Engage Your Community

Residents who are aware of and understand climate change vulnerabilities are less likely to be impacted by them and are more likely to support local projects that address them. Townsville, Australia, for example, has been implementing a collective social learning exercise in a workshop format to engage and educate the community for the past decade.

The workshop helps stakeholders create realistic outcomes and solutions to public challenges through an interactive visioning process. When complex information is shared in ways that make sense to local decision makers, it allows them to develop actionable, affordable, and equitable strategies.

Look for Knowledge Exchange Opportunities

You are not alone. There are local governments all over the world in varying stages of climate preparedness with which you can trade lessons learned. In South Africa, for example, eThekwini Municipality established the Central KZN Climate Change Compact[3] as a way for regional municipalities to pool resources and capacity to address climate change.

Compact members have different levels of institutional capacity and access to resources but have been able to leverage the compact to combat institutional inertia and garner political support. The compact is modeled on the Southeast Florida Regional Compact[4] that eThekwini Municipality was exposed to during an ICMA CityLinks™ partnership.

These compacts are a form of regional climate governance that commit local governments to working together on mitigation and adaptation activities.

Explore "no regrets" Strategies

Invest in projects that generate social and economic benefits independently of increasing your community's resilience to climate change. Boulder, Colorado, as one example, was able to provide green space and recreation for its residents while keeping critical infrastructure out of low-lying areas through its Greenways Program.

The city program sought to buy vulnerable land in flood plains for environmental protection, habitat restoration, flood mitigation, and increased storm water drainage capacity.

Track Your Progress

Climate change adaptation or mitigation projects need to be goal-directed, evidence-based, and cost-effective. Using performance management, data analysis, and project management tools to identify opportunities for improvement, and tracking the implementation of those plans is crucial to the short-and long-term success of climate change preparedness goals.

To support its greenhouse gas emissions reduction targets, Somerville, Massachusetts, uses MassEnergyInsight, a free, Web-based tool that can help local governments understand their energy use and reduce their carbon footprint. It delivers customized, easy-to-use reports on electricity, natural gas, and oil use.

Confronting Climate Change

Climate change is a global problem, yet many future solutions will be found at the local level. Local governments that work across community sectors and boundaries, as well as with each other, will be the leaders the world needs.

Common Climate Change Terminology

Adaptation: The process of adjusting to actual or expected type of weather and its effects in order to moderate harm or exploit beneficial opportunities. Adaptation activities build resilience to the unavoidable impacts of climate change.

Mitigation: Actions to reduce the amount of greenhouse gasses released into the atmosphere, to recapture greenhouse gasses currently in the atmosphere, and then to sequester them in ecosystems.

Urban Heat Island Effect: A phenomenon where the concentration of structures and waste heat from human activity causes the temperature in urban regions to be higher than their rural surroundings.

What Do These Places Have In Common?

Local governments used as examples in this article were all participants in ICMA's CityLinks Climate Adaptation Partnership Program, funded by the U.S. Agency for International Development.

The CityLinks model was designed by ICMA as a way to enable local government officials in developing and decentralizing countries to draw on the resources of their international counterparts to find sustainable solutions tailored to the real needs of their cities.

It is based on the premise that well-managed communities are the key to efficient service delivery, economic growth, sound management of resources, and political stability.

Climate Change Advice

Here is what representatives of the ICMA CityLinks cities had to say when asked: How do you begin to face climate change?

"So much of what people think about climate change is wrapped up in the 2030, 2050, or 2070 horizon and how warm is it going to be then, along with other factors that are even harder to discern, like how wet or dry it might be.

"Local government managers need to look at climate change through the lens of what they need to do long term, but they also need to be thinking of what does this practically mean for what we need to do in the next year, in the next five years.

"I think there are a wealth of examples from the past that we could choose from, where we maybe weren't as prepared as we could have been, and we know that climate change is going to exacerbate those issues.

"So [consider] what planning strategies we can employ that really set us up for success in that five- to seven-year horizon that we can achieve and then set another five- to seven-year horizon. Then, by the time we're at these future dates, we're hopefully much closer to the track we need to be on."

—Russell Sands, Watershed Sustainability and Outreach
Supervisor, Boulder, Colorado

"If you can find a city that you can communicate with you whether it's by Skype or e-mail, establish a link with that city. Learn about other projects it has already done, like creating a climate action plan, and it will provide a good base for you to move forward."

—Kerry Chambers, Chief Administrative Manager,
Portmore Municipal Council, Jamaica

"Understand what the nature of impacts are over a period of time. Some cities view climate change as a big thing, just an immense thing they're grappling with, but you can't build bridges with people by constantly telling them a doomsday scenario.

"Be strategic with what actions you can do over a period. Make sure that you can break down problems into a short-, medium-, and long-term approach. Constantly evaluate your actions in dealing with those problems as they are grouped in how they are improving and keeping you on track."

—Pradesh Ramiah, Climate Change Planner,
Gold Coast, Queensland, Australia

"Don't go looking for models of a city that has solved climate change or adaptation. I think one of the most interesting things about this partnership is that none of us can claim to be the experts.

"What we're doing is sharing challenges and maybe there's some things along the way that we're hopeful for or some small things that can be replicated. There isn't one city that is fully adapted or has even come close.

"Look for things that are useful and replicable but recognize that there is unpredictability and that's what resiliency is all about."

—Oliver Sellers-Gracia, Director of Sustainability
and Environment, Somerville, Massachusetts

NOTES

1. IPCC, 2013: Summary for Policymakers. In: Climate Change 2013: The Physical Science Basis. Contribution of Working Group I to the Fifth Assessment Report of the Intergovernmental Panel on Climate Change [Stocker, T.F., D. Qin, G.-K. Plattner, M. Tignor, S.K. Allen, J. Boschung, A. Nauels, Y. Xia, V. Bex and P.M. Midgley (eds.)]. Cambridge University Press, Cambridge, United Kingdom and New York, NY, USA.
2. USGCRP 2014, Third Climate Assessment.
3. USGCRP 2017, Fourth Climate Assessment.
4. http://www.coastalresettlement.org.

33. Local Government Climate Change and Evolution*

MINCH LEWIS

The climate is changing. Species survive if they can adapt. But no climate is changing faster than the climate for local governments. Governments have responded with a number of evolutionary survival strategies, some more successful than others. Can we take a lesson from nature?

Restructuring

Like monarch butterflies, many Local governments have changed their structure. Boards of supervisors have been replaced by county management systems, with elected executives or with professional managers. The metamorphosis can be as dramatic as the changes that produce a monarch butterfly.

Outside Investment

Capital funding stress has been reduced by privatizing infrastructure and urban reclamation projects with industrial development revenue bonds. Public/private Partnerships (P3's) are an evolving trend to apply the resources of the private sector to meet the needs of the public sector.

Government Consolidation

Local governments evolved (in a sense) when communication was limited to the distance a horse could travel in a day. Today, digital communication travels at the speed of light. Resources have migrated from urban cores to fertile suburban sites. Governmental consolidation brings resources back together in regional or metro governments. Nature judges' evolutionary changes on survival; humans' debate. For consolidation, there is a debate between "regionalists" and "localists."

*Originally published as Minch Lewis, "Local Government Climate Change and Evolution," *PA Times*, https://patimes.org/local-government-climate-change-evolution/ (August 18, 2017). Reprinted with permission of the publisher.

Shared Services

Some Local governments have evolved without disappearing. Improved technology, stronger professionalism and better communication have made it possible for local governments to capitalize on economies of scale and efficiencies. In a recent report for the New York State Department of State, the Maxwell School identified the history of service sharing and governmental consolidation. The report includes examples of both successful and unsuccessful "evolutions."

Eds and Meds

Economic forces in urban areas strongly support the expansion of educational and medical facilities. Every community has a hospital. Most have higher education institutions. Successful local governments are securing external funding for expanding both types of facilities. They provide badly needed employment opportunities as economic base enterprises—funds come from outside the local community and spurn a powerful "multiplier" economic boost inside the community. This evolutionary strategy requires careful management since Eds and Meds can "swallow cities" if other economic benefits do not offset property tax concessions.

The Hospitality Industry

National trends have indicated major growth in tourism and travel fuels local hospitality facilities. Local governments have courted hotels and destination tourist attractions to generate revenues from occupancy and sales taxes, both of which fall on non-local citizens, and incidentally, have "multiplier" effects the same as the Meds and Eds.

Infrastructure Projects

Urban centers with utility systems created in the last century face major maintenance costs. One strategy is to seek state and federal funds for projects to replace aging infrastructure. Once again, such projects also have a powerful "multiplier" impact on local economies. "Ready to go" projects may tap into new resources if the Trump administration moves infrastructure programs forward. The one trillion program may not be "stalled" forever. Other approaches rely on creative leadership to take advantage of latent opportunities like Birmingham's inland port expansion. The International City/County Management Association has published a guide on financing infrastructure projects.

Alternate Revenue Sources

Historically, colonial governments had been financed primarily from property taxes that were an indication of wealth. That strategy worked because the economic resources were located in urban centers. The centers morphed into industrial powerhouses. The workers who supported those industrial powerhouses lived in houses that were taxed at levels subsidized by the taxes on the industries. In some communities, tax rates were adjusted by class of property. In others, like New York State, burden was distributed to the commercial and industrial properties by use of assessment policy. When industry and commerce migrated to the suburbs, cities were forced to diversify their revenue sources. User fees, sales taxes and revenue sharing with state and federal aid substituted to create mendicant governments that no longer control their own revenue sources.

Gentrification

Hollowed out urban cores in some cities have been revitalized by transforming retail and commercial properties into residential havens for millennials and empty nesters. My column on millennials makes the point that new economic life can come from the next generation. As with other evolutionary changes in nature, there can be unintended consequences. Low-income residents can be displaced as the market value of central city sites skyrockets. On Chicago's Northshore, single-family bungalows on 30-foot lots have been replaced with million-dollar 6-story townhomes. The City wins taxes, but the original residents win relocation.

Innovation

Another way nature deals with stress is to innovate. Local governments can innovate both internally and externally. Internal innovation can lead to more efficient and effective management decisions by mining financial and operational data with creative software as promoted by many private vendors such as Forecast5 Analytics. External innovation can build customer satisfaction with access and transparency as the City of Syracuse is promoting.

Conclusion

The lesson we can take from nature is that evolution is the key to the future of local government. Evolution in nature and in government is risky—the outcome is uncertain. But the outcome of a refusal to evolve is certain: extinction in nature and irrelevance in government.

34. California's Capabilities to House Disaster Survivors*

Melynda Moran *and* Alan R. Roper

It is a hot summer evening and you and your loved ones are in your back yard mid-summer enjoying the hot California sun and warm summer breeze. Suddenly you smell the scent of something reminiscent to your childhood and campfires with mom and pop up at the lake. You peer over your eight-foot fence line and notice the once rolling hills and beautiful redwood tree line covered in a roaring blaze, donning an orange and red ember with billowing smoke. You rush to the front door to see emergency response vehicles and personnel running up and down the neighborhood, knocking on doors urging people to take what they can, giving them only five minutes to grab only what they can hold in their hands. This is very the moment when you are forced to evacuate your home with just minutes to spare before roads are cordoned off by fire and emergency first responders. This is the very moment you are told to leave your home behind before it is destroyed and everything you have come to know is either about to be destroyed or burned to the ground. Imagine your home being obliterated, your community ravaged, your family and friends completely separated for the foreseeable future without having an end in sight. This unimaginable scenario has turned into reality for many Californians in the past few years due to destruction and devastation caused by the wildfires. Communities are at a high-risk for wildfires throughout the state of California due to rapid climate change causing drought conditions throughout the state, and politics impacting funding and resources. Residents are often unaware of the dangers lurking in their very back yards and are urged to prepare both individually and as a community to prevent some of the dangers associated to wildfires and displacement caused in the aftermath.

Wildfires and the potential hazards that come along with them can be severe if not planned for, or managed properly. The damage left in the wake of these fires can be catastrophic, often leaving hundreds if not thousands homeless and without shelter, food or running water in most cases. Following a disaster such as this, the main priority for first responders is to save lives rather than property. It is essential for first responder personnel responding to a critical incident or natural disaster such as a wildfire to establish some type of life saving measures or casualty collection point for those survivors post-disaster. The State of California experienced a catastrophic fire season in 2018. High heat, shifting winds and dry bush were all contributing factors that lead to such a devastating fire

---

*Published with permission of the authors.

season in Northern California. Much of the destruction and damage left behind by these fires is indescribable unless experienced firsthand or seen by the human eye.

The Town of Paradise, located in Butte County, California, experienced more devastation from wildfires than any other community in the State of California. The Town of Paradise's landscape consisted mainly of wild brush, trees, shrubbery, grass and rolling hills overlooking Butte County and the Sacramento Valley. This desolate, small, and private community located between rolling hills and trees was considered home and a "paradise" to many. Residents of Paradise consisted mainly of retired, rural, prior military, peace-seeking individuals searching for a community in California that provided a safe haven from the urban-suburban lifestyle of the major cities.

Although the Camp Fire (Paradise) was devastating, it proved to be a learning experience for first responders, local governments, and the Federal Emergency Management Agency (FEMA) alike. One of main challenges the Camp Fire presented to first responders and Cal Fire personnel was the rural area habituated by individuals from all walks of life with little to no preparation for the destruction a wildfire of this magnitude could cause to an entire community. Many residents either lost their homes entirely or were unable to move back in whether their homes were still standing. The California Environmental Protection Agency (CALEPA) had to clear each lot to determine whether or not any dangers were still present on the property. This, of course, took a great deal of time and left the town of Paradise and surrounding areas faced with a major housing crisis for post-disaster survivors. In turn, this left many of the local areas such as parking lots, campsites, motels and hotels overrun with disaster survivors.

California's Ability to Provide Short and Long-Term Housing and Shelter Large Communities

After the devastating Camp Fire which virtually destroyed the town of Paradise and surrounding areas, research was conducted to assess California's ability to house a large amount of disaster survivors, and whether or not the California's draft plan to house residents of disaster stricken communities post 2018 disaster is effective today. The research was supported by survivor testimony, and statistics. The data was acquired through conducting interviews with subject matter experts employed in the emergency response career fields.

This study also identifies how lack of policy leading up the 2018 fire season has since influenced either change, or implementation of new policy and procedures for housing disaster survivors post-disaster. California appears to be better prepared to house and shelter large communities both short and long-term following the 2018 wildfire season in part due to the lessons learned following the destruction left behind by the wildfires during the 2018 season.

Measuring the Need for Emergency Housing by the Numbers

Disaster Survivor individual assistance numbers for the 2018 disaster and wildfire season are as follows. During 2018, there were several large-scale disasters and wildfires that claimed tens of thousands of homes throughout the State of California leaving just as many people in their wake looking for individual assistance, shelter, and housing. There were approximately 70,854 eligible disaster survivors in the State of California who applied for individual assistance. Of this number, approximately 2.3 percent of these survivors (eligible) were from Ventura County and had survived the Woolsey Fire disaster that claimed 1,643 structures and three lives. Approximately 3.7 percent of survivors hail from Lake County and suffered through the devastation of both the Pawnee and River Ranch Fires that destroyed upwards of 650 homes. 10.3 percent survived the Carr Fire in Shasta County that burned nearly 230,000 acres, destroyed over 1,600 structures, and claimed eight lives. Another 12.8 percent of California's disaster survivors who applied for individual assistance were from Los Angeles County, where the Hill Fire blazed through over 96,000 acres and destroyed almost 1,700 structures while claiming three lives. The Camp Fire, which blazed nearly all of Butte County, burned roughly 154,000 acres, destroyed almost 19,000 structures, and left 86 dead in its wake. 71.3 percent of California's disaster survivors in the year 2018 that applied and were found to be eligible for individual assistance were from the Butte County Fires (Camp Fire).

It was found that approximately 3,808 out of 70,854 (5.3 percent) people who applied for individual assistance were between the ages of 0–5 years. 9,845 out of 70,854 (13.8 percent) who applied were between the ages of 5–18 years of age whereas a staggering 42,071 out of 70,854 (59.3 percent) were between the ages of 19–64 years of age. The last age group of 65 and older had approximately 15,130 out of 70,854 (21.3 percent) of people who applied for individual assistance. The largest age group of disaster survivors affected was between 19–64 years of age with the second largest age group affected being that of senior citizens.

Of the 70,854 people affected by 2018 wildfire disasters, approximately 27,416 homeowners or renters reported damage to their homes and requested assistance. This represented approximately 38 percent of the 70,854 people affected by the disasters in California for 2018. Another 13,662 (19.2 percent) of the 70,854 people affected from the wildfires requested some type of shelter or temporary housing assistance. The majority of those in need of either home repair, shelter or housing came from those survivors from the Camp Fire in Butte County respectively, with survivors from the Hills Fire and Woolsey Fires right after them.

Research Findings

The researcher conducted numerous site visits and interviews to produce findings and recommendations. This included an in-depth analysis on wildfire disasters and disaster housing which was conducted relevant to wildfires that occurred in 2018 that left thousands of Californians displaced from their homes in their aftermath of destruction. Following the data collection and analysis process in this study, the researcher identified the following significant findings which provide helpful information for stakeholders and agencies involved in the disaster response and recovery.

Lack of Communication Amongst Collaborative Agencies. The agencies involved to include local, state and federal agencies weren't able to communicate effectively throughout the course of the response to the fires in Paradise California. This led to confusion and inability to make decisions often leaving the Federal Emergency Management

Agency (FEMA) to lead the way in the decision-making process. Additionally, the lack of communication between the collaboration of disaster response agencies led to increased time on deliverables and stalled recovery efforts when housing disaster survivors.

Lack of Pre-Selected Sites for Housing Disaster Survivors. The housing program had failures in that the state and local governments FEMA were not prepared to handle disasters of such a large magnitude. Local governments failed in their responsibilities to pre-identify sites that would eventually house large amounts of disaster survivors who were exposed when the wildfires struck, mostly in Butte County. There were not any site sections made by local governments so that when FEMA came in to take control of the recovery phase, the groundwork for site selection was never done. This is one of the first things that should have been pre-identified leading up to the magnitude of destruction left behind from the fires.

Local Environmental Laws and Regulations Cause for Initial Hold-Up of MHUs. FEMA temporary housing units (MHUs) are pre-staged in Texas. When these units were requested by California to assist in housing disaster survivors, they were shipped out, but held up at state lines due to local and environmental regulations and standards not yet being met for the housing units. This prevented the use for response to disaster sites, only making the recovery phase much more strenuous and trying for survivors.

Lack of Disaster Preparedness Training for Community Members. Local law enforcement, fire and emergency medical services (EMS) personnel all have disaster preparedness training and know what to do during a disaster. However, many community members do not receive this same training or similar that would be useful in the event of a disaster. Many of the subject matter experts expressed the increased need for disaster preparedness training amongst community members, particularly in rural communities and communities with large amounts of retirees and elderly communities in need of special attention.

Lack of Decision Making by Community Leaders, Heavily Reliant on FEMA for Decision Making. Many community leaders were not prepared for the type of disaster that occurred in Butte County and Paradise. When it came time to make decisions on what to do next, they often looked to FEMA and California Governor's Office of Emergency Services (CalOES) personnel to make these decisions. No one from the local government knew what to do. This can be chalked up as a lack of knowledge or training on disasters as well, but at an administrative level for the local government.

Lack of Disaster Response Plan for Evacuating Elderly Communities or Disabled Persons Care Facilities. The state and local government did not have a designated evacuation plan for elderly communities housing senior citizens or communities with disabled persons or concentrated care facilities for them. When the fires came, many did not have the strength or mindset to know what to do in these homes or care facilities, which presumably led to their untimely deaths. This is something the state needs to improve on in terms of training and preparedness.

California Does Not Have a Plan to House Disaster Survivors. California is completely reliant on the federal government to house disaster survivors and does not have their own disaster response plan for emergency housing. Without the federal government, the state would not be able to house the thousands of individuals affected by the wildfires during the 2018 wildfire season. As of this writing, there are still well over 1,000 people without shelter due to many of the barriers and incidents that held up the response and recovery to these disasters.

Lessons Learned and Recommendations:

The state's current disaster plans seem to revolve around federal assistance to ensure they are fully operative and do not necessarily seem to be on the right track as of right now. There are still many changes that need to be made to operations during disaster response and recovery efforts by the state in order to be fully capable to shelter or house disaster survivor communities big or small for that matter. If the state is still going to rely on FEMA to carry out their disaster plans or spearhead the housing issue, then they need to make some changes to their current practices. From just some of the important findings in this study, the researcher makes some recommendations to better assist the state in its response to disasters and housing survivors.

Recommendation One:

The framework design and structure at CalOES Response & Recovery should be divided into divisions organized by disaster type. CalOES responds and mitigates multiple disasters at once, with one leader making decisions for two different disasters. Each type of disaster should have its own Incident Command System (ICS) structure to enhance strategic decision-making skills and improve disaster response and recovery postures, which will ensure a timely and sound housing program for each specific disaster. CalOES will lead this framework design as it should be attainable within the next three to four months of this writing.

Recommendation Two:

Housing sites should be pre-identified in each county throughout the state on a quarterly basis. On a quarterly basis, vacant and available lots, housing units, and hotels that meet FEMA regulations for housing disaster survivors should be identified in a proactive measure to respond to housing disaster survivors. Pre-identifying potential housing locations can expedite the housing program for survivors and ensure a timely response to homeless disaster survivors. This project needs to be spearheaded via a multi-collaborative agency effort from local, state and federal agencies. The California Environmental Protection Agency (CalEPA) needs to have a hand in this as well as the local, city or municipal public works departments such as water and wastewater utility divisions.

Recommendation Three:

Local governments and communities should be provided more education and development pertaining to community disaster recovery and community disaster preparedness. The responsibility for this training should from local and state governments such as the California Office of Emergency Services. The training should consist of an annual preparedness and recovery training that is disseminated to city and county officials as well as first responders (i.e., police and fire personnel).

Recommendation Four:

Local governments and communities should be provided more education and training pertaining to community disaster recovery. Surrounding communities should be more supportive and preemptive to assisting disaster survivors. Allowing community involvement in planning for their communities and the surrounding will also enhance the housing program by having buy-in from the potential areas that will be housing these survivors. FEMA as the governing agency should disseminate the necessary disaster preparedness training then delegate this training to local and state agencies. From there this training could be utilized to train public entities and other constituents to ensure proper training and preparedness measures are taking place prior to disasters.

Recommendation Five:

The State of California should adopt a housing assistance program that supports individuals who may not qualify for FEMA housing assistance. This would allow a stronger recovery program for cities devastated by disaster. The housing assistance program should identify grants for survivors and a plan to house survivors such as pre-staged containers allowable for habitation, recreation vehicles, or even camps such as the ones utilized by CalFire and other first responders during disasters. This needs to be headlined by local and state agencies together to show that California is capable or can house disaster survivors and is not entirely reliant upon federal aid.

Recommendation Six:

Federal, state and local emergency mangers should be better trained and prepared in communication leading up to and during disasters. Research from this study suggests that emergency managers from the agencies above need to be able to disseminate information collectively and collaboratively though the joint information center. This needs to be a joint collaborative effort between all agencies. The local and state governments can obviously facilitate this training and have FEMA bring their expertise and knowledge into the discussion to enable constructive feedback and recommendations to better serve the disaster housing programs as well as individual assistance. The overall goal amongst the agencies needs is to ensure all disaster survivors' shelter and housing needs are met within a reasonable amount of time. One year later is not considered reasonable. A timeline to completion for a program such as this should be short, in fact, this should be taking place immediately on monthly basis at joint information centers and state operations centers for disaster relief. This needs to be integrated into monthly trainings.

REFERENCES

Deaton, L. (2018). Wildfire: No backing down even after a historic wildfire, residents in one Santa Rosa neighborhood continue to embrace the value of the fire-wise USA program. Retrieved on July 6, 2019, from https://www.nfpa.org/News-and-Research/Publications-and-media/NFPA-Journal/2018/July-August-2018/Columns/Wildfire.

Federal Emergency Management Agency. (2009). National Disaster Housing Strategy, Retrieved July 3, 2019, from https://www.fema.gov/pdf/emergency/disasterhousing/NDHS-core.pdf.

Federal Emergency Management Agency. (2018). National Disaster Recovery Framework. Retrieved August 4, 2019, from https://www.fema.gov/national-disaster-recovery-framework.

Leven, R. (2019). Natural Disasters Are Getting Worse: People with the least power are most at risk. Retrieved on August 10, 2019, from https://publicintegrity.org/environment/climate-change-natural-disasters/.

Martin, G. (2019). Losing Paradise: The "New Normal" of California Wildfires: More frequent, more intense, more destructive wildfires. Welcome to the new normal. Retrieved August 13, 2019, from https://alumni. berkeley.edu/california-magazine/spring-2019/losing-paradise-new-normal-california-wildfires.

Siegler, K. (2019). Morning Edition: More than one-thousand families still searching for homes six months after the campfire. Retried on July 17, 2019, from https://www.npr.org/2019/05/08/721057281/more- than-1-000-families-still-searching-for-homes-6-months-after-the-camp-fire.

Sylves, R.T. (2019). Disaster policy and politics: Emergency management and homeland security. Los Ange- les: Sage.

35. How Texas Is "building back better" from Hurricane Harvey*

Nicole Errett

For most Americans, the one-two punch of last fall's hurricanes is ancient history. But hard-hit communities in Texas, Florida and the Caribbean are still rebuilding.

I recently traveled with public health students from the University of Washington to southeast Texas, where the impacts of Hurricane Harvey last August are still felt today. With support from the Natural Hazards Center's Quick Response Grant Program, we wanted to understand how disaster recovery strategies can create long-term opportunities to promote healthy communities.

Through interviews with local health officials, we learned how Hurricane Harvey is still affecting many residents. As we often see during natural disasters, Harvey amplified pre-existing health and social stresses and inequities.

For example, greater Houston had only a paltry pre-storm supply of affordable housing. Now buyers and renters are competing to secure undamaged units. We heard about families who were living in homes with toxic mold because they couldn't afford to leave, and concerns that rising prices would drive people out on the street or force them to move to other cities and states. However, we also saw signs that communities were using Hurricane Harvey to springboard efforts to address persistent housing problems.

Turning Disasters into Opportunities

The default response after a major disaster is often to rebuild as quickly as possible. This typically means replicating what existed before the storm. But why not build back in a way that corrects long-standing problems?

Major disasters like Hurricane Harvey often bring influxes of resources and attention to communities that are struggling with health and social challenges. In a 2015 report, the Institute of Medicine found that many communities fail to fully leverage recovery resources to address pre-existing issues, such as access to health care.

The report urged communities to consider short- and long-term health impacts of their recovery decisions, known as a "health in all policies" approach to recovery. This

*Originally published as Nicole Errett, "How Texas Is 'building back better' from Hurricane Harvey," *The Conversation*, https://theconversation.com/how-texas-is-building-back-better-from-hurricane-harvey-90609 (March 30, 2018). Reprinted with permission of the publisher.

approach recognizes that health is connected to many other issues, including transportation, social networks and housing. By thinking about the health impacts of recovery strategies, municipal leaders can rebuild in a way that promotes stronger and more resilient communities.

For example, co-locating mental health professionals at sites where people are signing up for FEMA aid can help more residents get counseling and support. In the long term, decisions about land use in badly damaged neighborhoods can create spaces where people can exercise and socialize, which helps them to lead healthier and happier lives.

Leveraging Local Expertise to Build Back Better

The idea of incorporating health in all policies may sound sensible, but putting it into action after a hurricane, wildfire or tornado strike is easier said than done. As a former emergency manager in Baltimore, I know that working conditions after disasters are fast-paced and often chaotic. Communities are under political and social pressure to recover quickly, and health may not be at the top of their agendas.

Advance planning for recovery is important. And involving people who understand challenges to community health and well-being is essential. Local health departments, as well as community- and faith-based organizations, are often connected to at-risk populations. Involving these organizations in recovery planning and implementation can inform an approach that promotes community health and well-being. For example, they can identify opportunities to use recovery resources to meet pre-existing housing needs, or direct case management services to families that are already struggling.

Building Healthier Post–Harvey

Harvey caused US$125 billion in damages, making it the second-worst storm to strike the U.S. mainland after Hurricane Katrina in 2005. The storm flooded one-third of Houston, displacing more than 30,000 people from their homes.

During our trip to Texas we saw that pre-disaster recovery planning was paying off. As an example, Fort Bend Recovers was established in Fort Bend County, which covers 885 square miles in the Houston metro area, after major flooding on Memorial Day in 2016.

In Harvey's wake, plans developed by Fort Bend Recovers created a process for organizations, including local health and social services agencies, to rapidly reconvene to respond to community needs. Together they offered case management services, staffed mental health support lines, and convened emotional support groups. Such services can help individuals affected by the floods find housing and supplies, but also connect them with solutions for longer-term problems, such as finding affordable medical care.

Hurricane Season 2018 Is Coming

In order to truly "build back better," states and communities need to develop a plan for recovery in advance of the next disaster. Galveston County, on Texas' Gulf Coast, is using its Hurricane Harvey recovery experience to formalize a Long Term Recovery Group that brings together the local health department and other community- and faith-based organizations to address community health needs. But we also heard about other communities that still don't have a plan or mechanism for organizing recovery.

With support from the Robert Wood Johnson Foundation's New Connections Program, my research team is now reviewing state disaster recovery plans nationwide. We plan to identify whether and how states use the disaster recovery period to build back better. We hope to highlight recovery strategies that promote equitable access to affordable and safe housing, health care, and places and spaces that encourage healthy activity and foster social connections.

As climate change amplifies storms, floods and other extreme weather events, U.S. communities can expect more frequent and severe natural disasters in the years to come. By recognizing and planning for opportunities to build back better, they can make themselves more resilient against the next disaster.

36. Climate Change

Basic Information*

ENVIRONMENTAL PROTECTION AGENCY

Climate Change Is Happening

Our Earth is warming. Earth's average temperature has risen by 1.5°F over the past century and is projected to rise another 0.5 to 8.6°F over the next hundred years. Small changes in the average temperature of the planet can translate to large and potentially dangerous shifts in climate and weather.

The evidence is clear. Rising global temperatures have been accompanied by changes in weather and climate. Many places have seen changes in rainfall, resulting in more floods, droughts, or intense rain, as well as more frequent and severe heat waves.

The planet's oceans and glaciers have also experienced some big changes—oceans are warming and becoming more acidic, ice caps are melting, and sea levels are rising. As these and other changes become more pronounced in the coming decades, they will likely present challenges to our society and our environment.

Humans Are Largely Responsible for Recent Climate Change

Over the past century, human activities have released large amounts of carbon dioxide and other greenhouse gases into the atmosphere. Most greenhouse gases come from burning fossil fuels to produce energy, although deforestation, industrial processes, and some agricultural practices also emit gases into the atmosphere.

Greenhouse gases act like a blanket around Earth, trapping energy in the atmosphere and causing it to warm. This phenomenon is called the greenhouse effect and is natural and necessary to support life on Earth. However, the buildup of greenhouse gases can change Earth's climate and result in dangerous effects to human health and welfare and to ecosystems.

The choices we make today will affect the amount of greenhouse gases we put in the atmosphere soon and for years to come.

---

*Public document originally published as Environmental Protection Agency, "Climate Change: Basic Information," https://www.epa.gov/climate-research/human-health-and-climate-change-research (March 2020).

Climate Change Affects Everyone

Our lives are connected to the climate. Human societies have adapted to the relatively stable climate we have enjoyed since the last ice age which ended several thousand years ago. A warming climate will bring changes that can affect our water supplies, agriculture, power and transportation systems, the natural environment, and even our own health and safety.

Some changes to the climate are unavoidable. Carbon dioxide can stay in the atmosphere for nearly a century, so Earth will continue to warm in the coming decades. The warmer it gets, the greater the risk for more severe changes to the climate and Earth's system. Although it's difficult to predict the exact impacts of climate change, what's clear is that the climate we are accustomed to is no longer a reliable guide for what to expect in the future.

We can reduce the risks we will face from climate change. By making choices that reduce greenhouse gas pollution, and preparing for the changes that are already underway, we can reduce risks from climate change. Our decisions today will shape the world our children and grandchildren will live in.

What EPA Is Doing About Climate Change

EPA is taking a number of common-sense steps to address the challenge of climate change.

Collecting Emissions Data. EPA collects various types of greenhouse gas emissions data. This data helps policy makers, businesses, and the Agency track greenhouse gas emissions trends and identify opportunities for reducing emissions and increasing efficiency.

The Inventory of U.S. Greenhouse Gas Emissions and Sinks provides the United States' official estimate of total national-level greenhouse gas emissions. This report tracks annual U.S. greenhouse gas emissions since 1990. The Greenhouse Gas Reporting Program collects and publishes emissions data from individual facilities in the United States that emit greenhouse gases in large quantities.

Getting Reductions. EPA is reducing greenhouse gas emissions and promoting a clean energy economy through highly successful partnerships and common-sense regulatory initiatives.

- Developing Common-sense Regulatory Initiatives: EPA is developing common-sense regulatory initiatives, to reduce GHG emissions and increase efficiency. For example, EPA's vehicle greenhouse gas rules will save consumers $1.7 trillion at the pump by 2025, and eliminate six billion metric tons of GHG pollution.
- Partnering With the Private Sector: Through voluntary energy and climate programs, EPA's partners reduced over 345 million metric tons of greenhouse gases in 2010 alone—equivalent to the emissions from 81 million vehicles—and saving consumers and businesses of about $21 billion.
- Reducing EPA's Carbon Footprint: EPA is monitoring emissions from its own energy use and fuel consumption and working to reduce greenhouse gas emissions by 25 percent by 2020. Learn more about how we're greening EPA.

Evaluating Policy Options, Costs and Benefits

EPA conducts economy-wide analyses to understand the economic impacts and effectiveness of proposed climate policies. Learn more about EPA's economic analyses on climate policies and the associated costs and benefits.

Air Quality and Climate Change Research

Climate change can impact air quality and, conversely, air quality can impact climate change.

Changes in climate can result in impacts to local air quality. Atmospheric warming associated with climate change has the potential to increase ground-level ozone in many regions, which may present challenges for compliance with the ozone standards in the future. The impact of climate change on other air pollutants, such as particulate matter, is less certain, but research is underway to address these uncertainties.

Emissions of pollutants into the air can result in changes to the climate. Ozone in the atmosphere warms the climate, while different components of particulate matter (PM) can have either warming or cooling effects on the climate. For example, black carbon, a particulate pollutant from combustion, contributes to the warming of the Earth, while particulate sulfates cool the earth's atmosphere.

Researchers are working to:

- Develop methods to apply possible global-scale changes in air temperature and precipitation patterns to local-scale conditions that affect air quality.
- Understand the influence of climate change on fine particulate matter and other air pollutions.
- Identify co-benefits of reducing air pollutants that also reduce the impacts of climate change.
- Understand how mitigation options to reduce carbon dioxide, a greenhouse gas, can affect emissions of particulate matter, ozone, precursors, and other air pollutants.
- The scientific knowledge and tools developed by EPA are enhancing the ability of state and local air quality managers to consider climate change in their decisions to protect air quality and to reduce the impacts of a changing climate.

Ecosystems and Climate Change Research

Researchers at EPA are providing innovative ways to help communities and resource managers adapt to the impacts of climate change on ecosystems that are occurring across the nation. They are developing the scientific information and tools that can be used by states and communities to develop strategies to protect our vulnerable ecosystems from the impacts of climate change.

Many factors affect the ecosystems in which we live, work, and play, including land use, application of fertilizers and population growth. Ecosystems are further impacted by the changing climate that is resulting in extreme air and water temperatures and changes in the amount and type of precipitation.

We rely on the natural environment to provide us with food, clean water, and a multitude of natural resources. Understanding how climate change is affecting these resources now and how they may affect them in the future is an important part of EPA's research.

Researchers are working to:

- Assess the likelihood and effects of extreme events on ecosystems
- Develop ways to assess risk to near-coastal species and habitats
- Understand the vulnerability of wetlands and water quality to changes in the amount and timing of water flow
- Develop models and maps to evaluate the effects of climate change on water availability and water quality at basin and regional scales
- Improve models that help us understand the direct and indirect impacts of sea level rise on coastal wetlands

Research is focused on developing new approaches to prepare for, reduce, or adapt to climate change impacts on ecosystems. Preparation includes developing scenarios of plausible future conditions that can then be used to evaluate alternative responses. The results can be used to support decision making by states and communities in the face of a changing environment.

Energy and Climate Change Research

Changes in how we produce and use energy can have significant impacts on human health and affect air and water quality and other measures of environmental quality. Energy technologies are changing rapidly, improving efficiency and environmental sustainability. EPA researchers are improving our understanding of how changes in energy production and use can impact climate change and the environment and how climate change can impact energy production. The ways that energy is produced and used are changing in many areas, including:

- Growing numbers of vehicles that use electricity
- More electricity generation from wind and solar plants
- Substantial use of biofuels

It is important to understand how increasing or decreasing one source of energy can affect the other sources and lead to different consequences for the environment. Using wind power to generate electricity, for example, changes how and when electricity is needed from other types of power plants, which can affect the environment in multiple ways. For instance, biofuels do not generate as much carbon dioxide (CO_2) as gasoline, but production of crops for biofuels requires more land area and uses more water than production of the same amount of energy in the form of gasoline.

EPA, states, communities, and tribes need detailed projections of potential future air pollution emissions from energy sources to analyze strategies for meeting or maintaining the National Ambient Air Quality Standards. To address this need, researchers are developing modeling tools to study the nation's energy system with a focus on environmental changes related to energy production and use.

Energy Modeling Tools

GLIMPSE Model—GLIMPSE is a decision support modeling tool being developed by EPA that will assist states with energy and environmental planning through the year 2050. Users of GLIMPSE can explore the impacts of energy technologies and policies on the environment. For example, GLIMPSE can examine measures that promote energy efficiency, estimating the resulting energy savings, analyzing how emissions and air quality would be affected, and reporting how energy-related water use would change. Additional technologies that could be analyzed include electric and hydrogen fuel cell vehicles, wind and solar power, and carbon capture and sequestration.

An exciting feature is that users can specify energy, air quality, and water use goals within GLIMPSE, which then identifies cost-effective strategies for meeting those goals. For example, states could use GLIMPSE to develop air quality management strategies that also meet renewable electricity targets, energy security objectives, and factor in how droughts could affect power plant operations.

GLIMPSE Model

EPAUS9rT (Regional-scale representation of the U.S. system)—EPA has developed a database for use in the TIMES energy system model that accounts for environmental impacts related to energy production and use. TIMES is an energy system optimization model used by local and federal governments, national and international communities and academia. It helps decision makers understand how changes in the amount or cost of one type of energy (solar energy, for instance) can affect the rest of the energy system in complex ways. Understanding these changes allow us to better understand the environmental consequences of changes in technologies and costs in the energy sector. The EPA database, known as EPAUS9rT, allows users to examine these changes for nine regions across the U.S.

Human Health and Climate Change Research

Climate change is having direct and indirect impacts on the health of people. More extreme weather events, heat waves, spread of infectious diseases and detrimental impacts on air and water quality are having impacts on our health.

Research is underway to assess those most susceptible to the health impacts related to a changing climate and identify ways to reduce those impacts.

Researchers are working to:

- Identify and characterize communities and people at greatest risk to the impacts of climate change and air pollution.
- Assess the individual and synergistic impacts of climate change and air quality on human health.
- Develop approaches to assess the likelihood and effects of extreme events, including wildfires, floods, and heat waves, on human health.
- Identify potential societal and behavioral responses to human health risks from climate change.

37. Impacts, Risks and Adaptation in the United States*

U.S. GLOBAL CHANGE RESEARCH PROGRAM

These Summary Findings represent a high-level synthesis of the material in the U.S. Global Change Research Program report. The findings consolidate Key Messages and supporting evidence from 16 national-level topic chapters, 10 regional chapters, and 2 chapters that focus on societal response strategies (mitigation and adaptation). Unless otherwise noted, qualitative statements regarding future conditions in these Summary Findings are broadly applicable across the range of different levels of future climate change and associated impacts considered in this report.

1. Communities

Climate change creates new risks and exacerbates existing vulnerabilities in communities across the United States, presenting growing challenges to human health and safety, quality of life, and the rate of economic growth.

The impacts of climate change are already being felt in communities across the country. More frequent and intense extreme weather and climate-related events, as well as changes in average climate conditions, are expected to continue to damage infrastructure, ecosystems, and social systems that provide essential benefits to communities. Future climate change is expected to further disrupt many areas of life, exacerbating existing challenges to prosperity posed by aging and deteriorating infrastructure, stressed ecosystems, and economic inequality. Impacts within and across regions will not be distributed equally. People who are already vulnerable, including lower-income and other marginalized communities, have lower capacity to prepare for and cope with extreme weather and climate-related events and are expected to experience greater impacts. Prioritizing adaptation actions for the most vulnerable populations would contribute to a more equitable future within and across communities. Global action to significantly cut greenhouse gas emissions can substantially reduce climate-related risks and increase opportunities for these populations in the longer term.

---

*Public document originally published as U.S. Global Change Research Program, "Impacts, Risks, and Adaptation in the United States," https://nca2018.globalchange.gov/ (January 2020).

2. Economy

Without substantial and sustained global mitigation and regional adaptation efforts, climate change is expected to cause growing losses to American infrastructure and property and impede the rate of economic growth over this century.

In the absence of significant global mitigation action and regional adaptation efforts, rising temperatures, sea level rise, and changes in extreme events are expected to increasingly disrupt and damage critical infrastructure and property, labor productivity, and the vitality of our communities. Regional economies and industries that depend on natural resources and favorable climate conditions, such as agriculture, tourism, and fisheries, are vulnerable to the growing impacts of climate change. Rising temperatures are projected to reduce the efficiency of power generation while increasing energy demands, resulting in higher electricity costs. The impacts of climate change beyond our borders are expected to increasingly affect our trade and economy, including import and export prices and U.S. businesses with overseas operations and supply chains. Some aspects of our economy may see slight near-term improvements in a modestly warmer world. However, the continued warming that is projected to occur without substantial and sustained reductions in global greenhouse gas emissions is expected to cause substantial net damage to the U.S. economy throughout this century, especially in the absence of increased adaptation efforts. With continued growth in emissions at historic rates, annual losses in some economic sectors are projected to reach hundreds of billions of dollars by the end of the century—more than the current gross domestic product (GDP) of many U.S. states.

3. Interconnected Impacts

Climate change affects the natural, built, and social systems we rely on individually and through their connections to one another. These interconnected systems are increasingly vulnerable to cascading impacts that are often difficult to predict, threatening essential services within and beyond the Nation's borders.

Climate change presents added risks to interconnected systems that are already exposed to a range of stressors such as aging and deteriorating infrastructure, land-use changes, and population growth. Extreme weather and climate-related impacts on one system can result in increased risks or failures in other critical systems, including water resources, food production and distribution, energy and transportation, public health, international trade, and national security. The full extent of climate change risks to interconnected systems, many of which span regional and national boundaries, is often greater than the sum of risks to individual sectors. Failure to anticipate interconnected impacts can lead to missed opportunities for effectively managing the risks of climate change and can also lead to management responses that increase risks to other sectors and regions. Joint planning with stakeholders across sectors, regions, and jurisdictions can help identify critical risks arising from interaction among systems ahead of time.

4. Actions to Reduce Risks

Communities, governments, and businesses are working to reduce risks from and costs associated with climate change by taking action to lower greenhouse gas emissions and implement adaptation strategies. While mitigation and adaptation efforts have expanded substantially in the last four years, they do not yet approach the scale considered necessary to avoid substantial damages to the economy, environment, and human health over the coming decades.

Future risks from climate change depend primarily on decisions made today. The integration of climate risk into decision-making and the implementation of adaptation activities have significantly increased since the Third National Climate Assessment in 2014, including in areas of financial risk reporting, capital investment planning, development of engineering standards, military planning, and disaster risk management. Transformations in the energy sector—including the displacement of coal by natural gas and increased deployment of renewable energy—along with policy actions at the national, regional, state, and local levels are reducing greenhouse gas emissions in the United States. While these adaptation and mitigation measures can help reduce damages in a number of sectors, this assessment shows that more immediate and substantial global greenhouse gas emissions reductions, as well as regional adaptation efforts, would be needed to avoid the most severe consequences in the long term. Mitigation and adaptation actions also present opportunities for additional benefits that are often more immediate and localized, such as improving local air quality and economies through investments in infrastructure. Some benefits, such as restoring ecosystems and increasing community vitality, may be harder to quantify.

5. Water

The quality and quantity of water available for use by people and ecosystems across the country are being affected by climate change, increasing risks and costs to agriculture, energy production, industry, recreation, and the environment.

Rising air and water temperatures and changes in precipitation are intensifying droughts, increasing heavy downpours, reducing snowpack, and causing declines in surface water quality, with varying impacts across regions. Future warming will add to the stress on water supplies and adversely impact the availability of water in parts of the United States. Changes in the relative amounts and timing of snow and rainfall are leading to mismatches between water availability and needs in some regions, posing threats to, for example, the future reliability of hydropower production in the Southwest and the Northwest. Groundwater depletion is exacerbating drought risk in many parts of the United States, particularly in the Southwest and Southern Great Plains. Dependable and safe water supplies for U.S. Caribbean, Hawai'i, and U.S.-Affiliated Pacific Island communities are threatened by drought, flooding, and saltwater contamination due to sea level rise. Most U.S. power plants rely on a steady supply of water for cooling, and operations are expected to be affected by changes in water availability and temperature increases. Aging and deteriorating water infrastructure, typically designed for past environmental conditions, compounds the climate risk faced by society. Water management strategies that account for changing climate conditions can help reduce present and future risks to water security, but implementation of such practices remains limited.

6. Health

Impacts from climate change on extreme weather and climate-related events, air quality, and the transmission of disease through insects and pests, food, and water increasingly threaten the health and well-being of the American people, particularly populations that are already vulnerable.

Changes in temperature and precipitation are increasing air quality and health risks from wildfire and ground-level ozone pollution. Rising air and water temperatures and more intense extreme events are expected to increase exposure to waterborne and food-borne diseases, affecting food and water safety. With continued warming, cold-related deaths are projected to decrease and heat-related deaths are projected to increase; in most regions, increases in heat-related deaths are expected to outpace reductions in cold-related deaths. The frequency and severity of allergic illnesses, including asthma and hay fever, are expected to increase as a result of a changing climate. Climate change is also projected to alter the geographic range and distribution of disease-carrying insects and pests, exposing more people to ticks that carry Lyme disease and mosquitoes that transmit viruses such as Zika, West Nile, and dengue, with varying impacts across regions. Communities in the Southeast, for example, are particularly vulnerable to the combined health impacts from vector-borne disease, heat, and flooding. Extreme weather and climate-related events can have lasting mental health consequences in affected communities, particularly if they result in degradation of livelihoods or community relocation. Populations including older adults, children, low-income communities, and some communities of color are often disproportionately affected by, and less resilient to, the health impacts of climate change. Adaptation and mitigation policies and programs that help individuals, communities, and states prepare for the risks of a changing climate reduce the number of injuries, illnesses, and deaths from climate-related health outcomes.

7. Indigenous Peoples

Climate change increasingly threatens Indigenous communities' livelihoods, economies, health, and cultural identities by disrupting interconnected social, physical, and ecological systems.

Many Indigenous peoples are reliant on natural resources for their economic, cultural, and physical well-being and are often uniquely affected by climate change. The impacts of climate change on water, land, coastal areas, and other natural resources, as well as infrastructure and related services, are expected to increasingly disrupt Indigenous peoples' livelihoods and economies, including agriculture and agroforestry, fishing, recreation, and tourism. Adverse impacts on subsistence activities have already been observed. As climate changes continue, adverse impacts on culturally significant species and resources are expected to result in negative physical and mental health effects. Throughout the United States, climate-related impacts are causing some Indigenous peoples to consider or actively pursue community relocation as an adaptation strategy, presenting challenges associated with maintaining cultural and community continuity. While economic, political, and infrastructure limitations may affect these communities' ability to adapt, tightly knit social and cultural networks present opportunities to build community capacity and increase resilience. Many Indigenous peoples are taking steps to adapt to climate change impacts structured around self-determination and traditional knowledge, and some tribes are pursuing mitigation actions through development of renewable energy on tribal lands.

8. Ecosystems and Ecosystem Services

Ecosystems and the benefits they provide to society are being altered by climate change, and these impacts are projected to continue. Without substantial and sustained reductions in global greenhouse gas emissions, transformative impacts on some ecosystems will occur; some coral reef and sea ice ecosystems are already experiencing such transformational changes.

Many benefits provided by ecosystems and the environment, such as clean air and water, protection from coastal flooding, wood and fiber, crop pollination, hunting and fishing, tourism, cultural identities, and more will continue to be degraded by the impacts of climate change. Increasing wildfire frequency, changes in insect and disease outbreaks, and other stressors are expected to decrease the ability of U.S. forests to support economic activity, recreation, and subsistence activities. Climate change has already had observable impacts on biodiversity, ecosystems, and the benefits they provide to society. These impacts include the migration of native species to new areas and the spread of invasive species. Such changes are projected to continue, and without substantial and sustained reductions in global greenhouse gas emissions, extinctions and transformative impacts on some ecosystems cannot be avoided in the long term. Valued aspects of regional heritage and quality of life tied to ecosystems, wildlife, and outdoor recreation will change with the climate, and as a result, future generations can expect to experience and interact with the natural environment in ways that are different from today. Adaptation strategies, including prescribed burning to reduce fuel for wildfire, creation of safe havens for important species, and control of invasive species, are being implemented to address emerging impacts of climate change. While some targeted response actions are underway, many impacts, including losses of unique coral reef and sea ice ecosystems, can only be avoided by significantly reducing global emissions of carbon dioxide and other greenhouse gases.

9. Agriculture

Rising temperatures, extreme heat, drought, wildfire on rangelands, and heavy downpours are expected to increasingly disrupt agricultural productivity in the United States. Expected increases in challenges to livestock health, declines in crop yields and quality, and changes in extreme events in the United States and abroad threaten rural livelihoods, sustainable food security, and price stability.

Climate change presents numerous challenges to sustaining and enhancing crop productivity, livestock health, and the economic vitality of rural communities. While some regions (such as the Northern Great Plains) may see conditions conducive to expanded or alternative crop productivity over the next few decades, overall, yields from major U.S. crops are expected to decline as a consequence of increases in temperatures and possibly changes in water availability, soil erosion, and disease and pest outbreaks. Increases in temperatures during the growing season in the Midwest are projected to be the largest contributing factor to declines in the productivity of U.S. agriculture. Projected increases in extreme heat conditions are expected to lead to further heat stress for livestock, which can result in large economic losses for producers. Climate change is also expected to lead to large-scale shifts in the availability and prices of many agricultural products across the world, with corresponding impacts on U.S. agricultural producers and the U.S. economy. These changes threaten future gains in commodity crop production and put rural livelihoods at risk. Numerous adaptation strategies are available to cope with adverse impacts of climate variability and change on agricultural production. These include altering what is produced, modifying the inputs used for production, adopting new technologies, and adjusting management strategies. However, these strategies have limits under severe climate change impacts and would require sufficient long- and short-term investment in changing practices.

10. Infrastructure

Our Nation's aging and deteriorating infrastructure is further stressed by increases in heavy precipitation events, coastal flooding, heat, wildfires, and other extreme events, as well as changes to average precipitation and temperature. Without adaptation, climate change will continue to degrade infrastructure performance over the rest of the century, with the potential for cascading impacts that threaten our economy, national security, essential services, and health and well-being.

Climate change and extreme weather events are expected to increasingly disrupt our Nation's energy and transportation systems, threatening more frequent and longer-lasting power outages, fuel shortages, and service disruptions, with cascading impacts on other critical sectors. Infrastructure currently designed for historical climate conditions is more vulnerable to future weather extremes and climate change. The continued increase in the frequency and extent of high-tide flooding due to sea level rise threatens America's trillion-dollar coastal property market and public infrastructure, with cascading impacts to the larger economy. In Alaska, rising temperatures and erosion are causing damage to buildings and coastal infrastructure that will be costly to repair or replace, particularly in rural areas; these impacts are expected to grow without adaptation. Expected increases in the severity and frequency of heavy precipitation events will affect inland infrastructure in every region, including access to roads, the viability of bridges, and the safety of pipelines. Flooding from heavy rainfall, storm surge, and rising high tides is expected to compound existing issues with aging infrastructure in the Northeast. Increased drought risk will threaten oil and gas drilling and refining, as well as electricity generation from power plants that rely on surface water for cooling. Forward-looking infrastructure design, planning, and operational measures and standards can reduce exposure and vulnerability to the impacts of climate change and reduce energy use while providing additional near-term benefits, including reductions in greenhouse gas emissions.

11. Oceans and Coasts

Coastal communities and the ecosystems that support them are increasingly threatened by the impacts of climate change. Without significant reductions in global greenhouse gas emissions and regional adaptation measures, many coastal regions will be transformed by the latter part of this century, with impacts affecting other regions and sectors. Even in a future with lower greenhouse gas emissions, many communities are expected to suffer financial impacts as chronic high-tide flooding leads to higher costs and lower property values.

Rising water temperatures, ocean acidification, retreating arctic sea ice, sea level rise, high-tide flooding, coastal erosion, higher storm surge, and heavier precipitation events threaten our oceans and coasts. These effects are projected to continue, putting ocean and marine species at risk, decreasing the productivity of certain fisheries, and threatening communities that rely on marine ecosystems for livelihoods and recreation, with particular impacts on fishing communities in Hawai'i and the U.S.-Affiliated Pacific Islands, the U.S. Caribbean, and the Gulf of Mexico. Lasting damage to coastal property and infrastructure driven by sea level rise and storm surge is expected to lead to financial losses for individuals, businesses, and communities, with the Atlantic and Gulf Coasts facing above-average risks. Impacts on coastal energy and transportation infrastructure driven by sea level rise and storm surge have the potential for cascading costs and disruptions across the country. Even if significant emissions reductions occur, many of the effects from sea level rise over this century—and particularly through mid-century—are already locked in due to historical emissions, and many communities are already dealing with the consequences. Actions to plan for and adapt to more frequent, widespread, and severe coastal flooding, such as shoreline protection and conservation of coastal ecosystems, would decrease direct losses and cascading impacts on other sectors and parts of the country. More than half of the damages to coastal property are estimated to be avoidable through well-timed adaptation measures. Substantial and sustained reductions in global greenhouse gas emissions would also significantly reduce projected risks to fisheries and communities that rely on them.

12. Tourism and Recreation

Outdoor recreation, tourist economies, and quality of life are reliant on benefits provided by our natural environment that will be degraded by the impacts of climate change in many ways.

Climate change poses risks to seasonal and outdoor economies in communities across the United States, including impacts on economies centered around coral reef-based recreation, winter recreation, and inland water-based recreation. In turn, this affects the well-being of the people who make their living supporting these economies, including rural, coastal, and Indigenous communities. Projected increases in wildfire smoke events are expected to impair outdoor recreational activities and visibility in wilderness areas. Declines in snow and ice cover caused by warmer winter temperatures are expected to negatively impact the winter recreation industry in the Northwest, Northern Great Plains, and the Northeast. Some fish, birds, and mammals are expected to shift where they live as a result of climate change, with implications for hunting, fishing, and other wildlife-related activities. These and other climate-related impacts are expected to result in decreased tourism revenue in some places and, for some communities, loss of identity. While some new opportunities may emerge from these ecosystem changes, cultural identities and economic and recreational opportunities based around historical use of and interaction with species or natural resources in many areas are at risk. Proactive management strategies, such as the use of projected stream temperatures to set priorities for fish conservation, can help reduce disruptions to tourist economies and recreation.

38. Climate Change Adaptation*

U.S. Department of Agriculture

CCPO is leading USDA efforts to identify how climate change is likely to affect our ability to achieve mission, operations, and policy and program objectives. Through adaptation planning, USDA will develop, prioritize, implement, and evaluate actions to minimize climate risks and exploit new opportunities that climate change may bring. By integrating climate change adaptation strategies into USDA's programs and operations, USDA better ensures that taxpayer resources are invested wisely, and that USDA services and operations remain effective in current and future climate conditions.

Climate Change Program Office

The Climate Change Program Office (CCPO) coordinates USDA's responses to climate change, focusing on implications of climate change on agriculture, forests, grazing lands, and rural communities. CCPO ensures that USDA is a source of objective, analytical assessments of the effects of climate change and proposed response strategies both within USDA and for our partners. CCPO is also responsible for coordinating activities with other Federal agencies, interacting with the legislative branch on climate change issues affecting agriculture and forestry, and representing USDA on U.S. delegations to international climate change discussions. CCPO's responsibilities include:

- Analysis, planning, research coordination, and the development of climate change response strategies;
- Providing liaison with other Federal agencies;
- Informing the Department of scientific developments and policy issues relating to the effects of climate change on agriculture and forestry, and recommending responsive courses of action; and
- Ensuring that recognition of the potential for climate change is fully integrated into USDA's research, planning, and decision-making processes.

Climate Change: Mitigation

The U.S. agriculture and forestry sectors can play an important role in limiting the build-up of greenhouse gases (GHG) in the atmosphere. Conservation and land

---

*Public document originally published as U.S. Department of Agriculture, "Climate Change Adaptation," https://www.usda.gov/oce/climate_change/ (2020).

management practices can reduce emissions of carbon dioxide, methane, and nitrous oxide associated with crop and livestock production; increase the quantity of carbon stored in soils and above ground vegetation; and generate renewable fuels that recycle carbon dioxide from the atmosphere.

Adaptation

The effects of climate change are complex and far-reaching, and while the scope, severity, and pace of future climate change impacts are difficult to predict, it is clear that changes could have important effects on producers and on the ability of USDA to fulfill its core mission. Adaptation refers to the process of finding ways to prepare for and flexibly respond to changes in climate. USDA is developing a multi-pronged approach toward adaptation, including research, education, extension, risk management, and strategic planning.

CCPO works across USDA to help ensure that climate change adaptation is integrated into USDA programs, policies and operations. CCPO also provides data, tools and information to assist land managers, stakeholders and USDA agencies and mission areas with adaptation assessments, planning and implementation.

Climate Change, Global Food Security, and the U.S. Food System

Climate change is likely to diminish continued progress on global food security through production disruptions that lead to local availability limitations and price increases, interrupted transport conduits, and diminished food safety, among other causes.

Climate change can affect food availability, access, utilization, and the stability of each of these over time. Constrictions at any point can lead to food insecurity through the activities of the food system, including food production, transportation, and storage.

Climate Change, Global Food Security, and the U.S. Food System is a peer-reviewed scientific assessment that identifies climate change effects on global food security. The assessment is a contribution to the U.S. National Climate Assessment.

Quantifying Greenhouse Gas Fluxes in Agriculture and Forestry

America's farm, ranch and forest managers are stewards of the land, and have long recognized the significance of managing soil health, plant productivity and animal nutrition. Conservation practices and other management changes can reduce greenhouse gas (GHG) emissions and increase carbon storage while improving soil health, crop or livestock productivity, and resilience to drought and other extreme weather. This report lays out methods for estimating changes in GHG emissions and carbon storage at a local scale. The methods in the report will be used to develop user-friendly tools for farmers, ranchers, forest landowners and other USDA stakeholders to help them evaluate the GHG benefits of a wide variety of management practices.

National Greenhouse Gas Inventory

Periodically, USDA produces an updated inventory of GHG emissions and carbon storage for the agriculture and forestry sectors. These reports are consistent with the annual emissions reporting done by EPA, but provide an enhanced view of the data regionally and by land use.

U.S. Agriculture and Forestry Greenhouse Gas Inventory: 1990–2013

In 2013, agricultural greenhouse gas sources accounted for about 9 percent of total U.S. greenhouse gas emissions. The U.S. Agriculture and Forestry Greenhouse Gas Inventory: 1990–2013 was developed to provide a comprehensive assessment of the contribution of U.S. agriculture and forestry to greenhouse gas emissions and carbon sequestration. It provides an in-depth look at greenhouse gas emissions and carbon sequestration at the state and regional scales.

Climate Change Science Plan

The U.S. Department of Agriculture (USDA) Climate Change Science Plan (the Science Plan) provides a guide for the Department and its stakeholders to enable clear and consistent consideration of current and potential investments in climate change science activities. This Science Plan presents an overview of the critical questions facing the Department's agencies as they relate to climate change and offers a framework for assessing priorities to ensure consistency with USDA's role in the Federal Government's broader U.S. Global Change Research Program (USGCRP) and related efforts. This document identifies important roles and responsibilities for USDA agencies and areas of needs and dependencies wherein USDA agencies are reliant on other programs for cooperation.

The vision articulated by USDA for FY 2010–2015 calls for the Department "to expand economic opportunity through innovation, helping rural America thrive; to promote agriculture production sustainability that better nourishes Americans while also helping to feed others throughout the world; and to preserve and conserve our Nation's natural resources through restored forests, improved watersheds, and healthy private working lands." Climate change has the potential to disrupt USDA efforts to meet these core obligations and responsibilities to the Nation.

USDA's Strategic Plan specifically addresses the challenges of climate change and the opportunities associated with addressing greenhouse gas emissions. The USDA Strategic Plan further calls on the Department to lead efforts to mitigate and adapt to climate change. The plan calls for the Department to capitalize on opportunities presented by the Nation's efforts to develop markets for ecosystem services and mitigate climate change. The Plan's second strategic goal is to ensure that our national forests and private working lands are conserved, restored, and made more resilient to climate change.

39. Climate Research*

NATIONAL OCEANIC AND
ATMOSPHERIC ADMINISTRATION

National Oceanic and Atmospheric Administration (NOAA) is an agency that enriches life through science. Our reach goes from the surface of the sun to the depths of the ocean floor as we work to keep the public informed of the changing environment around them.

From daily weather forecasts, severe storm warnings, and climate monitoring to fisheries management, coastal restoration and supporting marine commerce, NOAA's products and services support economic vitality and affect more than one-third of America's gross domestic product. NOAA's dedicated scientists use cutting-edge research and high-tech instrumentation to provide citizens, planners, emergency managers and other decision makers with reliable information they need when they need it.

From supercomputers and state-of-the-art models to observations and outlooks, we provide data, tools, and information to help people understand and prepare for climate variability and change. NOAA Climate.gov provides timely and authoritative information about climate. We promote public understanding of climate science and climate-related events through videos, stories, images, and data visualizations; we make common data products and services easy to access and use; and we provide tools and resources that help people make informed decisions about climate risks, vulnerability, and resilience.

Climate Change Impacts

Impacts from climate change are happening now. These impacts extend well beyond an increase in temperature, affecting ecosystems and communities in the United States and around the world. Things that we depend upon and value—water, energy, transportation, wildlife, agriculture, ecosystems, and human health—are experiencing the effects of a changing climate.

Water. Changes to water resources can have a big impact on people's lives. In some regions, particularly in the western United States, drought is an important factor affecting communities. Less snow accumulation in the mountains is important in the West and Alaska, where the snowpack stores water for later use. In the Midwest and northeastern

*Public document originally published as National Oceanic and Atmospheric Administration, "Climate Research," https://www.noaa.gov/climate (2020).

states, the frequency of heavy downpours has increased. In many regions, floods and water quality problems are likely to be worse because of climate change.

Food. Our food supply depends on climate and weather conditions. Although agricultural practices may be adaptable, changes like increased temperatures, water stress, diseases, and weather extremes create challenges for the farmers and ranchers who put food on our tables.

Health. Human health is vulnerable to climate change. The changing environment is expected to cause more heat stress, an increase in waterborne diseases, poor air quality, and diseases transmitted by insects and rodents. Extreme weather events can compound many of these health threats.

The environment. Ecosystems are also affected by climate change. Habitats are being modified, the timing of events such as flowering and egg laying are shifting, and species are altering their home ranges.

Changes are also occurring to the ocean. The ocean absorbs about 30 percent of the carbon dioxide that is released into the atmosphere from the burning of fossil fuels. As a result, the ocean is becoming more acidic, affecting marine life. Rising sea levels due to thermal expansion and melting land ice sheets and glaciers put coastal areas at greater risk of erosion and storm surge.

Indo-Pacific Ocean Warming Is Changing Global Rainfall Patterns

Rainfall declines may affect U.S. West Coast and parts of the East Coast.

New research by NOAA and a visiting scientist from India shows that warming of the Indo-Pacific Ocean is altering rainfall patterns from the tropics to the United States, contributing to declines in rainfall on the United States west and east coasts.

In a study published this week in the journal *Nature*, researchers report a doubling in the size of a warm pool of water spanning the western Pacific and eastern Indian Ocean in recent years. This Indo-Pacific warm pool in what is already the warmest part of the global ocean is expanding each year by an area the size of California.

The expansion is changing a key weather and climate feature called the Madden-Julian Oscillation, which is characterized by a band of rain clouds that move over the tropical ocean from the Seychelles off Africa toward India and into the Pacific Ocean, influencing everything from monsoons in India to heat waves and flooding in the United States.

Rainfall patterns are changing around the globe due to warming of the Indo-Pacific Ocean that is altering the Madden-Julian Oscillation—a weather maker that influences weather from India to the United States. The shining sun depicts areas of declining rainfall while the rain clouds show where rainfall is increasing. Credit: Roxy M. Koll, Indian Institute of Tropical Meteorology, et al., *Nature*.

Warming Ocean Driving Change in Key Climate Pattern

The changes in the behavior of the MJO have brought a decline in rainfall to the central Pacific, the west and east coasts of the United States, north India, east Africa and the Yangtze basin in China. These same changes are causing an increase in rainfall over northern Australia, the Amazon basin, southwest Africa and Southeast Asia, researchers conclude.

"NOAA is part of coordinated international efforts to extend the range of accurate weather forecasts out to lead times of two to four weeks and the MJO is one of the most important keys to the success of this enterprise," said Michael McPhaden, a senior scientist at NOAA's Pacific Marine Environmental Lab and co-author of the study. "Our research provides a critical benchmark for determining which computer models to trust for extended range weather forecasting, based on their ability to simulate the observed behavior of the MJO in changing the climate."

Though the entire Indo-Pacific Ocean has warmed, the warmest waters are over the west Pacific, creating a temperature contrast that drives moisture from the Indian Ocean to the west, enhancing cloud formation. This has changed the life cycle of the MJO. The length of time these clouds linger over the Indian Ocean has shrunk by four days from an average of 19 to 15 days. Over the west Pacific, the clouds now reside five more days. It is this change in the residence of MJO-driven clouds that is altering weather patterns around the globe, researchers found.

"Climate model simulations indicate that continued warming of the Indo-Pacific Ocean is highly likely, which may further intensify these changes in global rainfall patterns," said Roxy Mathew Koll, lead author of the study with the Indian Institute of Tropical Meteorology who worked with McPhaden while visiting PMEL for the last year. "This means that we need to enhance our ocean observational arrays to monitor these changes accurately and update our climate models to skillfully predict the challenges presented by a warming world."

The study is part of a collaboration between NOAA and India's Ministry of Earth Sciences, facilitated by the National Academy of Sciences with funding from NOAA's Climate Program Office Climate Variability and Predictability Program. In addition to McPhaden, Chidong Zhang, also of NOAA PMEL, is a co-author of the research.

A Year Locked in Ice

Unprecedented international expedition to explore the central Arctic gets underway.

The most ambitious research expedition ever to target the central Arctic got underway as the German icebreaker RV Polarstern pulled out of Tromso on September 20, destined for an ice floe where it will serve as a drifting base for hundreds of scientists during the next 13 months.

More than 10 years after CIRES scientist Matthew Shupe conceived of the idea, the Multidisciplinary Drifting Observatory for the Study of Arctic Climate (MOSAiC) has become a $150 million voyage of discovery led by the Alfred Wegener Institute, with significant funding by the U.S. Department of Energy and other U.S. agencies. More than 400 scientists from 19 countries, including some of the world's top Arctic researchers, will participate.

Years of Planning Help Ease a Hectic Departure

This is the first time a modern research icebreaker will operate in the direct vicinity of the North Pole year-round, including the nearly six-month long polar night during winter. In terms of the logistical challenges involved, the total number of participants, the number of participating countries, and the available budget, MOSAiC represents the largest Arctic expedition in history.

"It's really amazing to see all the composure here during a really stressful time," said Shupe, the U.S. co-lead on the massive expedition, as dozens of scientists worked to install equipment on board just hours before Polarstern's departure. "I am really energized by all these people and energy moving in the same direction. I see this around every corner of the ship."

Researchers will be conducting experiments and collecting data from the atmosphere, ice and ocean with instruments on board the Polarstern, and from locations up to several miles away, to explore the physical, chemical, and biological processes that drive the Arctic atmosphere, sea ice, ocean, and ecosystem. Results from the mission will help scientists improve models and forecasts of local, regional, and global weather and climate.

In total, scientists and funding agencies from 19 nations are involved. The United States represents the second-largest national funder with support from the National Science Foundation, Department of Energy, National Oceanic and Atmospheric Administration, and NASA. The NOAA contingent is comprised primarily of CIRES scientists from NOAA Research's Earth System Research Laboratory.

First Challenge: Where Do You Park an Icebreaker?

After departing Tromsø, 350 miles north of the Arctic Circle, the ship will position itself so that it freezes into drifting ice as the polar night descends. Research during the roughly six months of darkness will present challenges on top of those delivered by the frigid Arctic winter. Special lights, night-vision goggles to watch for polar bears, and activities designed to maintain a healthy daily schedule in the close confines of the ship are some of the adaptations scientists will have to make.

The expedition will be resupplied by four icebreakers from Sweden, Russia and China.

What Happens in the Arctic Doesn't Stay in the Arctic

For the Alfred Wegener Institute's Markus Rex, leader of the MOSAiC expedition, the Arctic is the "kitchen" for weather in the northern hemisphere. Extreme weather conditions like outbreaks of cold Arctic air in winter, or heat waves in summer, are linked to the changes in the Arctic, he said. Given that Arctic change is likely to have a global impact, research to improve climate models is of utmost importance.

"There aren't any reliable prognoses of how the Arctic climate will develop further or what that will mean for our weather," said Rex. "Our mission is to change that." The National Oceanic and Atmospheric Administration is an American scientific agency within the United States Department of Commerce that focuses on the conditions of the oceans, major waterways, and the atmosphere.

40. Greenland's Rapid Melt Will Mean More Flooding*

Arielle Samuelson

The Greenland Ice Sheet is rapidly melting, having lost 3.8 trillion tons of ice between 1992 and 2018, a new study from NASA and the European Space Agency (ESA) finds. The study combined 26 independent satellite datasets to track global warming's effect on Greenland, one of the largest ice sheets on Earth, and the ice sheet melt's impact on rising sea levels. The findings, which forecast an approximate 3 to 5 inches (70 to 130 millimeters) of global sea level rise by 2100, are in alignment with previous worst-case projections if the average rate of Greenland's ice loss continues.

Changes to the Greenland and Antarctic ice sheets are of considerable societal importance, as they directly impact global sea levels, which are a result of climate change. As glaciers and ice sheets melt, they add more water to the ocean. Increasing rates of global warming have accelerated Greenland's ice mass loss from 25 billion tons per year in the 1990s to a current average of 234 billion tons per year. This means that Greenland's ice is melting on average seven times faster today than it was at the beginning of the study period. The Greenland Ice Sheet holds enough water to raise the sea level by 24 feet (7.4 meters).

The paper, published Dec. 10 in *Nature*, is the result of an international collaboration between 89 polar scientists from 50 scientific institutions supported by NASA and ESA. The Ice Sheet Mass Balance Inter-comparison Exercise, or IMBIE, used well-calibrated data from 13 NASA and ESA satellite missions to create the most accurate measurements of ice loss to date. The team found that half of the loss is tied to surface ice melting in warmer air. The rest of the loss is the result of factors such as warmer ocean temperatures, iceberg calving and the ice sheet shedding ice into the ocean more quickly.

"There are climate projections that are based on models of varying levels of complexity and observations, but they have large uncertainties. Our study is purely an observational one that tests those uncertainties. Therefore, we have irrefutable evidence that we seem to be on track with one of the most pessimistic sea level rise scenarios," said Erik Ivins, second author and lead scientist at NASA's Jet Propulsion Laboratory in Pasadena, California.

Greenland is home to the only permanent ice sheet outside Antarctica. The sheet covers three-fourths of Greenland's land mass. But in the last 26 years, Greenland's

---

*Public document originally published Arielle Samuelson, "Greenland's Rapid Melt Will Mean More Flooding," https://www.nasa.gov/feature/jpl/greenlands-rapid-melt-will-mean-more-flooding (Dec. 11, 2019).

melting ice has added 0.4 inches (11 millimeters) to sea level rise. Its cumulative 3.8 trillion tons of melted ice is equivalent to adding the water from 120 million Olympic-size swimming pools to the ocean every year, for 26 years.

"As a rule of thumb, for every centimeter rise in global sea level, another 6 million people are exposed to coastal flooding around the planet," said Andrew Shepherd, lead author and scientist from the University of Leeds in the United Kingdom. "On current trends, Greenland ice melting will cause 100 million people to be flooded each year by the end of the century, so 400 million in total due to sea level rise."

In addition to storm surges and high tides that will increase flooding in many regions, sea level rise exacerbates events like hurricanes. Greenland's shrinking ice sheet also speeds up global warming. The vast expanse of snow and ice helps cool down Earth by reflecting the Sun's rays back into space. As the ice melts and retreats, the region absorbs more solar radiation, which warms the planet.

The new study will contribute to the evaluation and evolution of sea level rise models used by the Intergovernmental Panel on Climate Change in evaluating risks to current and future populations. The results of the study currently appear consistent with the panel's worst-case projections for sea level rise in the next 80 years.

"The full set of consequences of future melt from the Greenland Ice Sheet remain uncertain, but even a small increase in sea level can have devastating effects on ports and coastal zones, cause destructive erosion, wetland flooding, and aquifer and agricultural soil contamination with salt," said Ivins.

This is the third IMBIE study on ice loss as a result of global warming. IMBIE's first report in 2012 measured both Greenland and Antarctica's shrinking ice sheets, finding that the combined ice losses from Antarctica and Greenland had increased over time and that the ice sheets were losing three times as much ice as they were in the early 1990s. Antarctica and Greenland continue to lose ice today, and that rate of loss has accelerated since the first IMBIE study.

41. Ice in Motion

*Satellites Capture Decades of Change**

KATE RAMSAYER

New time-lapse videos of Earth's glaciers and ice sheets as seen from space—some spanning nearly 50 years—are providing scientists with new insights into how the planet's frozen regions are changing.

At a media briefing Dec. 9 at the annual meeting of the American Geophysical Union in San Francisco, scientists released new time series of images of Alaska, Greenland, and Antarctica using data from satellites including the NASA–U.S. Geological Survey Landsat missions. One series of images tells illustrates the dramatic changes of Alaska's glaciers and could warn of future retreat of the Hubbard Glacier. Over Greenland, different satellite records show a speed-up of glacial retreat starting in 2000, as well as meltwater ponds spreading to higher elevations in the last decade, which could potentially speed up ice flow. And in Antarctic ice shelves, the view from space could reveal lakes hidden beneath the winter snow.

Using images from the Landsat mission dating back to 1972 and continuing through 2019, glaciologist Mark Fahnestock of the University of Alaska Fairbanks, has stitched together six-second time-lapses of every glacier in Alaska and the Yukon.

"We now have this long, detailed record that allows us to look at what's happened in Alaska," Fahnestock said. "When you play these movies, you get a sense of how dynamic these systems are and how unsteady the ice flow is."

The Columbia Glacier, for example, was relatively stable when the first Landsat satellite launched 1972. But starting in the mid–1980s, the glacier's front began retreating rapidly, and by 2019 was 12.4 miles (20 kilometers) upstream. In comparison, the Hubbard Glacier has advanced 3 miles (5 km) in the last 48 years. But Fahnestock's time-lapse ends with a 2019 image that shows a large indentation in the glacier, where ice has broken off.

"That calving embayment is the first sign of weakness from Hubbard Glacier in almost 50 years—it's been advancing through the historical record," he said. If such embayments persist in the coming years, it could be a sign that change could be coming to Hubbard, he said: "The satellite images also show that these types of calving embayments were present in the decade before Columbia retreated."

The Landsat satellites have provided the longest continuous record of Earth from

---

*Public document originally published by Kate Ramsayer, "Ice in Motion: Satellites Capture Decades of Change," https://www.nasa.gov/feature/goddard/2019/ice-in-motion-satellites-capture-decades-of-change (Dec. 10, 2019).

space. The USGS has reprocessed old Landsat images, which allowed Fahnestock to hand-pick the clearest Landsat scenes for each summer, over each glacier. With software and computing power from Google Earth Engine, he created the series of time-lapse videos.

Scientists are using long-term satellite records to look at Greenland glaciers as well. Michalea King of Ohio State University analyzed data from Landsat missions dating back to 1985 to study more than 200 of Greenland's large outlet glaciers. She examined how far the glacier fronts have retreated, how fast the ice flows, and how much ice glaciers are losing over this time span.

She found that Greenland's glaciers retreated an average of about 3 miles (5 km) between 1985 and 2018—and that the most rapid retreat occurred between 2000 and 2005. And when she looked at the amount of glacial ice entering the ocean, she found that it was relatively steady for the first 15 years of the record, but then started increasing around 2000.

"These glaciers are calving more ice into the ocean than they were in the past," King said. "There is a very clear relationship between the retreat and increasing ice mass losses from these glaciers during the 1985-through-present record." While King is analyzing ice lost from the front of glacier, James Lea of the University of Liverpool in the United Kingdom is using satellites data to examine ice melting on top of Greenland's glaciers and ice sheets, which creates meltwater lakes.

These meltwater lakes can be up to 3 miles (5 km) across and can drain through the ice in a matter of hours, Lea said, which can impact how fast the ice flows. With the computing power of Google Earth Engine, Lea analyzed images of the Greenland ice sheet from the Moderate Resolution Imaging Spectroradiometer (MODIS) on the Terra satellites for every day of every melt seasons over last 20 years—more than 18,000 images in all.

"We looked at how many lakes there are per year across the ice sheet and found an increasing trend over the last 20 years: a 27 percent increase in lakes," Lea said. "We're also getting more and more lakes at higher elevations—areas that we weren't expecting to see lakes in until 2050 or 2060."

When these high-elevation meltwater ponds punch through the ice sheet and drain, it could cause the ice sheet to speed up, he said, thinning the ice and accelerating its demise.

It doesn't always take decades worth of data to study polar features—sometimes just a year or two will provide insights. The Antarctic ice sheet experiences surface melt, but there are also lakes several meters below the surface, insulated by layers of snow. To see where these subsurface lakes are, Devon Dunmire of the University of Colorado, Boulder, used microwave radar images from the European Space Agency's Sentinel-1 satellite. Snow and ice are basically invisible to microwave radiation, but liquid water strongly absorbs it.

Dunmire's new study, presented at the AGU meeting, found lakes dotting the George VI and Wilkins ice shelves near the Antarctic Peninsula—even a few that remained liquid throughout the winter months. These hidden lakes might be more common than scientists had thought, she said, noting that she is continuing to look for similar features across the continent's ice shelves.

"Not much is known about distribution and quantity of these subsurface lakes, but this water appears to be prevalent on the ice shelf near the Antarctic peninsula," Dunmire said, "and it's an important component to understand because meltwater has been shown to destabilize ice shelves."

• *D. International* •

42. Fighting Climate Change*

Sadhu Aufochs Johnston

More and more local governments around the world are rising to the climate change challenge. Many are pushing to decarbonize their energy, building, transport, and waste systems and developing their resilience to the rise in sea levels and extreme precipitation and heat.

For the past 17 years, I have been deeply involved in the efforts of two cities—now, as city manager for Vancouver, British Columbia, and before that, as Chicago's chief environmental officer. These cities are both global leaders in addressing climate change. More importantly, they are using their innovative efforts to make themselves into better places to live, work, and play.

Early in 2019, our newly elected council joined hundreds of other cities from around the world to declare a Climate Emergency. In April of this year, it unanimously approved an ambitious set of next steps intended to align Vancouver's work with efforts to limit global warming to 1.5 degrees. That call to action is a recommitment to taking steps to be a global leader, as well as confirmation that we must act now to protect our communities from the rapidly changing climate.

In Vancouver, we have used the commitment to taking action to help drive our economic growth. We have partnered with entrepreneurs to develop a fast-growing, job-creating "green economy" business sector, and we are home to 20 percent of Canada's clean-tech companies. Jobs and population in our community have each grown by more than a third since 1990, while our carbon emissions have decreased in that same time by about 7 percent.

Vancouver has successfully branded itself as a highly desirable place for young, innovative talent to find work and build companies. A 2015 study by Brand Finance, based in Toronto, found that Vancouver has one of the strongest brands, valued at $31 billion, and that the city is uniquely associated with being clean, green, and environmentally sustainable.[1]

Three Lessons for Local Governments

In my close work with mayors and councils, city departments, business community leaders, environmental activists, community-based leaders, universities, philanthropies,

---

*Originally published as Sadhu Aufochs Johnston, "Fighting Climate Change," *PM Magazine*, https://icma.org/articles/pm-magazine/book-review-fighting-climate-change (July 2019). Reprinted with permission of the publisher.

urban planners, architects, engineers, and residents, I've learned three lessons about how local governments can take action and have a significant impact in addressing climate change.

1. Innovate, Innovate, Innovate.

When local governments began to tackle climate change, no one knew how much they could do. It was assumed that national governments would have the greatest impact. But it turns out that cities and counties can do, and have done, much more than anyone imagined possible. The Global Covenant of Mayors has carbon-reducing commitments from more than 9,000 local governments with 800 million residents. More than 600 cities around the world measured and reported their emissions to CDP (www.cdp.net/en) and disclosed more than 8,000 urban sustainability actions.

In Vancouver, we are working toward achieving our goal to be 100 percent renewably powered before 2050 by reducing our energy usage and switching from fossil fuels to renewable energy sources such as wind, solar, and hydropower. The largest source of carbon pollution is burning natural gas for space and water heating in buildings, so with strong support of council and the community, we have put in place a world-pioneering Zero Emission Building Plan for all new construction to ensure that new buildings are energy efficient and use no fossil fuel by 2030.

We struggled with the fact that we don't control the sources of that energy, so we built Canada's first sewer heat recovery system that harvests heat from a significant sewer line to provide heat to a neighborhood, thereby enabling residents and businesses to reduce their carbon emissions by 70 percent. To produce our own renewable energy, we are harvesting methane from the landfill and partnering with FortisBC, our gas utility, to clean the gas and put it into the fossil gas distribution system. Each of these solutions required taking an innovative approach to our challenges.

2. Connect, Connect, Connect.

Back in 2008, while in Chicago, I was charged with addressing the rising summer heat using green technologies, but I didn't know which cities and counties I could learn from, so I helped to start a peer-to-peer network, the Urban Sustainability Directors Network (USDN, www.usdn.org) to find out what people in other cities were doing—to get the inside scoop, the questions and failures, not just the messages for public consumption.

And it worked: USDN now has more than 200 city and county members in North America. The city-to-city information sharing and collaboration have been extraordinarily robust and inspiring, and in 2018 the network members identified 14 high-impact "must do" practices for local governments.[2] I was learning so much from that network of North American cities that five years ago I helped to start another peer-cities network, the Carbon Neutral Cities Alliance (CNCA, carbonneutralcities.org), of 20 vanguard cities in 10 countries that are global leaders in decarbonization.

CNCA had the same purpose: Share inside information about innovations and collaborate on research and experiments. Many other city-based networks, such as C40[3] and 100 Resilient Cities[4] have been started in just the past decade. All of them demonstrate the great value that is created when cities exchange information and insights and band together to learn, collaborate, and advocate. In the twenty-first century, no city alone can fully address the challenges of decarbonization and strengthening climate resilience.

3. Embrace Bold, Transformational Ideas and Vision.

It's critical for cities to have a clear vision about where they want to go. These visions are built on ideas about what cities can and should be. As mentioned earlier, Vancouver's city council has declared that we will be 100 percent renewably powered by 2050. It's hard to imagine a city without the noise and pollution that comes from burning gas and diesel, but we are more than 30 percent of the way there already, and our plan will get us there.

In the process, we are using demonstration projects, neighborhood working groups, clean-energy conferences, and social-media campaigns to inspire our residents and businesses. The big ideas underpinning this vision—a green city, a competitive city, a renewable-energy city, an equitable city—are bold because they are quite different from the ideas on which most modern cities have been built. They represent a radical change in our thinking about what Vancouver and other cities can become—and these ideas for urban transformation are taking hold across the globe. Of course, this work must be done with a strong lens on equity to ensure that everyone, especially low-income people and traditionally under-represented people, are involved with and can benefit from these changes.

Life After Carbon

Vancouver is not alone in following this ambitious pathway. Cities large and small, wealthy and poor, on every continent are innovating and connecting in response to climate change. The vigor, impact, and transformational direction of this urban movement has been fully documented in a book, Life After Carbon: The Next Global Transformation of Cities by Peter Plastrik and John Cleveland (Island Press, 2018).

The authors look closely at 25 cities worldwide—including Austin, San Francisco, Copenhagen, London, Shanghai, Melbourne, Cape Town, Mexico City, and, yes, Vancouver—and explain how they have become "climate innovation laboratories" at the leading edge of systemic urban change. These cities "have come to understand themselves, their place in the world, in a new way and act boldly on their changed awareness."

The book describes the rise and impact of a global urban "Rebel Alliance." It's a network of networks; a new urban capacity of countless city officials, community activists, professionals, corporate leaders, scholars, and others—"a self-organizing, tireless swarm with no commander-in-chief, following the 'North Star' of climate action."

Most usefully, Life After Carbon identifies four big transformative ideas that are at the heart of the many climate innovations cities have developed—and shows how these ideas are being applied worldwide. In this set of new ideas, cities are understood to be primary drivers of:

- Economic innovation and growth, meaning they can turn the world's emerging renewable-energy economy into business and jobs.
- Environmental quality, human health, and social inclusion—values that reach beyond an economic standard of living.

- Restoration of nature inside and outside of cities; turning back to nature to provide environmental, social, health, and economic benefits.
- Preparation for and adaptation to uncertainties and risks in ways that build civic capacity and social cohesion.

"Gradually," note the authors, "transformational ideas are becoming a new standard for cities—not just a toolbox of innovations but a radically different way of thinking about, a model for, city development and urban achievement around the world."

Plastrik and Cleveland know what they are talking about—having worked in and alongside many cities. They helped to build the USDN and CNCA networks and have written insightful reports about cities' climate innovations. Life After Carbon presents an inspiring account of actual urban change that could not have been written just 10 years ago; there simply wasn't enough going on then.

But today, the story of cities' transformative journeys makes compelling reading for local government leaders everywhere. My experiences in Vancouver and Chicago and in various city-based networks have taught me that, as Life After Carbon puts it, "The successor to the modern city is busy being born."

If your council is considering declaring a climate emergency and getting in on this action, I urge you to pick up a copy of this book to see what other cities are doing and how they're doing it.

Notes

1. https://vancouver.ca/news-calendar/brand.aspx.
2. https://www.usdn.org/public/page/137/USDN-High-Impact-Practices.
3. https://www.c40.org/.
4. https://www.100resilientcities.org/.

43. Cities and Climate Change*

United Nations Environment Programme

Climate change is a global phenomenon that largely impacts urban life. Rising global temperatures causes sea levels to rise, increases the number of extreme weather events such as floods, droughts and storms, and increases the spread of tropical diseases. All these have costly impacts on cities' basic services, infrastructure, housing, human livelihoods and health. At the same time, cities are a key contributor to climate change, as urban activities are major sources of greenhouse gas emissions. Estimates suggest that cities are responsible for 75 percent of global CO_2 emissions, with transport and buildings being among the largest contributors.

Only with a coordinated approach and action at the global, regional, national and local levels, can success be achieved. It is essential, therefore, to make cities an integral part of the solution in fighting climate change. Many cities are already doing a lot by using renewable energy sources, cleaner production techniques and regulations or incentives to limit industrial emissions. Cutting emissions will also reduce local pollution from industries and transport, thus improving urban air quality and the health of city dwellers.

In cooperation with partners, UNEP assists national and local governments by raising awareness, organizing workshops and trainings, developing evaluation tools and involving cities in international meetings on climate change. One of these collaborations is a Joint Work Programme between UNEP, the World Bank, UN–Habitat, under the facilitating role of Cities Alliance to address cities and climate change. With a focus on developing countries, this partnership aims to support local and national governments in urban adaptation and mitigation processes. One of the main outputs of this cooperation is an online knowledge center which provides information on cities and climate change.

As member of the Climate Neutral Network which brings together 19 partner cities and numerous organizations, UNEP provides its expertise on environmental issues. The network's objective is to make the shift to a low-emissions and eventually climate neutral society. Also the Environment and Climate Change Outlook (ECCO) project conducted by UNEP's Division of Early Warning and Assessment (DEWA) provides a global methodology which enables sub-regional and national level authorities to conduct vulnerability and impact assessments for adaptation to climate change.

The Global Initiative for Resourcwe Efficient Cities is a UNEP-led initiative launched in June 2012 at the Rio+20 Summit. The initiative currently works with different

---

*Public document originally published as United Nations Environment Programme, "Cities and Climate Change," https://www.unenvironment.org/explore-topics/resource-efficiency/what-we-do/cities/cities-and-climate-change (2020).

stakeholders to promote energy efficient buildings, efficient water use, sustainable waste management and other activities. UNEP and its partners aim to assist cities in combining greater productivity and innovation with lower costs and reduced environmental impact.

Integrated Environmental Planning

Unplanned rapid urban growth leads to overexploitation of natural resources and destruction of fragile ecosystems in the city and beyond. The urban poor are the most vulnerable to such environmental degradation. Yet in many cities the environmental dimension is not considered in urban planning processes. Therefore, UNEP, with support of the Cities Alliance, is developing a practical methodology for better integrating environmental concerns in strategic planning at the city level.

Cities and Climate Change

Flooding, heat waves, tornados: for many communities around the world, climate change is already a reality. About 75 percent of global CO2 emissions originate from cities, with transport and buildings being among the largest contributors. In addition to efforts at the global and national level, local authorities are already leading the way in finding local solutions to these challenges. UNEP together with its partners supports cities in accounting and reducing their emissions and assessing their climate vulnerability. Learn more

Linking Global Agenda to Local Action

UNEP is working closely with UN–Habitat on sustainable urban planning and management. Since 2007 a joint Partnership Framework is in place. Concrete joint activities between the two international organizations are laid out in biennial Implementation Plans. Activities include joint work on Climate Change assessments, ecosystem-based adaptation in coastal cities as well as cooperation in related urban sectors such as transport, buildings and construction.

Sustainable Buildings and Climate Initiative (SBCI)

SBCI was launched in 2006 as a partnership between the UN and the building sector. It promotes and supports sustainable building practices on a global scale with a focus on energy efficiency and GHG emission reduction. It brings together stakeholders involved in the sector on the local, national, and international level. Furthermore, the initiative develops tools and strategies to better evaluate and implement sustainable building practices, such as the Common Carbon Metric.

Sustainable Social Housing Initiative (SUSHI)

UNEP's Sustainable Social Housing Initiative promotes sustainability in social housing programs. In Bangkok and São Paulo SUSHI assessed the status of social housing programs, policies, market initiatives and voluntary actions and identified barriers for the implementation of sustainable building practices. A guideline with tools and strategies to overcome these constraints is being finalized. A follow-up phase for SUSHI is currently underway.

Sustainable Buildings Policies in Developing Countries (SPoD)

The SPoD project aims to assist governments at national and local levels to develop policy tools in support of mainstreaming sustainable construction and building approaches, resulting in reduced carbon footprints from buildings. SPoD provides a Quick-Scan Tool for governments to evaluate relevant policy measures according to existing barriers and opportunities at national and local level. This approach is being tested and verified in two pilot locations.

Urban Clean Development Mechanism (CDM)

One of the outcomes of UNEP's cooperating with the City of Gwangju (Republic of Korea) is to explore the feasibility of developing a methodology for a Clean Development Mechanism at city-wide level. The study has identified barriers and opportunities for cities and CDM and provides a list of recommendations for reforms to the CDM for better uptake and application at the city level.

Joint Work Programme

UN–Habitat, UNEP, the World Bank and Cities Alliance have joined forces in taking on the issue of cities and climate change. The joint work program aims to contribute to a more coordinated and focused response to issues, which cities are facing, in particular in developing countries. Initiatives of the JWP include developing a global standard on greenhouse gas emissions originating from cities, editing a joint position paper on cities and climate change, the harmonization of approaches to urban risk assessments and the development of an online knowledge center on cities and climate change.

UN-Habitat Partnership

Due to their complementary mandates in the fields of sustainable urban development and the global environment, UN–Habitat and UNEP have a long history of cooperation. Together, they have developed a joint work program to mainstream environmental considerations into urban policymaking, to incorporate urban perspectives into environmental policymaking, and to highlight the linkages between local and global environmental issues.

Under this partnership, UNEP and UN–Habitat aim to provide improved and expanded services to local and national governments in the field of urban environment.

UNEP and UN–Habitat cooperate to enable cities to better assess and prioritize local environmental concerns and to have a voice in national and global environmental debates, in particular in such areas as climate change. Helping countries and cities to implement global standards, agreements and conventions enables them to better link local issues to global concerns. UNEP and UN–Habitat conduct joint activities on:

- Cities and climate change assessments
- Ecosystem-based adaptation in coastal cities
- Harnessing the mitigation potential of buildings, housing and construction
- Low carbon cities: the transport and urban planning dimension.
- Gwanju City Cooperation

In the context of the Urban Environmental Accords, signed by more than a hundred cities to achieve sustainable development at city level, UNEP is cooperating with the City of Gwangju (South Korea). The initiative aims at developing and documenting approaches and tools for cities to promote green growth, resource-efficiency and the development of low carbon cities. Expected outputs include the development of a global framework to assess the environmental performance of cities and to explore the feasibility of developing a methodology for a Clean Development Mechanism at city-wide level.

44. Mapping Mangrove Management

Lessons Learned from Mexico*

Astrid J. Hsu

Between land and sea, one will often find mangrove forests hugging the coasts of tropical countries. These humble ecosystems play a vital role in sustainability and socio-economic livelihood but are threatened by high rates of deforestation and poor management. While gaps to efficient management of these ecosystems remain, partnerships among university researchers, nongovernmental groups, and government agencies are working together to bridge solutions.

This chapter introduces mangroves, their importance to society—especially in light of climate change, and their economic value. It then describes the global state of mangroves and addresses some of the existing barriers to successful mangrove management, before focusing on Mexico (home to 7 percent of the world's mangroves) and their leadership in mangrove conservation (Bunting et al., 2018). Following is a firsthand account of an international and interdisciplinary approach to mangrove management: this account details a rising effort across different levels and sectors of Mexican government to fulfill international commitments towards mangrove conservation. From this case study, lessons that can be applied to other case studies are then highlighted.

Services Worth Conserving

Mangrove ecosystems provide far more than meet the eye. These coastal habitats are critical hubs of biodiversity, nursery habitats for commercial fisheries, natural water filtration systems, and buffers from storms and erosion (Bowman, 1917; Millennium Ecosystem Assessment, 2005; Costanza et al., 2014). Mangroves have also emerged as a formidable force in climate change adaptation and mitigation by sequestering carbon dioxide—a main driver of climate change—and storing them for millennia, earning the trees recognition as a source of "blue carbon" (Murdiyarso et al., 2015; Ezcurra et al., 2016). Though they make up less than one percent of forests worldwide, mangroves contribute to over three percent of carbon extraction of all forests and account for 14 percent of the carbon captured by the world's oceans (Alongi D., 2012; Makowski and Finkl, 2018). Together, these benefits are worth approximately 100,000 USD per hectare annually (Mukherjee et al., 2014). In Mexico, mangroves cover approximately 775,555

*Published with permission of the author.

ha of land; thus, these forests and their services are valued up to 77 billion USD per year (CONABIO, 2017)!

The Global State of Mangroves and Monitoring Them

Despite the international recognition of the value of mangroves' valuable ecosystem services, these forests continue to be threatened on a global scale. Deforestation of these coastal habitats continues to occur as the result of aquaculture, agriculture, urban sprawl, and large-scale tourism (Sandilyan and Kathiresan, 2012; Friess and Webb, 2013). Combined with climate change and other threats, deforestation has caused worldwide loss in mangrove coverage of over 35 percent in the last 30 years, with some regions losing as much as 80 percent of their mangroves (Duke et al., 2007).

A loss of mangroves not only means losing the capacity to remove carbon from the air, but also releasing thousands of years-old carbon stored in their soils back into the atmosphere, as the uprooted trees exposes the soil (where most of the carbon is stored) to air. In a single year, countries can release up to 3,410 Gigagrams of carbon dioxide from deforestation, roughly equivalent to the per capita carbon emission of Latin America (Atwood et al., 2017).

To date, monitoring efforts have simply recorded the loss of mangroves. The most regular estimates occur only on local scales, with Mexico as a leader in estimating the country's mangrove extent every five years (CONABIO, 2017). This lag time in between estimates prevents decision makers from making real-time choices to conserve these habitats, as detailed knowledge of the current extent and state of mangroves is instrumental to the design of protected areas, the assignment of land use categories, and the evaluation of ecosystem services.

Recently, initiatives such as the Global Mangrove Watch (GMW) have made tangible steps towards monitoring global mangrove extent on an annual basis. However, the satellite imagery used is presently at a 30-meter resolution (each pixel in a photo represents 900 square meters). While the resolution of these mangrove maps and the frequency at which the maps are updated may be sufficient for international decisions, both higher resolution and frequency of update may be required for more regional mangrove management. This is because more detailed information can indicate immediate mangrove threats with greater accuracy so that both reactive and proactive action can be taken in a timely manner.

Mexico's Role in Mangrove Conservation

Mexico, one of the top five countries in terms of mangrove extent, has been recognized as a leader in mangrove conservation, and is advanced in prioritizing mangroves and their role to mitigate climate change impacts (Bunting et al., 2018). Mangroves are designated as a protected habitat in the country; thus, Mexico's *National Commission for the Knowledge and Use of Biodiversity* (CONABIO) monitors and updates the extent of the habitat within its borders every five years (CONABIO, 2017). In 2015, Mexico and over 150 other countries put forth their Nationally Determined Contributions (NDCs), a document that details a country's voluntary commitment to curbing climate change impacts in their own country, and establishes targets for a country's carbon emissions. NDCs are the heart of the historic United Nations Framework Convention on Climate Change's Paris Agreement, yet mangroves are largely left out: Mexico is only one of 45 countries that mentions mangroves and one of the 27 countries that mentions blue carbon in their NDCs (Gallo et al., 2016).

In addition to ratifying the Paris Agreement and including mangroves in their NDC, Mexico is also party to the *United Nations Environmental Programme Conference on Protection of the Marine Environment from Land-Based Activities*, the *Man and the Biosphere Programme* of 1968, the *Convention of Biological Diversity* of 1992, and the *Ramsar Convention* of 1971 (Macintosh and Ashton, 2002; Slobodian & Badoz, 2019). Being party to these international commitments further signifies Mexico's historical dedication an sense of responsibility to mangrove conservation.

These varied commitments are just one reason why several Mexican agencies maintain an interest in monitoring mangroves. Because mangroves find their home at the fuzzy border between land and sea, both land and water-focused government agencies are invested in these habitats (Friess et al., 2016). As a protected resource, a forest, and a critical source of blue carbon, mangroves find themselves in overlapping jurisdiction among government agencies such as the *National Commission of Protected Areas (CONANP)* and the *National Commission of Water (CONAGUA)*. Thus, the question remains: in order to achieve international commitments, how can we encourage participation among national and local governments to improve efficiency in mangrove conservation?

A Case Study: Building Upon a Scientific Partnership

Since 2009, researchers from *the Scripps Institution of Oceanography* at the *University of California, San Diego* (*UCSD*) in San Diego, California, have worked closely with the *Centro para la Biodiversidad Marina y la Conservación* (*CBMC*), a nongovernmental agency located in La Paz, Baja California Sur, Mexico, on a variety of marine conservation issues in the Gulf of California. This work has long included mangroves, and in 2017, the two organizations looked towards drones as a novel way of collecting mangrove data. The organizations then established a collaboration with *Engineers for Exploration* (*E4E*), also at *UCSD*. Together the three organizations formed a team with the objective to develop technologically current methodologies, build government capacity in drone applications, and foster cross-sector collaborations for mangrove management.

At the time, because the team was working in protected areas, they needed permission from the local office of *CONANP* in La Paz to conduct their research. As they planned their operations, the team provided a letter to *CONANP* detailing their planned activities. Additionally, and perhaps even more crucially, the team extended an invitation for *CONANP* to join them in the field. As they returned to Baja California Sur to further collect data and test their methods, the team and their project garnered interest in the municipality of La Paz. They soon met with the Regional Director of *CONANP–Baja California Sur* and shared the project's overview, progress, and challenges. The team also presented their protocol on drone operations in mangroves, and *CONANP* expressed their own interest to collaborate with the team in training *CONANP* members on drone techniques and to participate in collecting aerial imagery of mangroves. The team then met with *CONANP* officials based in nearby Magdalena Bay, showcasing their field methods to the officials and guiding *CONANP* in a hands-on drone demonstration over local mangroves. Word concerning the team's work continued to be shared within *CONANP*, and the team was soon asked by the head director of *CONANP* for a meeting with *CONANP*'s Wetland Commission. At that meeting, the team worked with government members to identify agencies that played a role in mangrove management. This conversation led to a subsequent meeting with members of those identified agencies, *CONAGUA* and the *National Institute of Statistics and Geography* (*INEGI*), and the dialogue proved to be a step towards increasing communication and efficiency across multiple government agencies on mangrove conservation.

With the synergy of cross-sectoral conversations and the great interest in the team's applied drone methods, the team set forth to train the government officials so that agencies themselves can implement these tools as they see fit. The team proceeded to design a basic curriculum on their drone methodologies that also incorporated knowledge of flight skills and planning. In 2019, the team held workshops to train members from the Mexican government, students, and other academics on drone operations in Sian Ka'an National Park, Yucatan; La Paz, Baja California Sur; and Mexico City. These workshops trained over 70 people, but more importantly, acted as a scaffold to seed collaborations amongst government agencies regarding mangrove conservation. Particularly in regard to the workshop in Mexico City, division directors from different agencies came together to learn more about the team's project and how to work together for mangrove conservation. The list below represents the agencies that joined the workshops and their interest in doing so:

National Commission of Protected Areas (*CONANP*): This government agency manages all of Mexico's protected areas. Wetlands that lie within protected areas are closely monitored. *CONANP*—and its subsequent Wetland Commission—is also responsible for fulfilling commitments outlined in international agreements such as the Ramsar Convention, Sustainable Development Goal 14, and Aichi Biodiversity Goals.

National Commission of Water (*CONAGUA*): *CONAGUA* manages all the waterways of Mexico, and this occasionally intersects with wetlands. Additionally, *CONAGUA* has the responsibility to define the boundaries of Mexico's wetlands (Slobodian & Badoz, 2019).

National Institute of Statistics and Geography (*INEGI*): *INEGI* is a key player in mangrove conservation as they are responsible for updating all the maps of Mexico, including national maps of mangrove extent. They have a national commitment to increase the resolution of the nation's validated maps, and in that way, *INEGI* is a driving force to monitoring mangroves at higher resolutions. Without these verified maps, the ability for *CONANP*, *CONAGUA*, or other agencies to proceed with management dependent on these maps is severely limited.

Secretariat of Agrarian, Land, and Urban Development (*SEDATU*): This agency manages the land for agriculture, land, and urban development, and wetlands are of interest because this agency develops land use policies. As such, *SEDATU* monitors how wetlands are used and how much area is being converted to other uses, i.e., agriculture or urban development.

Together, the workshop attendees identified the goals of each agency, acknowledged challenges to achieving those goals, and divided up roles and responsibilities to further the generation of collaborative knowledge regarding mangrove conservation.

There are other significant federal agencies in Mexico, such as the *National Forest Commission* (*CONAFOR*) and the *National Institute of Ecology and Climate Change*

(*INECC*), that were not identified in this case study. This is not to say that these agencies are not involved in other manners. The case study presented here is continually evolving, and details of these relationships are outside the scope of this chapter.

Challenges Worth Overcoming

Challenges to collaboration are inherent, as different agencies often have different priorities and different organizational structure. Navigating the bureaucracy within a single agency can be difficult in and of itself, and this complexity can easily be compounded across agencies.

One example of this is data sharing. Agencies often collect data to better inform their decision making. In this case study, the data collected was the extent of mangrove habitats and the local threats to these ecosystems. *CONABIO*'s data is powered by *INEGI*, but their data is only updated once every five years, and organizations such as *CONANP* and *CONAGUA* are looking for maps that are updated more quickly and with higher resolution. Due to the lack of communication among agencies, each independently set out to map the nation's mangroves. Efforts were essentially tripled as these three agencies (*INEGI*, *CONANP*, and *CONAGUA*) worked towards the same end goal. Without identifying how the agencies can communicate with each other, incompatibility will remain a challenge to streamlining across agencies and efficient resource management.

Throughout this case study, it was critical to work closely with local organizations and offices. Especially since *UCSD* is a U.S. organization, collaborating with *CBMC* was essential to achieving the project's objectives. Their expertise and insight on local field operations facilitated the collection of data and directly contributed to the success of the team's field expeditions. More critically, *CBMC* played a large role in establishing dialogue with the local *CONANP* office in La Paz, and later, the national *CONANP* office in Mexico City. A strong partnership with local groups is absolutely instrumental and cannot be underscored enough for effective conservation.

The Age of Big Data

Society now lives in the age of big data, and the value of information has skyrocketed. As such, data sharing can be leveraged for collaboration. This is because entities are all eager for data that can help achieve organizational priorities, and thus data sharing is often provides incentive for collaboration. Furthermore, data sharing acts as tremendous facilitator as it also streamlines efficiency in such that all entities have the latest and best available information.

Just as people talk in different languages, data can also appear in a variety of forms. It is paramount for agencies and organizations to format their data in a manner that can easily "speak" with other data. In regards to mangrove-related data, data best practices are available through ocean biogeographic information system (OBIS, https://obis.org/manual/nodes/) and Darwin Core (https://dwc.tdwg.org/terms/). Checking with the scientific community as well as one's collaborators to ensure that best data practices are implemented across participating entities can save quite a bit of time, energy, and headache down the road.

Sharing data is just one form of communication, and highlights the need for agencies to be well connected among levels—from their local office to their national office—as well as amongst each other.

Transferrable Lessons

The case study presented here is not a recipe. Each situation regarding collaboration has its own unique constraints, challenges, and culture that must be taken into account when approaching interdisciplinary and cross-sectoral implementation. Regardless of the topic at hand, navigating the political system, defining a common goal for all involved, and framing roles and responsibilities are key. It is of the utmost importance to leave room for conversations in which each stakeholder can voice their goals and relevant challenges to achieving them and can be empowered to contribute in a meaningful way. This process can be broken down into the following steps:

- Identify a lead organization (leadership characteristics can be found in Macintosh and Ashton, 2002)
- Express relevant agency goals and the challenges
- Identify overlaps in goals among agencies
- Identify potential solutions and/or resources available to develop a solution
- Define actionable steps by designating roles and responsibilities to each agency
- Set a deadline and a subsequent meeting

By taking the steps above, the team and its multiple government partners streamlined collaboration in developing a national strategy for the inventory and conservation of Mexico's wetlands. *CONANP* was identified as the lead organization, other relevant agencies were identified and invited to contribute to the conversation, and the common goal across agencies was defined as fulfilling mangrove conservation targets as set forth by international commitments. Ultimately, as scientists, the team seeks to empower decision makers with access to the most accurate and updated science. Likewise, decision makers and local community members have the responsibility to communicate their information needs and how their lack of information impacts society. It is then that an interdisciplinary community can come together and progress towards a more sustainable world.

References

Alongi, D.M. (2012). Carbon sequestration in mangrove forests. Carbon management, 3(3), 313–322.

Atwood, T. B., Connolly, R. M., Almahasheer, H., Carnell, P. E., Duarte, C. M., Lewis, C.J. E., ... & Serrano, O. (2017). Global patterns in mangrove soil carbon stocks and losses. Nature Climate Change, 7(7), 523.

Bowman, H.H.M. (1917). Ecology and physiology of the red mangrove. Proceedings of the American Philosophical Society, 56(7), 589–672.

Bunting, P., Rosenqvist, A., Lucas, R., Rebelo, L. M., Hilarides, L., Thomas, N., ... & Finlayson, C. (2018). The global mangrove watch—a new 2010 global baseline of mangrove extent. Remote Sensing, 10(10), 1669.

Comisión Nacional para el Conocimiento y Uso de la Biodiversidad (CONABIO). (2017). Manglares de México: actualización y exploración de los datos del sistema de monitoreo (1970/1980–2015). CONABIO, Mexico City.

Costanza, R., Pérez-Maqueo, O., Martinez, M. L., Sutton, P., Anderson, S. J., & Mulder, K. (2008). The value of coastal wetlands for hurricane protection. AMBIO: A Journal of the Human Environment, 37(4), 241–249.

Duke, N. C., Meynecke, J. O., Dittmann, S., Ellison, A. M., Anger, K., Berger, U., ... & Koedam, N. (2007). A world without mangroves?. Science, 317(5834), 41–42.

Ezcurra, P., Ezcurra, E., Garcillán, P. P., Costa, M. T., & Aburto-Oropeza, O. (2016). Coastal landforms and accumulation of mangrove peat increase carbon sequestration and storage. Proceedings of the National Academy of Sciences, 113(16), 4404–4409.

Friess, D. A., Thompson, B. S., Brown, B., Amir, A. A., Cameron, C., Koldewey, H. J., & Sidik, F. (2016). Policy challenges and approaches for the conservation of mangrove forests in Southeast Asia. Conservation Biology, 30(5), 933–949.

Friess, D. A., & Webb, E.L. (2014). Variability in mangrove change estimates and implications for the assessment of ecosystem service provision. Global ecology and biogeography, 23(7), 715–725.

Gallo, N. D., Victor, D. G., & Levin, L.A. (2017). Ocean commitments under the Paris Agreement. Nature Climate Change, 7(11), 833.

Hammer, D. A., & Bastian, R.K. (1989). Wetlands ecosystems: natural water purifiers. Constructed wetlands for wastewater treatment: municipal, industrial and agricultural, 5.

Kivaisi, A.K. (2001). The potential for constructed wetlands for wastewater treatment and reuse in developing countries: a review. Ecological engineering, 16(4), 545–560.

Lugo, A. E., & Snedaker, S.C. (1974). The ecology of mangroves. Annual review of ecology and systematics, 5(1), 39–64.

Macintosh, D. J., & Ashton, E.C. (2002). A review of mangrove biodiversity conservation and management. Centre for tropical ecosystems research, University of Aarhus, Denmark.

Makowski, C., & Finkl, C.W., eds. (2018). Threats to Mangrove Forests: Hazards, Vulnerability, and Management (Vol. 25). Springer.

Millennium Ecosystem Assessment. Current State and Trend Statement: Coastal Systems. (2005). Available at http://www.millenniumassessment.org/documents/document.288.aspx.pdf.

Mukherjee, N., Sutherland, W. J., Dicks, L., Huge, J., Koedam, N., & Dahdouh-Guebas, F. (2014). Ecosystem service valuations of mangrove ecosystems to inform decision making and future valuation exercises. PloS one, 9(9), e107706.

Murdiyarso, D., Purbopuspito, J., Kauffman, J. B., Warren, M. W., Sasmito, S. D., Donato, D. C., ... & Kurnianto, S. (2015). The potential of Indonesian mangrove forests for global climate change mitigation. Nature Climate Change, 5(12), 1089.

Sandilyan, S., & Kathiresan, K. (2012). Mangrove conservation: a global perspective. Biodiversity and Conservation, 21(14), 3523–3542.

Slobodian, L. N., Badoz, L., eds. (2019). Tangled roots and changing tides: mangrove governance for conservation and sustainable use. WWF Germany, Berlin, Germany and IUCN, Gland, Switzerland. xii+280pp.

Acknowledgments

I would like to acknowledge P. Ezcurra, J. Kim, C. Pereira, and J. Fu for their time and effort to provide feedback on this chapter; the Gulf of California Marine Program for the field opportunities; the members of the Aburto Lab, Centro para la Biodiversidad Marina y la Conservación, and Engineers for Exploration for the research support; and the National Commission of Protected Areas (CONANP) for letting me be a part of the conversation. This work would not have been possible without funding from the Pew Charitable Trusts and the National Geographic Society.

45. A Case for Transition Shelters*

Gabby V. Moraleda

Historical data suggests that a mere 15 percent of the people affected by disasters are reached by all forms of combined assistance and can recover. The remaining 85 percent are left on their own to rebuild their homes and lives. Surely, difficult for those who do not have the means

Understandably, humanitarian shelter gets priority.

Foreign/International aid and diaspora donations are primarily designated for food, medicines and short-term shelter. In the absence or shortage of covered spaces (ex. basketball courts), tents (or tent-like shelters) have become the most convenient and visible structures in evacuation areas. Tents are portable, relatively easy to setup and reasonably priced—becoming the quickest way to provide a roof over one's head. Not durable, limited functionality but given the situation, the most practical.

These tents, by their very nature and given their technical specifications, are meant for a few weeks of stay only. Temporary in nature—for emergency. Beyond that, their value and utility diminish, substantially. Its continued use exposes the people living in them—the elderly, infants, handicapped and nursing mothers to more harm than good. In the normal course of recovery, it is envisioned that if homes are livable after a disaster, then the people are ushered back into their permanent homes. If homes are severely damaged, they are moved to transition shelters, fitted for better living—up to a point in time when the homes are repaired.

Building back better permanent houses is a straight-forward proposition. Financing is readily available from usual lending sources backed by government mortgage institutions. In the Philippines, access to these funds can be through the Social Security System (SSS) and the Government Service Insurance System (GSIS) housing loans in conjunction with PAGIBIG's Home Development Mutual Fund. Most of these lenders have structured lending protocols skewed in favor of low-risk borrowers, basically their contributing members. If you can demonstrate the capacity to pay (i.e., have a regular job), these lenders will lend you. After the appropriate building permits have been properly secured, repair/rebuilding can take several months.

In other words, the upper and middle-income groups have a clear pathway to recovery.

The case for low-income, high-risk families (marginal farm workers and fishermen) is different. Quite the opposite. They have no one to run to. No parameters to work with and no access to lenders.

---

*Published with permission of the author.

They are left on their own to source funds, if they can, from friends, family members—local and overseas. The obvious consequence is that if they are unable to secure funds, they linger in a "state of limbo," the default option, and stay in humanitarian shelters for an "extended" period of time. This can be "forever." When this happens, migration becomes the one avenue left—as in the case of Typhoon Haiyan and the Marawi siege.

Inequity, even in disasters.

As such, it is clear, transition shelter presents itself as the vital link—from humanitarian shelter to permanent housing—the only option open, not for those who can afford but for the poor and underprivileged. Unless these better built shelters are made available, the people will remain in deplorable emergency-living conditions.

Without a doubt, there are fundamental fiscal policy and operational considerations—specially when destruction is widespread and extensive as in Tacloban. For one, the magnitude alone can be overwhelming, overpowering and consuming—and when help is nowhere in sight. Private donations generally taper off after a week of giving. Whose primary responsibility is it then to rebuild—government, the diaspora, the international community or themselves? No one seems to have a definite answer—or even paying attention.

And, since time is of the essence, "speed of delivery" is a second major factor. Time does not stand still. When bureaucracy seeps in, gridlock happens, and everything is pushed back—or out. As a result, a great majority are left unattended, alone to fend for themselves for months, if not years. Indeed, a sad plight repeatedly heard off and ignored.

The starting (humanitarian) and end (permanent) points of the shelter recovery process are, in a way, "covered." It is in place and defined. The middle (transition) phase, the most critical, is not. It is no wonder the responses of the "community" in past major disasters have been consistently lacking and inadequate.

The pursuit of aggressive transition shelter solutions and settlements becomes compelling. For without it, the defenseless will always be left out in the dark, remain homeless, hopeless and will stay in makeshift shelters—vulnerable, if not perish, when the next disaster strikes.

The Assumptions

As we chart out our best options, it is wise to review four (4) simple assumptions that have guided our approaches and proposed solutions. These are;

First, we must be cognizant of the fact that in these changing times, in the context and reality of climate change—*nature always wins*. Given its strength, it takes anything along its path. There is no way around this. For disaster volunteer groups—be forewarned, it is a myth to believe otherwise.

Second, in the face of any impending disaster (super typhoons) and the context of crudely built homes, on "no build or hazard zones" and are unable to withstand nature—the first line of "defense" is—*to run to safer/higher ground*, to places of (temporary) refuge. Evacuation to safe areas and structures is the first order of business. This is the most logical thing to do, no ifs and buts.

Third, given the repetitiveness and increasing strength of typhoons, and to the extent we can, we must realize—*man can only mitigate* or minimize the risks, through better building technologies, common sense engineering solutions in flood control/water management including the adoption of environmentally-based solutions such as erosion prevention, among others. These interventions are technologically sound, readily available from experienced engineers and can be put in place, way before a disaster strikes. No rocket science needed.

And fourth, *"prevention" pays off*—or costs related to "upgrading" or retrofitting poorly built homes with inferior materials to conform with acceptable standards are worth the expense. A dollar spent in prevention equates to four dollars in rebuilding—a $1: $4 ratio, validating the classic principle that "an ounce of prevention is worth a pound of cure."

If you look at it closely, literally, figuratively and profoundly, the task at hand is really to find or build *places of refuge*—safe, secure shelters that can withstand the storms that are sure to come.

The sad experiences of the past must not be repeated. Unfortunately, it is. The prolonged misery we continually witness in each disaster is a raison d'etre to put on each of our shoulders the burden and tremendous challenge to respond—collectively.

A Work in Progress: Portable Container Vans, Bamboo Homes and Available Spaces

Haiyan is a game changer. It is a first and certainly not the last. Our interest paper "After Haiyan: Where?" highlighted the following points:

1. That, there is an urgency to start discussions on how we can, at least, start a rebuilding and renewal program that shall prepare the nation.

2. In the short run, there is a need to move the evacuees from emergency centers to habitable "transition homes and communities" before the next rainy season. Retrofitted container vans are a possibility because they are portable and reusable.

3. We foresee the need to "challenge" the boundaries of engineering and architectural science and explore its boundaries to "Build Better Than Before" solutions.

As detailed out (parts of our paper are quoted below), container vans as transition shelters have become a desired solution. Strength, portability and reuse are its strengths. With compact, configurable, and Lego brick-like properties, the vans can withstand the fiercest of storms.

It is envisioned that 40 × 8 foot containers be used having a total area of 320 square feet (or, 30 square meters) for these living quarters to make a decent livable space for a household of five (5) persons. Container dimensions are 10 feet high and vary from 10, 20, 30 and 40 feet long so they can be modularly combined. They are structurally sound, being able to load up to 20 tons of cargo and stacked up 9-high. These can be locked with a mechanism side-by-side and on top of each other such as can be observed on container ships.

Containers are cost effective. They need to undergo sandblasting, painting, cutting window openings, and conversion of steel gates to maintenance free pvc doors. Interior features of the containers are R-15 fiberglass insulation on the ceiling and sides conforming to container corrugation, finish-painted ceiling and side walls of riveted ½-inch marine plywood, 2 white pvc windows of 2 ft × 4 ft, and 12 CFL overhead lights/switches, wiring for 12 outlets. In addition, foldable bunk beds, and tables and space separators will be installed. The specific layout of these temporary container shelters within or around the city shall be such as to minimize obstructions and interference to rapid reconstruction of the Tacloban commercial districts.

The locations and configurations of these shelters will be environmentally sound and conform to space planning standards. Access roads need to be included in the site preparation as well as electrical connections to each container shelter with power to be provided by the local utility.

These refurbished container vans will not be fitted with toilets and bathrooms. Instead, a communal system will be provided in a central location to centralize water supply and delivery and a septic tank for disposal of biohazard wastes. Fresh water shall be drawn from deep wells, where available and pumped into a 10,000-gallon elevated water tank. From the tank, water delivery will be piped into dedicated lines for drinking water and another line for washing, bathing and laundry needs. Large garbage bins will also be provided for solid wastes destined for landfill and composting. Moreover, inhabitants will be taught to segregate biodegradable, recyclable and true wastes.

Assuming that land, containers and most importantly, funds, are available, these temporary village shelters can be completed in six (6) months on a compressed schedule to create a quick and welcome response to this disaster and well ahead of the next devastation storm that can be expected in approximately eight (8) months. As these container vans are planned to transition beneficiaries to permanent homes, it is imperative that a long-term viable housing project be simultaneously put in place.

A second option is to use bamboo.

The plant, actually a grass, is pretty abundant in the countryside and easy to cultivate. It can be farmed and commercially grown. Bamboo is used for food, charcoal, furniture and construction—as scaffolding. Its roots hold the soil, prevents erosion and is a climate change agent. For some time now, bamboo has been on the radar screen as a possible construction material. To this day, there are pro and con discussions on its technical properties as a substitute for steel. In the last few years, a Non-Governmental Organization (NGO) has adopted treated bamboo for home construction. It is pioneering its use for shear walling and roofing frames or the cement-bamboo framing technology. They claim model homes built out of bamboo can withstand above normal wind loads and conforms with the National Structural Code of the Philippines.

A second NGO supplies the treated bamboo. The company is making a strong pitch in the housing and construction industry for its regular usage. They are confident with their findings on the properties, structural strength and usefulness of bamboo—to a point they have invested in a treatment plant in Negros. With the 2 NGO's, the supply chain is taking shape.

The third option is to utilize available spaces in schools, churches—even shopping malls as transition shelters. It is sensible because in most towns and cities, they are in existence. No need to build, just design and assign space.

These buildings are equipped with the necessary hygiene facilities and running water, essential for daily living. The engineering challenge is to evolve functional designs that will convert available spaces into a "mix use" and provide "zones" as living quarters for extended stay. For structures that have daily and heavy "consumer traffic" such as shopping malls, they may offer some resistance. Churches and schools, inherent places of refuge and learning may be more "flexible" in configuring their workspace to accommodate the modified living needs of these transients.

Finding Financing

By the sheer size of the problem, finding funds remain the biggest barrier to implementation. In spite of the global prosperity, we find the usual sources of financing—the international community of donors, are seemingly running out of funds. The reason for this is the high incidence and intensity of disasters worldwide as a result of climate change and conflict—i.e., more to serve with limited funds. Notwithstanding the geo-political realities, there is growing perception, the have's (industrialized nations) are gradually "distancing" themselves from the have not's (developing counties) in disaster response—unable to hear the plea, that universally held development tenets are no longer valid when viewed in context of recurring disasters.

In itself, an imminent "disaster"—on the horizon?

In this day and age of natural disasters and political turmoil, development implies disaster planning. Both are two (2) sides of the same coin, with a caveat—disaster planning must drive development.

This situation undoubtedly has created a scare and put pressure on countries prone to disasters (those in the typhoon belt) to search for creative ways outside the norm to raise the necessary funds. Though still very raw and tentative, in recent discussions, there are three ideas (3) that have been put forth.

The first is to tap the local government units (LGU) Internal Revenue Allotments (IRA). The IRA is the LGU's yearly share of the national revenue. This can go anywhere upwards from

P120 Million for a first-class municipality. At least five (5 percent) percent of the IRA is mandated to fund disaster response and preparedness—or at least P 6 Million is available each year. The LGU's can leverage these disaster funds and are allowed to borrow on it. So, assuming only half or P 3 Million is allotted for preparedness—using this amount, the LGU can secure a substantial loan, say P15 Million, which could be smartly used for transition shelters. The loan can securely be paid off in 5 years—without compromising their financial status.

Another idea is to tap the increasing overseas dollar remittances to share in the burgeoning cost of disaster recovery. The idea behind is to engage the participation of the U.S. diasporas of the most vulnerable nations. The suggestion is to take a small piece of the remittance fees and/or tag on an additional amount for this purpose. Somewhat akin to asking donations when you pay at a Safeway counter.

The last one is to partake in the "rounding off" receipts—when the rates are mathematically expressed beyond 2-decimal places. This can be significant when you factor the huge amounts of annual remittances.

Overall, the plan is to lodge these cumulative funds into some sort of a "Rainy Day" fund—for disaster preparedness. The administrative and legal details have not been ironed out. They need to be. However, this should not stop us from pursuing these mutually independent courses of action—with focus, passion and a sense of mission.

46. Incentivizing Collaborative Governance for Climate and Disaster Adaptation*

Maria Fe Villameiro-Mendoza
and Joaquin Jay Gonzalez III

The discipline of Public Administration has moved beyond the State and now encompasses market and civil society in its embrace. It has moved from "governing" or State or bureaucracy-centric paradigm to "governance," which is now concerned with managing the affairs of society, giving to each domain, e.g., government, business, civil society organization, the role/s it can do best (Carino 2008, Reyes et al. 2015). It has changed its focus from bureaucracy only, to that of collaboration of various stakeholders in the context of the network society, presumably to bring about better quality public services.

Public administrators have also blurred the lines between the people, the private sector and the government. Although bureaucracies still remain, public administrators have begun to recognize, considering "wicked problems" and complicated development challenges, that more can potentially be achieved by collaboration and networking (Morse and Stephens 2012).

Governance has also evolved to various forms, from conflictual and adversarial to consensus building to collaborative networks. Collaborative governance has emerged as a response to the failures of downstream implementation and to the high cost and politicization of regulation. It has developed as an alternative to the adversarialism of interest group pluralism and to the accountability failures of managerialism (especially as the authority of experts is challenged). More positively, one might argue that trends toward collaboration also arise from the growth of knowledge and institutional capacity beyond the monopoly of the State. As knowledge becomes increasingly specialized and distributed and as institutional infrastructures become more complex and interdependent, the demand for collaboration increases. The common metric for all these factors may be, as Gray (1989) has pointed out, the increasing "turbulence" faced by policy makers and managers (Ansell and Gash 2008, 544).

This chapter adopts a "simplified" framework of collaborative governance, i.e., the finer variables anchored on the policy process, which is a cyclical and iterative process of policy problem (re) definition, policy formulation, implementation, and evaluation (Mendoza 1998). It usually "starts" with a trigger or a policy problem that would be

---

*Published with permission of the authors.

solved, an analysis of policy alternatives and solutions, and an adoption of a preferred solution. In these processes, collaborative governance will be uncovered initially from the process of policy formulation to implementation. Collaborative environmental governance has been used to enhance collective community action for better climate change and disaster resilience (see Bodin 2017, Ulibarri 2019).

The Galing Pook Awards

The Galing Pook Foundation is a leading resource institution that incentivizes innovation, sustainability, citizen empowerment, and excellence in local governance. It rewards excellence in local governance through the recognition, sharing of information and support of efforts to replicate best practices at the local level. It recognizes innovation and excellence in local governance through its pioneering program called the Galing Pook (GP) Awards. The Awards started in October 21, 1993, under the joint initiative of the Department of the Interior and Local Government's Local Government Academy, the Ford Foundation, and other individual advocates of good governance from the academe, civil society and the government. The Asian Institute of Management carried on the awards program until 2001. Earlier in 1998, the Galing Pook Foundation was formed as a juridical institution to sustain the program (*www.galingpook.org*).

Since 1994, more than 250 programs have already won recognition. The Galing Pook winners are chosen each year from a wide array of programs from local governments after undergoing a rigorous multi-level screening process. The winning programs are selected based on, among others, whether the programs: (a) led to positive results and impacts on the community they serve; (b) promoted people's participation and empowerment; (c) showcased innovation, transferability and sustainability; and (d) epitomized efficiency of program service delivery. The weights for these criteria are in the GP website (*www.galingpook.org*). The 2018 Galing Pook winners are a mix of mainly environmental, socio-cultural, educational and economic programs. Three of these most outstanding programs are environmental management programs providing better climate adaptation and disaster resilience: Bindoy, Negros Occidental's From Ridge to Reef Program, Del Carmen, Surigao Del Norte's Mangrove Management Program, and Iloilo City's Iloilo-Batiano River Development Program.[1]

Bindoy's From Ridge to Reef Program

Out of 10,975 hectares of forestland in Bindoy, only 1,420.92 hectares of natural forest remained in 2010 caused by illegal tree cutting and the use of *kaingin*[2] method. In 1998, the Department of Environment and Natural Resources (DENR) declared that the Mantalip Reef was devastated due to dynamite fishing, *muro-ami*,[3] and compressor fishing with the use of cyanide. These alarming trends prompted the municipality to launch the Ridge to Reef Program to implement social and technical approaches to address the degradation of upland and coastal ecosystems by adopting alternative strategies for farmers and fishermen to earn their living while preserving the environment.

Given that 70 percent of its population consists of farmers and fisherfolk, the municipality launched a campaign to educate its constituents on the need to preserve the environment, which serves as their main source of livelihood. The program applied two approaches, upland resource management and development, and coastal resource management and development. For the upland, farmers and other stakeholders were consulted on what crops to plant, and farmers were given cash incentives ranging from PhP1,000–5,000 per ($20-$100) hectare to plant timber, bamboo, and coffee.

In partnership with the DENR and the National Greening Program (NGP), the municipality achieved increased forest cover from 1,420.92 hectares in 2010 to 5,420.92 hectares in 2018. Moreover, 2,828 hectares of timber plantations, 200 hectares of agroforestry, 620 hectares of coffee plantations, 125 hectares of native trees, and 85 hectares of bamboo plantations were revitalized. Its 75 hectares dedicated for cacao and rubber had an 86 percent survival rate. There was also an increased appearance of bird species, which initially disappeared prior to the implementation of the program.

The coastal resource management and development efforts led to the creation of a 65-hectare marine sanctuary covering five (5) coastal barangays. To revive the Mantalip Reef, the municipality collaborated with the World Bank and mobilized PhP 1.5 million ($30,000) funding support for the construction of the Mantalip guardhouse and patrol boat. This was part of the municipality's efforts in providing 24/7 protection of the 46-hectare Mantalip Reef. The guardhouse was also expanded to accommodate a visitors' area and was later developed as an eco-tourism destination in 2008.

The presence of the Black-spotted Snapper, commonly known as *alumahan* (Tagalog) or *labongan* (Visayan), which had not appeared for more than eight years, was a positive indication of the municipality's success in its conservation efforts. Bindoy also deputized 42 sea rangers in all six coastal barangays to monitor any illegal fishing activities. Local fisherfolk were able to coordinate with and report any illegal activities to the sea rangers and the Bantay Dagat (literally means Guardians of the Sea) using a telephone hotline.

With the strict enforcement of the law against illegal fishing and kaingin, the municipality observed an increase in fish catch from 1–2 kgs in 2010 to 4–5 kgs in 2016. There was also an improved hard coral cover from 43.6 percent in 2012 to 59.5 percent in 2017.

In 2012, the municipality of Bindoy partnered with an NGO, Rare Philippines, to implement a social marketing campaign on marine conservation. Called the Pride campaign, various activities were undertaken to help fisherfolk change their traditional ways of fishing, which were harmful to the environment. These included games, information materials, and community events, which were designed to promote deeper understanding on the value of preserving coastal resources as well as modify harmful fishing practices. Social marketing was incorporated in local festivities such as the Fisherfolks' day and Libod Sayaw[4] festival to generate broad participation. The Pride campaign culminated in the creation of their own mascot called "Lovie," representing the resurgence of the Black-spotted Snapper following Bindoy's conservation efforts.

The environmental conservation efforts of Bindoy municipality received several citations such as the 2018 Gawad Tugas Award for Region VII Biodiversity Conservation and Management, 2017 Ocean Hero Award for Best Managed Marine Protected Area in the Philippines, among others.

Del Carmen Mangrove Management Program

Housing the largest contiguous mangrove forest cover in the Philippines, with approximately 1,900 fishing households, the Municipality of Del Carmen depends on its mangrove for livelihood. Covering 27 kilometers in length and at least 500 meters in width, the mangrove block is the habitat of various species especially the endangered Philippine saltwater crocodile as well as the Philippine Cockatoo. However, due to the heavy reliance on these marine resources, there were rampant mangrove cutting, gleaning and dynamite fishing that threatened to endanger the mangrove ecosystem.

The Municipality of Del Carmen launched Siargao It Up! The Del Carmen Mangrove Management Program in 2013 in the hope to transform mangrove cutters into fisherfolk, and illegal fishers into boat guides in order to preserve the mangrove forest, and at the same time maximize its tourism potential. The program partnered with various organizations and the private sector in the operationalization of the program, which includes capacity building activities, community organizing, educational advocacy campaigns, and funding for livelihood innovations.

A Mangrove Management Plan was formulated with the participation of various stakeholders to systematically implement activities that will address mangrove cutting and illegal fishing. The plan was also science-based as the municipality partnered with scientists to effectively preserve the mangrove forest. Another highlight of the plan was the monitoring and evaluation mechanism set in place to measure the success of the various activities.

Leading to its inception in 2013, the municipality and various organizations in 2012 conducted numerous information, education, and communication (IEC) campaign activities, using various media including film to inform people of the hazards of mangrove cutting and illegal fishing as well as its long-term impact to the livelihood of the communities. To complement these awareness-raising activities, continuous organizing, and training of people's organizations (POs) on alternative sources of livelihood were conducted in the nearby mangrove and coastal areas.

Through its partnership with people's organizations, the municipality conducted regular mangrove planting and rehabilitation in partnership with the DENR. The program also developed innovative approaches to mangrove rehabilitation such as the use of mangrove propagules with coconut husks. It was found that the mangrove had a 90 percent survival rate with the coconut husks instead of polyethylene plastic bag and had a better and stable root system. A nursery was established for a stable supply of mangrove propagules to support the rehabilitation program. The use of this simple innovative technology resulted in an average mangrove survival rate of 80 percent per area planted. Bantay Dagat activities also led to a 200 percent fish stock increase.

The program also paved the way for the development of the community-based mangrove tours that provided alternative livelihood to 248 beneficiaries, who are either illegal mangrove cutters and fisherfolk and those affected by commercial fishing. Mangrove eco-guides were also trained in 2016 with the support of Shore It Up and MPIC Foundation for them to be Department of Tourism (DOT)-certificate holders. A Mangrove Protection Information Center (MPIC) was established to serve as the tourism receiving center or the jump off point for the mangrove forest tourism tours where educational and art installations were placed about the mangrove forest, its importance and preservation.

In addition, plastic paddleboats were provided to the illegal mangrove cutters with less production cost. These boats can easily be maneuvered in waterways because they are lightweight. They have cheaper materials that can be sourced out locally and relatively with lower cost. Its flexibility and elasticity allow boat makers to develop a more complex boat design, which is more appropriate to the target fishing grounds.

The various initiatives under the program led to the drastic reduction of illegal activities, 95 percent threat reduction of mangrove cutting as well as 90 percent decrease in illegal fishing based on a report of Bantay Dagat from 2014–2018. Household family income rose from PhP4,000–5,000 in 2014 to PhP8,000–10,000 in 2018.

Through the success of the program, the Municipality of Del Carmen received several key recognitions such as DILG Seal of Good Local Governance for 2016, 2017, and 2018; GGGI Climate Champion for Mangrove Management for 2015; and DOT/ATOP 2nd Best Tourism Event of Pearl Awards in 2014.

Iloilo-Batiano River Development Project

Due to rapid urbanization, the number of occupants along the Iloilo riverbank increased and as a consequence, this has resulted in unregulated conversion of riverbanks into fishponds, indiscriminate cutting of mangroves, unregulated waste disposal and informal settlements. The Iloilo River Master Plan was formulated in 2003 under the auspices of the Iloilo River Development Council to engage the people to revive as well as preserve the Iloilo River. The council, which was renamed to Iloilo-Batiano River Development Council (IBRDC) and chaired by the city mayor, provided the venue for interaction and coordination of programs for the rehabilitation of Iloilo River.

In 2011, two river summits were conducted to serve as the platform for future consensus-based action planning, decision-making as well as the formulation of the Council's objectives and strategies. Dialogue between agencies and stakeholders took place and emerging issues and integrated courses of action were discussed. Recognizing that people's participation and empowerment requires information, the Council embarked on a massive social marketing, information and education campaign.

For this purpose, the Iloilo-Batiano River Development project was developed. It is a collaboration among national agencies, non-government organizations, academe and the city government to rehabilitate the Iloilo River. It benefited more than 50 thousand residents from 35 barangays living along the Iloilo River in terms of improved health, ecological sustainability, and sense of security and livability. The project was also successful in the relocation of informal settlers along the riverbank as well as in the removal of fish pens which resulted in increased fish population, prevention of soil erosion, and preservation of the mangrove's high biodiversity index.

The project also attracted the construction of circumferential and radial roads and the establishment of convention centers, hotels, and condominiums which spurred local economic development, created more jobs and livelihood activities, increased income, and improved quality of life. As part of development of waterway, the Esplanade provided the needed access to Iloilo River and brought a sense of pride and ownership among Ilonggos.[5] Today, it serves not only as a major tourist destination but also as a venue for many outdoors recreation and healthy lifestyle activities as well as community assemblies.

To ensure the sustainability of the Council, a city ordinance institutionalizing the Iloilo-Batiano River Development Council is currently being drafted. The proposed ordinance will highlight the roles and responsibilities of the city government, member agencies and stakeholders as well as the mechanisms, policies and procedures for the integrated management of the Iloilo-Batiano River System.

The Iloilo-Batiano River Development Council and its accomplishments have been acknowledged through various awards and recognitions such as the 2010 Gold Livcom Award for the "Iloilo River Development Projects," 2011 Special Award for the "Advancing the Iloilo River Development Initiatives Through Integrated Sustainable Management," among others. Among its international partners include the Rivers of the World Foundation, International River Foundation, International Council for Local Environmental Initiatives, CITYNET, Urban Environmental Accord, Brehmen Overseas Research and Development Association, and the U.S. Agency for International Development. The close collaboration with these organizations exemplified the strong public-private partnership that the project was able to achieve.

Stakeholders, Leaders and the Governing Structure

True to form, powered by collaborative governance, these outstanding local governance programs led to positive results and impacts on the community they serve; promoted people's participation and empowerment; showcased innovation, transferability and sustainability; and epitomized efficiency of program service delivery, the four main criteria of the Galing Pook Awards.

The programs addressed complicated development problems ranging from environmental degradation, land tenure security and anemic cultural heritage presence. The stakeholders involved leaders, who functionally are not exclusive to the local chief executives (mayors), but also inclusive of community-based people's organizations (Del Carmen), development councils (Iloilo), youth associations (Loboc), task forces (Cagayan de Oro), and program managers (Bindoy). They to a great extent embraced the shared responsibility of finding solutions to the development problem/s they are faced with. These leaders are more open to share-rule, more innovative in their approaches and are risk-takers, particularly in confronting the vulnerability of their decisions against the prevailing status quo. In our local parlance, they are *bukas* (open), *matino* (ethical), *magaling* (excellent), may *puso* (with heart) for public service.

Other stakeholders include among others, the culprits and beneficiaries of the programs, themselves, They also include the Bantay Dagat, the scientific community, the academe, non-government organizations involved in social marketing, transforming mindsets, education and skills training, the private sector, including development financial institutions, and other national and local government agencies.

Approaches

Early on, the leaders have realized that the complicated problems they face cannot be solved overnight by one sector alone, but by almost everyone in the city or municipality. They conducted dialogues, consultations, summits, and forums to go to the core of the matter. They consulted, collaborated, cooperated and communicated to define the problem, offer solutions and chart strategies and directions. The Cagayan de Oro Housing Summit, for one, informed the city government to align the objectives of the program to effectively meet the needs of the beneficiaries, address the housing problem and synergize efforts of all sectors in the city. The San Nicolas Heritage Conservation Project "talked" with the people to retrace their rich cultural tradition, relive and ensure that the children and the next generation will know, remember and appreciate.

Carrots and sticks were employed particularly with the environmental protection and management programs in Bindoy and Del Carmen, e.g., the strict implementation of the laws with sanctions and punishments against erring fisher folks, mangrove cutters, and kaingeros; while at the same time, giving them incentives for planting trees and securing the forests and the coastal resources. In addition, they are given orientation sessions, skills training and the like so that they will have alternative livelihood.

Social marketing, valuing nature and transformation of mindset from culprit or destroyer to agent of change, were also common in most of the programs. Informal settlers were given security of land tenure for a fee while educating them to be more conscious of their rights and responsibilities as productive members of the society.

The private sector has been an important player not only in financing projects but also as co-decision maker (Iloilo and Bindoy). Unintended effects of co-regulation of natural resources and co-implementation of social emancipation and heritage conservation projects with the private sector, non-government organizations and the scientific community and academe prove to be many and positive.

Conclusions, Lessons, and Implications

In place for the last three to fifteen years, these 2018 GP winners delivered quality public services and brought about positive effects in their localities. Directly, they contributed to forest and coastal resource regeneration; mangrove protection; emancipation of a number of informal settler households; increased employment; land use regulation along the riverbanks; provided alternative livelihood; increased production and harvest. Indirectly, they have inculcated better appreciation and valuation of nature; reclaimed dignity as a person; spurred economic, social and cultural development in the area. These could not have happened if there were only one or few problem solvers and the vision to a better quality of life today and in the future were not shared by most of the stakeholders concerned.

Their journey, however, is not a walk in the park and did not happen overnight. It was difficult to change mindsets, and transform illegal fisher folks, mangrove and forest cutters, informal settlers and pathetic cultural scenes into guardians of the forest, the sea and other natural resources; productive members of the society; or robust cultural champions, aware of their rich cultural heritage. These programs have shown that change and transformation are possible when leaders are beyond themselves, collaboration in the governance of development projects is at work, and a collective and shared engagement between and among various stakeholders is present.

More researches are however needed to find ways to make collaborative governance a way of life not only in the best local governance programs in Galing Pook, but in the thousands of other municipalities and cities out there. The Philippines has 81 provinces, 145 cities 1489 municipalities and 42,036 villages (www.dilg.gov.ph). The 10 GP winners annually are just drops in the bucket and there is a need to inspire thousands of other local government units out there to share, collaborate and work together, to achieve their vision for an excellent place and prosperous planet, with other stakeholders of the society. The complicated tasks cannot be done alone.

NOTES

1. Excerpts from the *2019 Galing Pook Magazine*, featuring the 2018 Galing Pook Winners, sent by email to the members of the National Selection Board.

2. *Kaingin* is basically the slash and burn method employed in shifting agriculture cultivation of forestlands into something else. It is believed to be worse than illegal logging in that no trees or seeds are left after the fire (www.odi.org/publications/752-kaingin-philippines-it-end-forest).

3. *Muro-Ami* Fishing, otherwise known as reef hunting, is one of the cruelest, most cataclysmic forms of illegal fishing that destroys the coral reefs and exploits children.

This practice consequently destroys corals which take whole lifetimes to form and causes the deaths of some of these unfortunate children (studyhippo.com/essay-muro-ami).

4. The term *libod* means, "to make rounds" in the dialect, and *sayaw*, means, "dance." *The Libod Sayaw Festival* is celebrated in the town of Bindoy as a thanksgiving for the skills and kind deeds of its patron saint, Saint Vincent Ferrer, the builder of one of the Catholic Churches in Bindoy (*Libod Sayaw Festival of Bindoy–Buglasan Festival–Negros…*buglasanfestival.com/…/libod-sayaw-festival-bindoy).

5. *Ilonggos are the natives of Iloilo.*

REFERENCES

Ansell, Christopher, and Gash, A. (2008). "Collaborative Governance in Theory and Practice." *Journal of Public Administration Research and Theory*, Vol. 18, Issue 4.

Bodin, Örjan. (2017). "Collaborative environmental governance: Achieving collective action in social-ecological systems." *Science* 18 Aug 2017.

Carino, Ledivina V. (2008). "State, Market, and Civil Society in Philippine Public Administration," Philippine Journal of Public Administration, 52 (2008/2–4), 139–166.

Galing Pook Foundation. (2019). *Galing Pook Magazine: The Galing Pook Awards 2018*: Ten Outstanding Local Governance Programs. www.galingpook.org.

Gray, Barbara. (1989). Collaborating: Finding common ground for multi-party problems. San Francisco, CA: Jossey-Bass.

Mendoza, Maria Fe V. (1998). PM 241: Public Policy and Program Administration. UP Open University.

Morse, R., and Stephens, J. (2012). "Teaching Collaborative Governance: Phases, Competencies, and Case-Based Learning." *Journal of Public Affairs Education*. 18 (3): 565.

Reyes, Danilo Dela Rosa et al., eds. (2015). *Introduction to Philippine Public Administration in the Philippines: A Reader Volume 1*, National College of Public Administration and Governance University of the Philippines Diliman.

Ulibarri, N. (2019). "Collaborative governance: a tool to manage scientific, administrative, and strategic uncertainties in environmental management?" *Ecology and Society* 24(2):15.

www.galingpook.org.

47. Climate Change Justice and Environmental Litigation in the Philippines*

Alder K. Delloro *and* Joaquin Jay Gonzalez III

Climate Change is one of the gravest threats to human rights of our generation. It poses serious risk to the fundamental rights to life, health and an adequate standard of living of individuals and communities across the world (UNEP 2015). It is a global phenomenon that affects the economic, socio-cultural, ecological and other vulnerabilities of countries (Mendoza 2014 citing World Bank 2010). The United Nation's Intergovernmental Panel on Climate Change (IPCC) warns in its most recent Fifth Assessment Report that warming of the climate system is unequivocal and that atmospheric concentrations of carbon dioxide have increased to levels unprecedented in the past 800,000 years. Most notably, the IPCC has concluded that human influence has been the dominant cause of global warming since the mid–20th century (IBA 2014).

In the midst of the post 2015 Development Agenda and the 17 Sustainable Development Goals, which serve as the framework of policies and programs for development in the next 30 years and the 2015 Paris Agreement on Climate Change, addressing the risks and hazards of climate change has become an imperative for which the survival of the human race hinges.

The 1987 Philippine Constitution mandates the preservation of a healthy environment and ecological balance. Thus, Section 16, Article II on the Declaration of Principles and State Policies of the Constitution, provides that:

> Section 16. The State shall protect and advance the right of the people to a balanced and healthful ecology in accord with the rhythm and harmony of nature.

The Philippines is presumably the first country in the world to enshrine in its Constitution the right of the people to a balanced and healthful ecology in accord with the rhythm and harmony of nature, and the correlative duty of the State to protect and advance that right (Davide Jr. 2012: 594).

The Philippine Response to Climate Change

In response to what has essentially become a global crisis, the Philippine government has enacted the Climate Change Act of 2009 that provides the policy framework

---

*Published with permission of the authors.

within which to systematically address the growing threats on community life and its impact on the environment.

The Climate Change Act establishes an organizational structure, the Climate Change Commission, and allocates budgetary resources for its important functions. These functions include:

- The formulation of a framework strategy and program, in consultation with the global effort to manage climate change,
- The mainstreaming of climate risk reduction into national, sector and local development plans and programs,
- The recommendation of policies and key development investments in climate-sensitive sectors, and
- The assessments of vulnerability and facilitation of capacity building.

The Climate Change Commission later crafted the National Climate Change Framework Strategy: 2010–2022 in 2010 and the National Climate Change Action Plan: 2011–2028 in 2011.

The national climate change framework strategy has been translated into a National Climate Change Action Plan, which prioritizes food security, water sufficiency, ecological and environmental stability, human security, climate-smart industries and services, sustainable energy as well as knowledge and capacity development as the strategic direction for 2011 to 2028. For easy reference, below is the list of the Philippine policy response to climate change:

1990–1995

- Inter-Agency Committee on Climate Change established (1991)
- Philippines signs UN Framework Convention on Climate Change (1994)

1995–2000

- 1st Philippine National Communication (1999)
- Philippine Clean Air Act (1999)

2001–2005

- Philippine Government signs Kyoto Protocol (2003)

2006–2010

- Biofuels Act (2006)
- Presidential Task Force on CC (2007)
- Presidential Proclamation of Climate Change Consciousness Week (2008)
- Renewable Energy Act (2009)
- Climate Change Act (2009)
- Philippine National REDD Plus Strategy (2010)
- National Framework Strategy on Climate Change (2010)

- Philippine Disaster Risk Reduction and Management Act (2010)
- The Philippine Strategy on Climate Change Adaptation (2010)

2011–2014

- National Climate Change Action Plan for 2011 to 2028 (2011)
- Cabinet Cluster on Integrity of the Environment and Climate Change Adaptation and Mitigation (2011)
- People's Survival Fund Act (2012)
- Integrating DRR-CCA in Comprehensive Land Use Plans of Local Government (2013)
- Guidelines in Tagging/Tracking Government Expenditures for Climate Change in the Budget Process (national level 2013 and local level 2014)
- Executive Order No. 174: Institutionalization of the GHG Inventory Management and Reporting System (2014)

2015–2020

- Philippine Green Jobs Act (2016)
- Philippines signs the 1995 Paris Agreement under the United Nations Framework Convention on Climate Change (2017)
- Climate-related policies and measures as discussed in 11 Chapters of the Philippine Development Plan 2017–2022

Climate Change Justice as the Higher-Order Strategy

According to the International Bar Association (IBA 2014), in its Climate Change Justice and Human Rights Report, mitigation and adaptation policies both raise justice issues:

> The central goal of mitigation policies is to limit GHG emissions but efforts to do so must take into account development goals in poorer countries. Moreover, certain measures designed to assist mitigation, such as the Clean Development Mechanism (CDM) developed under the Kyoto Protocol and the UN's programme of Reducing Emissions from Deforestation and Forest Degradation (REDD+) have raised their own human rights concerns in practice. And while many least developed countries (LDCs) have now drafted national adaptation programmes of actions (NAPAs) under the UNFCCC process—identifying activities to address their most urgent adaptation needs—the needed funding from other nations has been slow to appear. Resources devoted to both mitigation and adaptation strategies therefore need to be allocated with an understanding of and appreciation for, the ways in which they impact human rights. Indeed, the parties to the UNFCCC themselves stated, in a 15 March 2012 report on the Cancun conference, that they 'should, in all climate change-related actions, fully respect human rights' [IBA 2014: 4].

Thus, the Task Force on Climate Change Justice and Human Rights of the International Bar Associations adopts the following definition of climate justice:

> To ensure communities, individuals and governments have substantive legal and procedural rights relating to the enjoyment of a safe, clean, healthy and sustainable environment and the

means to take or cause measures to be taken within their national legislative and judicial systems and, where necessary, at regional and international levels, to mitigate sources of climate change and provide for adaptation to its effects in a manner that respects human rights [IBA 2014: 2].

Climate change justice or climate justice recognizes that climate change will disproportionately affect people who have less ability to prevent, adapt or otherwise respond to increasingly extreme weather events and rising sea levels. A climate-justice agenda embraces a conscious recognition of the development imbalances brought into relief by climate change. Climate justice seeks to combine the climate change discussion with human rights in a way that is equitable for the most climate-vulnerable groups (IBA 2014).

Climate justice is a struggle that considers justice as the basis of any solution. It supports climate solutions found in the practices and knowledge of those already fighting to protect and defend their livelihoods and the environment. Moreover, it also pertains to the struggle that insists on a genuine systematic transformation in order to tackle the real causes of climate change. (Hoodwinked in the Hothouse 2007: 26). Accordingly, climate justice addresses four key themes: root causes, rights, reparations and participatory democracy.

Climate justice can therefore be viewed as the higher-order strategy to address the challenges of climate change, alongside with mitigation and adaptation as it provides the substantive legal and procedural rights to these conventional strategies.

Climate Change Impact: The Philippine Perspective

Rincon and Virtucio, Jr. (2008) describe the Philippines as part of the western rim of the Pacific Ring of Fire, a belt of active volcanoes and major earthquake faults, and typhoon belts with a total discontinuous coastline of 32,400 kilometers, the longest in the world. Thus, the country is especially vulnerable to the adverse impacts of climate change. In fact, the Philippines has ranked fourth in the Global Climate Risk Index 2020 for the ten countries most affected from 1999–2018 (annual averages) and first in the Global Climate Risk Index 2013 for the ten most affected countries in the advent of Typhoon Haiyan which inflicted the Philippines with over Thirteen Billion Dollars (US$ 13 Billion) in economic loss and six thousand (6,000) deaths (Kreft, *et al.* 2015, Eckstein *et al.* 2020).

The Rules of Procedure for Environmental Cases

In the exercise of its auxiliary power to promulgate rules and regulations to enforce and protect Constitutional rights, the Philippine Supreme Court through Administrative Matter No. 09-6-8-SC promulgated the Rules of Procedure for Environmental Cases (rules). The rules lay down procedures governing the civil, criminal and special civil actions in all trial courts regarding environmental cases, with a view to protecting and advancing the constitutional right of the people to health and to a balanced and healthful ecology, and providing a simplified, speedy and inexpensive procedure for the enforcement of environmental rights under the Philippine law.

The rules empower the courts to issue environmental protection orders as an immediate action to protect the environment and the communities affected. Other remedies and orders direct government agencies to protect, preserve or rehabilitate the environment. The rules also enable communities to petition for the suspension or stoppage of destructive, environmental and development activities through the Citizen's Suit provision.

To summarize, the following are the innovations introduced in the rules:

- Citizen Suits—giving the right to ordinary citizens to initiate legal action to enforce their right to the life sources (a.k.a. environmental right);
- Consent Decrees;
- Temporary Environmental Protection Orders (TEPO) in cases of threat of serious damage to the environment (or life sources);
- *Writ of Kalikasan* or the writ of nature;
- *Writ of Continuing Mandamus*;
- Protection against harassment countersuits (i.e., SLAPP suits—Strategic Lawsuits Against Public Participation); and
- Adoption of the Precautionary Principle.

What is especially notable about the Rules of Procedure for Environmental Cases are the two special civil actions added to the existing rules of court in the Philippines, namely:

1. *Writ of Kalikasan*; and
2. *Writ of Continuing Mandamus*.

The Writ of Kalikasan: Philippine-Made

The *writ of kalikasan* is available when the environmental damage is of such magnitude that it prejudices the life, health, or property of inhabitants in two or more cities or provinces. The *writ* is issued by either the Supreme Court or the Court of Appeals within three days after the filing of the application. No docket or filing fee is required upon the filing of the complaint or petition.

Former Philippine Chief Justice Reynato Puno explains that while the *writ of habeas corpus* originated in England as a legal recourse for those wrongly detained and the *writ of amparo* came from Latin America to address its own brush with human rights violations, the *writ of kalikasan* is proudly Philippine-made to deal with cases in the realm of ecology.

The Writ of Continuing Mandamus

The Rules of Procedure for Environmental Cases integrated another procedure that was adopted and first introduced by the Supreme Court in the Manila Bay case. Through this *writ*, the court can direct the appropriate government agency to perform its mandate for the protection of the environment. This directive of the court is continuing, persisting and almost perpetual as it is enforceable until the judgment of the court is fully satisfied.

The Prospect of Climate Justice in the Philippines

A careful examination of landmark environmental cases in the Philippines shows that the Supreme Court has practically obliterated the legal obstacles in pursuing environmental cases and climate change litigation such as the issues on justiciability, *locus standi* and separation of powers.

As the concept of climate justice is anchored on the rule of law concept, the mechanisms and structures in the Philippine judicial system are supportive of this higher-order strategy in addressing the effects of climate change. The Supreme Court's jurisprudential pronouncements on environmental cases as well as its rules and procedures to enforce environmental domestic laws and international treaties are manifestations that climate justice as a remedy to combat climate change can be harnessed as a sound public policy.

Conclusion and Some Lessons

Climate change is a global phenomenon that poses real and imminent peril to the planet and all its inhabitants. It affects the economies and socio-cultural, ecological, and other vulnerabilities of countries and is thus necessarily a development issue which has greater consequences for the least developed counties like the Philippines. With poverty still looming in the country, a significant portion of its population does not possess adequate resources to insulate themselves from the potential dangers of climate change. The role of the State and the bureaucracy to address the challenges of climate change has therefore become more important than ever. As mentioned, the Philippine government has enacted and implemented numerous and significant responses to climate change primarily to mitigate and adapt with the climate change. More importantly, the judiciary, in general, and the Supreme Court, in particular, have taken an active stance to champion the cause for the environment pursuant to its mandate to be the guardian of the Constitution which provides a clear policy of the State to protect the environment.

The concept of climate justice is discussed as the third-order strategy, along with mitigation and adaptation, to address the issues of climate change. It is anchored on the rule of law concept which seeks to provide substantive legal and procedural rights relating to the enjoyment of a safe, clean, health and sustainable environment. Climate justice provides for the means to take or cause measures to be taken within the country's legislative, executive and judicial systems to mitigate sources of climate change and provide adaption to its effects in a manner that respects human rights.

The Philippine jurisprudence on environmental cases shows that the Philippine judicial system has breakthroughs which have successfully translated into helpful public policies and good practices which redress unjust distribution of power that weakens environment protection, and expanded access to justice and effective participation by anyone who considers himself or herself a steward of nature.

Moreover, a strong and independent judiciary is necessary to effectively pursue climate change justice in a country. In the Philippines, the Supreme Court has shed its restraint-based approach with the promulgation of rules of procedure for expeditious environmental litigation as well as for effectively managing environmental cases, an exercise of policymaking which is traditionally a domain of the legislature.

Indeed, climate change is a bigger issue than most of the ordinary citizenry understand it to be. The State and the bureaucracy, through the judiciary, play an important role in addressing the challenges of climate change especially so that it is a development issue that poses more risks to the poor, marginalized and disadvantaged members of our society. In fact, climate change threatens the very existence of the Philippines as it continues to be one of the most vulnerable countries to its debilitating effects. In the midst of these challenges, we will find a judiciary having the capacity to harness environmental justice and take advantage of its immense power of judicial review to ensure that the constitutional mandate to protect the environment is pursued even if it means striking down the acts of the executive and the legislature as unconstitutional or contrary to law. Thus, the changing tides in the Philippine judiciary has paved the way to an innovative solution like climate justice, one that addresses the challenges of climate change and gives meaning to the ends of human rights and environmental justice—a path that will hopefully lead towards sustainable development and a resilient Philippines.

References

Angara v. Electoral Commission, 63 Phil. 139, 158 (1936).

Davide Jr., Hilario G. (2012). "The Environment as Life Sources and the Writ of Kalikasan in the Philippines." *Pace Environment Law Review*. Volume 29, Issue 2 Winter. Pages. 591–561.

Eckstein, David et al. (2020). *Global Climate Risk Index 2020*. Germanwatch e.V. Berlin.

Hoodwinked in the Hothouse. (2007). https://www.tni.org/en/publication/hoodwinked-in-the-hothouse.

In Re Sotto 46 O.G. 2570 (1995).

Infotech Foundation, et. al. Vs. COMELEC, G.R. No. 159139, (2004).

International Bar Association. (2014). *Climate Change Justice and Human Rights Report: Achieving Justice and Human Rights in an Era of Climate Disruption*. (London: IBA).

Jacobson v. Massachusetts, 197 U.S. 22 (1905).

Kreft, S., Eckstein, D., Junghans, L., Kerestan, C. and Hagen, U. (2015). *Global Climate Risk Index 2015*. Germanwatch e.V. Berlin.

Lopez v. Roxas, 17 SCRA at 761 (1966).

Mendoza, Maria Fe V. (2014). "Private Sector: Engagement in Climate Change Mitigation and Adaptation: Implications on Good Governance." Paper Presented at the 3rd International Conference on ASEAN Connectivity: Current Issues and Prospects towards ASEAN Community held on 17 November 2014 at the Mahasarakham University, Thailand.

MMDA Vs. Concerned Citizens of Manila Bay, G.R. Nos. 171947–48, December 18, 2008.

Muskrat v. United States, 219 U.S. 346 (1911).

National Climate Change Action Plan: 2011–2028.

National Climate Change Framework Strategy: 2010–2022.

Oposa Vs Factoran, G.R. No. 101083 July 30, 1993.

People v. Alarcon, 69 Phil. 265 (1939).

Resident Marine Mammals vs. Reyes, G.R. Nos. 180771 & 181527, April 21, 2015.

Rincon, Maria Fernanda G. and Felizardo K. Virtucio, Jr. (2008). Climate Change in the Philippines: A Contribution to the Country Environmental Analysis. Presented at the Country Environmental Analysis (CEA) Consultative Workshops held in Manila, Philippines on June 16–17, 2008 and on November 18–19, 2008.

U.S. v. Bustos, 37 Phil. 731 (1918).

United Nations Environment Programme. (2015). Climate Change and Human Rights. https://www.unenvironment.org/resources/report/climate-change-and-human-rights.

48. Fostering Resilience in Water Supply Management*

JAKE ROM D. CADAG, SERGIO ANDAL, JR.,
EVELYN SAGUN *and* JULIE-ANN ROSS DEUS

Access to clean water is a critical aspect of development of any cities and communities. Without water, or with less access to it, many human activities intended for economic development and livelihood of people, and other purposes are restricted. Lack of access to clean water also increases the possibility of disease outbreaks and other health issues which could threaten the lives of people and economies of countries and cities. Thus, lack of access to water is a global development concern which could undermine many efforts for development particularly in the health sector. At the local level (i.e., cities and communities), water utilities play an important role in the delivery of water and other water services. The ever-increasing demand for water due to growing population and increased economic activities particularly in the urban areas, and water scarcity due to decreasing supply from the water sources, are some of the challenges for many water utilities operating in the cities and communities.

The delivery of water and other water services by water utilities becomes more challenging in times of disaster or hazard occurrence. During and after a disaster event, in most cases, the daily operation of water utilities is affected, and employees are restricted in performing their duties and responsibilities. And in the event of major disaster associated with human-induced and natural hazards such as strong tropical cyclone and high-intensity earthquakes, the water supply facilities are usually physically damaged. Drought and excessive precipitation, and other slow-onset and long-term hazards associated with climate change also threaten the delivery of water and other water services. All these natural hazards could physically damage many water supply facilities (i.e., intake boxes, pipes, reservoirs or water tanks) and contaminate water supply due to entry of contaminants through the damaged pipes and other facilities resulting to failure or poor delivery of water to the population by water utilities. This chapter provides insights on the impacts of disasters and climate change to water utilities and in their delivery of water and sanitation services in the context of the Philippines. Best practices from two cities in the country exemplifying efforts for resilience in water supply management are also provided.

---

*Published with permission from the authors.

Water, Disasters and Climate Change

Water is an essential aspect of every person's survival and of every country's development. It is a "primary element" in a person's diet and is required in many essential human activities such as agriculture and many economic activities in the urban areas (Cassardo and Jones, 2011). Unfortunately, there are over 2 billion people around the world that do not have access to safe drinking water, and at least 4 billion people experience water scarcity for at least a month every year (UNESCO World Water Assessment Programme, 2019). And based on the recent report by United Nations Children's Fund (UNICEF) and World Health Organization (WHO) (2019) on the progress on household drinking water, sanitation and hygiene in the period 2000–2017, this global water problem is more prevalent in the developing countries particularly in the urban poor communities and remote rural areas where poverty, malnourishment, lack of access to education and other development issues are also widespread.

Further, lack of access to clean and safe water also compromises public health due to increased chance of disease outbreaks associated with many water-borne diseases (e.g., diarrhea, cholera, typhoid, etc.). In that situation, the health condition of people especially the physically vulnerable people, e.g., children, pregnant women, older people, persons with disability, etc., is put at risk. Lack of access to water also means that Water, Sanitation and Hygiene (WASH) practices are also restricted which is important in preventing the spread of viruses such as the Corona Virus Disease 2019 (CoViD-19) and many similar infectious diseases. To address this global development problem on access to water, several international strategies and frameworks have already been adopted and implemented by governments and development partners to address lack of access to water. The Sustainable Development Goal 6 (SDG 6) i.e., ensuring access to water and sanitation for all is one of the global efforts that have made great progress in terms of reducing lack of access to water of many people around the world.

The development efforts on water, however, are also challenged by the increasing number of disasters associated with natural hazards particularly climate-related hazards. Communities affected by disasters often experience water shortage due to disruption on many water supply facilities such as water tanks, pipelines and transmission lines, water sources, etc. (PAHO, 2002). Scientific studies are also in agreement that climate change would cause water scarcity due to extreme weather and climate conditions. In fact, climate-change related hazards such as extreme temperature, excessive precipitation and sea-level rise are already affecting many parts of the world (International Panel on Climate Change, 2014).

USAID-SURGE Project in the Philippines

The United States Agency for International Development (USAID) recognizes the challenges posed by disasters and climate change to the development of the Philippines, particularly its secondary cities. Through the Strengthening Urban Resilience for Growth with Equity (SURGE) Project, USAID promotes resilient, sustainable and inclusive growth in highly urbanized cities and their adjacent areas in the Philippines. These cities are Batangas, Legazpi and Puerto Princesa in Luzon, Iloilo and Tagbilaran in the Visayas, and Cagayan de Oro, General Santos and Zamboanga in Mindanao.

The SURGE Project has three objectives: (1) improve local capacity in inclusive and resilient urban development; (2) improve environment for local economic development; and (3) expand economic connectivity and access between urban and rural areas. SURGE is the flagship project of USAID's Cities Development Initiative (CDI). CDI is a crucial component of the broader Partnership for Growth with Equity (PFG), a white House initiated partnership between the U.S. Government and the Government of the Philippines whose aim is to shift the Philippines to a sustained and more inclusive growth trajectory on par with other high-performing emerging economies.

Since 2015, USAID-SURGE has been providing technical assistance to water utilities in the CDI partner cities and adjacent areas, and Marawi City to ensure access to safe water of the population. This support is provided to water utilities of different categories, i.e., water districts, Rural Waterworks and Sanitation Associations (RWSAs), and Local Government Unit–led Waterworks (LGU-led water utilities). Private water utilities in partner CDIs are also engaged in some activities. Specifically, the technical assistance of SURGE to partner water utilities include, but are not limited to:

- Mainstreaming DRR-CCA in water and sanitation planning.
- Geo-resistivity surveys and geo-physical assessments to identify location of viable water sources.
- Water safety planning to ensure supply of quality water from source to consumer's tap.
- Ring-fencing, Strategic/Business planning to improve management and financing of water operations.
- Business continuity planning to manage and reduce impacts of hazard and disaster risks.
- Geo-resistivity surveys and geo-physical assessments to identify location of viable water sources.
- Diagnostic assessment, hydraulic modeling and water supply system designing, which serve as basis of expansion, upgrading and improvement.
- Non-revenue water assessment as basis of water supply system upgrading and improvement.
- Communication planning to improve current water and sanitation practices of consumers and communities.
- Establishing partnerships among water operators for peer to peer mentoring and sharing of good water and sanitation practices.
- Preparation of pre-feasibility studies, terms of references, formulation of water and sanitation ordinances, and creating environment for private sector to participate in water and sanitation projects.

USAID-SURGE facilitated these activities to improve many aspects of operation of water utilities. Several plans (e.g., water safety and business continuity plans) and technical studies (e.g., geo-resistivity studies, mini-master plans, hydraulic modeling, and water supply system designs) were produced and are now being used by partner water utilities. These outputs, and continued technical assistance by USAID-SURGE, will result to increase access to sustainable and resilient water and sanitation services in the CDI partner cities, adjacent areas, and Marawi City.

Disaster and Climate Resilience in Water Supply Management in the Philippines

In the last decade, the Philippines has adopted several disaster risk reduction and climate change adaptation (DRR-CCA) measures through national and local policies. These policies have introduced radical measures shifting the country's disaster DRR-CCA strategies from reactive to being more proactive (see Disaster Risk Reduction and Management Act of 2010 [Republic Act 10121] and Climate Change Act of 2009 [Republic Act 9729]). The overall goal of those DRR-CCA policies and programs is to foster resilience in the country's development programs. Specifically, these DRR-CCA policies aim to make every person and organization in the public and private sectors more prepared to disasters and climate change. Many water utilities having been affected repeatedly by disasters and continuously threatened by climate change-related hazards have responded and exerted efforts to foster resilience in their water supply management.

Water utilities in the Philippines are categorized according to their geographical scope of operation, and nature of business operation. A water utility may belong to any of the following categories:

- Water District is a local corporate entity that operates and maintains a water supply system in one or more provincial cities or municipalities. It is classified as a government-owned and controlled corporation (GOCC).
- LGU-run Waterworks is a water utility managed by the Local Government Unit to provide water supply services to the local population.
- Private Water Service Provider is a water utility carried out by a private concessionaire.
- Rural Waterworks and Sanitation Association (RWSA) is a non-stock and non-profit associations that provides water services to people in one or more barangays in the rural areas. RWSAs are community-based water utilities with usually 50–1000 household water connections.
- Barangay (village) waterworks and sanitation association (BAWASA) is an organization of water supply and sanitation beneficiaries at a community level. This is often smaller than RWSA.

Fostering resilience in water supply management is highly encouraged among water utilities regardless of their category. And this can be done in several ways and at different levels of engagement. But the most common starting points include the setting of key performance indicators in the strategic/ business plans of water utilities that measure interventions and milestones for resilient water and sanitation services. One of the key resilience indicators is the presence of relevant plans such as Water Safety Plan (WSP) and Business Continuity Plan (BCP). Firstly, WSP is a management tool that uses a comprehensive assessment and risk management approach to ensure delivery of clean water from the water sources (or catchment areas) to consumers. WSP allows identification and analysis of the potential hazards that may affect the water supply system and operations of the water utility. Specifically, WSP aims to prevent or minimize contamination of water sources, remove contamination through treatment and prevent re-contamination during storage, and ensure distribution and handling of drinking-water. WSP is a cost-effective, management-oriented, preventive approach to safe drinking-water (World Health

Organization, 2017). The Philippine government through the Department of Health supported this effort and issued an Administrative Order (AO) requiring all drinking-water service providers in the country to develop and implement water safety plan within three years after the issuance of the order.

Further, a BCP is a plan that guides an organization to continue operating while responding to or recovering from any interruptions. This plan is prepared in advance (e.g., before any emergencies or disaster events), and usually involves inputs from many concerned personnel and stakeholders. For water utilities, the BCP's overall goal is to maintain solid operations (i.e., financially, managerially, and functionally) during and after disaster events (Water Research Foundation, 2013). This plan integrates disaster mitigation and prevention, emergency preparedness and response, business continuity, and recovery and rehabilitation in the design of water supply and sanitation system of water utilities. The overall purpose of the BCP then is to pull all existing plans together and use it as basis of concerted actions to respond and recover from any emergencies or disasters. The next sections elaborate on the experiences of USAID-SURGE CDI partner cities in integrating disaster preparedness and resilience in their development planning.

Integrating Climate and Disaster Risk Assessment in Water Safety Planning for Marawi City, Philippines

Marawi City is an Islamic city in the Province of Lanao del Sur in the southern Mindanao. It is under the political jurisdiction of Bangsamoro Autonomous Region in Muslim Mindanao, and serves as the educational and trading center in the region. The city's projected population for 2020 is 217,616. It is situated on the shores of Lake Lanao and straddles the zone where Agus River, a major river in the region, begins. Water supply services in Marawi City are provided by the Marawi City Water District (MCWD), a self-sustaining Government Owned and Controlled Corporation (GOCC) operating since 1973 (Marawi City Water District, 2019). MCWD used to supply water to 43 out of 96 communities in the city. But after the Siege of Marawi, a five-month-long armed conflict in the city in 2017, many water supply facilities of MCWD were physically damaged which resulted to reduction in the number of areas served. Presently, MCWD serves 19 communities in the city with a total of 1,619 water consumers only. The degraded state of water supply facilities after the siege resulted to several challenges in the delivery of water services by MCWD particularly in ensuring the quality of water.

In 2019, as part of the larger efforts of USAID to support the reconstruction of Marawi City, USAID-SURGE Project assisted MCWD in crafting their WSP aimed at providing continues supply of safe water to their customers and help increase the number of people with access to safe drinking water in the City. Central to the workshops and seminars, and field mapping activities facilitated by USAID-SURGE Project with MCWD and the Local Government Unit of Marawi City is climate and disaster risk assessment and analysis. The WSP technical working group of MCWD identified several hazards, which include biological, physical and chemical hazards and the corresponding severity and impact of these to public health. The most common hazard is contamination of water due to presence of harmful pathogens such as bacteria, viruses, protozoans, and helminths with damaged and leaking pipes as entry points. These contaminants exacerbate and make water unsafe for drinking when proper maintenance and safety procedures of water supply management are not regularly checked and addressed.

But the bigger threats to the water supply services of Marawi City Water District are the occurrence of natural hazards, which have the potential to cause physical damage to their facilities and disruption of operations. The results of the climate and disaster risk assessment suggests that Marawi City is threatened by several natural hazards particularly hydrometeorological and geophysical hazards, and extreme climate change stimuli. Many water supply facilities in Marawi City is also likely to be (and has been) affected by rain-induced flooding and landslide and earthquake-related hazards. The facilities most exposed to these hazards are pipelines and water pumping stations. The proximity to fault lines (i.e., Mindanao Fault and Lanao Fault System) and previous seismic activities in the area also indicate high exposure to seismic hazards of water supply facilities. Some of the potential impacts of flooding and seismic hazards to water supply facilities include, but are not limited to the following (PAHO, 2002):

• Structural damage to infrastructure
• Rupture of mains and pipes
• Obstruction in water intake points and transmission pipes
• Contamination due to increased siltation or turbidity of water
• Disruption of power, communications and road systems
• Water shortage due to obstruction in water sources
• Temporary shortage of personnel
• Lack of access to equipment, spare parts for repair and maintenance

In addition, based on the current climate change projection provided for the Province of Lanao Del Sur including Marawi City, the region is likely to experience extreme weather and climate events in the mid–21st century (2036–2065) based on the baseline data from 1971–2000 (PAGASA, 2018). This include increasing temperature for all seasons and potential decrease in rainfall in some months. This scenario could result to drought and may be compounded and eventually aggravated by regional climate event such as El Niño phenomenon (Yumul et al, 2010). The frequency of extreme events that may be experienced in the coming decades is also likely to increase, i.e., number of days with temperature exceeding 35 degree Celsius and number of dry days with rainfall less than 2.5 millimeter are likely to increase in 2006–2036 and 2036–2065.

Business Continuity Planning for Resilient Water Supply Management in Legazpi City, Philippines

Legazpi City is located in the eastern coast of the Province of Albay in the Bicol Region. It is a component city with a population of 212,221 (projected total population for year 2020). Legazpi City is situated on the foot of Mayon Volcano, a very active stratovolcano and world-renowned for its near-perfect cone shape. The geographical location of the city makes it susceptible to many types of hydrometeorological and geophysical hazards such as volcanic hazards, tropical cyclones, earthquakes, extreme climate conditions and many secondary and associated hazards (e.g., storm surge, flooding, tsunami, etc.). These hazards are also the main threats to delivery of water and other water services in the city which are provided by a GOCC-run water utility. Since 1981, water supply in

Legazpi City is provided by the Legazpi City Water District (LCWD). Currently, LCWD serves 52 out of 70 communities in the city with a total of at least 21,841 water supply connections. Like all other water utilities in the Philippines, LCWD is committed to deliver reliable and affordable water services to meet customers' needs and with due regard to sustainable development.

In the last two decades, however, the commitment to improve delivery of water by LCWD was repeatedly challenged by the occurrence of major hazards and disasters. Recent experiences of disasters in the city had caused considerable physical damage to water supply facilities and hampered daily operation of employees of LCWD. In 2006, during and after Tropical Cyclone Durian (local name *Typhoon Reming*), rain-induced landslide, lahar and flood caused major damages to pipelines and water sources (e.g., springs and water collector canals) which cut off at least 1,000 households in three (3) communities. Major water transmission pipelines were washed away flash floods causing water interruption to almost all the consumers for at least two (2) days. Finally, water service connections along coastal areas were damaged by the storm surge resulting to salt water intrusion in the pipeline system. And each time a disaster like Tropical Durian occurs in Legazpi City, the business operation of LCWD is interrupted resulting to poor delivery of water and other services to customers. And this disaster situation is likely to happen again as climate change progresses and climate-related hazards become more extreme.

To address the potential impacts of occurrence of natural hazards particularly climate-related hazards in the delivery of water and other services in Legazpi City, USAID-SURGE Project assisted LCWD in the formulation of hazard-specific Business Continuity Plan (BCP). Since 2019, several workshops and seminars were facilitated by USAID-SURGE Project to craft the BCP of LCWD for frequent hazards such as severe wind, flooding and lahar flow. The BCP document which is the key output of the activity provides a standardized response and recovery protocol in the event of emergencies or disasters to avert, mitigate and minimize human and physical damages and ensure minimal disruption to all aspects of water utility operations. The plan highlights the importance of emergency management procedure into the organization to effectively prepare for, respond to, or recover from the impacts of specific hazards, i.e., severe wind, flooding and lahar flow. The BCP also establishes standard operating procedures to direct the mobilization of resources in the most efficient and orderly manner. And as a result of BCP, LCWD now have a well-structured operational emergency protocols which specify roles and functions of all responsible personnel in the event of emergencies. This BCP has already been applied and tested by LCWD in the recent tropical cyclones that have affected Legazpi City in 2019 and this 2020.

Fostering Resilience in Water Supply Management

Disaster resilience is defined as the "*ability of a system, community or society exposed to hazards to resist, absorb, accommodate, adapt to, transform and recover from the effects of a hazard in a timely and efficient manner, including through the preservation and restoration of its essential basic structures and functions through risk management*" (United Nations Office for Disaster Risk Reduction, 2017). A key aspect of resilience, therefore, is the capacity of individuals or public and private organizations to learn from their experiences of disasters and use existing knowledge to better prepare for the future. The efforts of water utilities in Marawi City and Legazpi City on water safety planning and business continuity planning capture such elements of resilience.

The integration of climate and disaster risk assessment of Marawi City paved the way for a more comprehensive planning process for water safety. Threats to water supply system are ranked and necessary strategies and actions to address them are prioritized. The risk mitigating measures of MCWD are also revisited and additional strategies are proposed to ensure that all potential threats (i.e., disasters and climate change) to water supply system are recognized and included in the disaster preparedness plan. Likewise, the business continuity planning in Legazpi City exemplifies a good practice in terms of emergency response and early recovery. This ensures that the mission essential functions (i.e., minimum financial, managerial and technical functions required to deliver water services) of LCWD are performed before, during and after disaster. These efforts on fostering resilience in water supply management are thus key to ensure access to safe water of the population.

REFERENCES

Cassardo, C., Jones, J.A.A (2011). Managing Water in a Changing World. Water, 3, 618–628.

International Panel on Climate Change (2014). Climate Change 2014: Synthesis Report. Contribution of Working Groups I, II and III to the Fifth Assessment Report of the Intergovernmental Panel on Climate Change. IPCC, Geneva, Switzerland.

Legazpi City Water District (2019). Business Continuity Plan for strong wind, flooding and lahar flow. Legazpi City, Philippines.

Marawi City Water District (2019). Water Safety Plan of Marawi City Water District (MCWD). Marawi City, Lanao Del Sur, Philippines.

PAGASA (Philippine Atmospheric Geophysical and Astronomical Services Administration) (2018). Observed Climate Trends and Projected Climate Change in the Philippines. PAGASA, Quezon City, Philippines. PAGASA Quezon City, Philippines.

PAHO (Pan American Health Organization) (2002). Emergencies and Disasters in Drinking Water Supply and Sewerage Systems: Guidelines for Effective Response. Division of Sanitary Engineering and Environmental Health in Emergencies and Disasters.

UNESCO World Water Assessment Programme (2019). The United Nations world water development report 2019: leaving no one behind. United Nations Educational, Scientific and Cultural Organization, Paris, France.

United Nations Children's Fund (UNICEF) and World Health Organization (WHO) (2019). Progress on household drinking water, sanitation and hygiene 2000–2017: Special focus on inequalities. United Nations Children's Fund (UNICEF) and World Health Organization (WHO), New York, USA.

United Nations Office for Disaster Risk Reduction (2017). 2009 UNISDR Terminology on Disaster Risk Reduction. United Nations General Assembly, Geneva, Switzerland.

Water Research Foundation (2013). Business Continuity Planning for Water Utilities: Guidance Document. Water Research Foundation, Colorado, USA.

World Health Organization (2017). Guidelines for drinking-water quality: fourth edition incorporating the 1st addendum. World Health Organization, Geneva, Switzerland.

Yumul, G. P., Dimalanta, C.B., Servando, N.T., Hilario, F.D. (2010) The 2009–2010 El Niño Southern Oscillation in the Context of Climate Uncertainty: The Philippine Setting. Philippine Journal of Science, 139 (1): 119–126.

49. Bridging the Gaps

Disaster Risk Reduction, Climate Change
Adaptation and Development Planning*

JAKE ROM D. CADAG, SERGIO ANDAL, JR.,
and JULIE ANN ROSS DEUS

In 2015, the seventeen (17) Sustainable Development Goals (SDGs) were adopted by United Nations to guide its member states in achieving sustainable development. Countries and localities (i.e., cities and communities) swiftly acted and made plans to achieve the specific targets for each development goal. On the same year that SDGs were implemented, several disasters associated with natural hazards particularly climate-related hazards devastated many parts of the world. Riverine flooding in India, wildfire in Russia, landslide in Guatemala, and drought in Indonesia and the Philippines are among the most devastating disasters in 2015. These disasters have had considerable negative impacts to many aspects of the society particularly of those affected regions or cities that they undermine many efforts, if not all, for sustainable developments. Scientific studies from both the academic and government institutions (e.g., International Panel for Climate Change or IPCC) point to climate change as one of the drivers of those disasters.

The Philippines is one of the most affected countries in the world by disasters associated with natural hazards particularly climate-related hazards, i.e., tropical cyclone, rain-induced flooding and landslides, storm surge, and drought. And like many other countries, the Philippines development goals were pushed back by many major disasters in the last decades. Each time a major disaster happens, i.e., heavy flooding, many essential functions in the cities (and of the cities) i.e., transportation, trading, education, cultural activities, etc., are paralyzed. And since 2016, according to the World Risk Index report, the Philippines is consistently included in the top 10 countries in the world with highest disaster risk (Welle and Birkman, 2016).

The Philippines has made advances to address disasters by enacting laws for disaster risk reduction and climate change adaptation and integrating them in the country's development framework. And the overall goal of such efforts is to ensure sustainable development without or with less interruptions due to disasters and climate change impacts. But practitioners on the ground particularly in the localities and cities (e.g., local government authorities, development partners and civil society organizations) observe gaps in mainstreaming DRR-CCA in development planning affecting the effectiveness and efficiency

---

Published with permission from the authors.

09

of local development efforts. And this is an important concern because the success of DRR-CCA and development efforts is measured on how effective the cities and communities can implement them. This chapter tackles these gaps between DRR-CCA and sustainable development in the context of secondary cities in the Philippines. Case studies exemplifying good practices on how to address those gaps are also presented.

USAID-SURGE, DRR-CCA and Development Planning

As stated in the previous chapter, the U.S. Agency for International Development's Strengthening Urban Resilience for Growth with Equity has been providing technical assistance to the Cities Development Initiative (CDI) cities in mainstreaming disaster risk reduction and climate change adaptation (DRR-CCA) in the development planning. The "mainstreaming" of DRR-CCA to development planning means that hazards and disasters that threaten the cities are fully considered in the strategies for development. For example, infrastructure development and expansion of urban growth centers must not result to increased exposure to hazards of people and properties, or further degradation of the environment through massive deforestation. USAID-SURGE facilitated several activities to help cities in planning for DRR-CCA and local development. Some of the specific activities include workshops and seminar on disaster and climate risk assessment, Geographic Information System (GIS) and community-based participatory hazard and vulnerability mapping, comprehensive land use planning (CLUP) and local climate change action planning (LCCAP).

SDGs, the successor of the Millennium Development Goals (2000–2015), is the current international framework that guides most countries of the world to achieve their development goals for 2015–2030. SDGs, in resemblance to MDGs and other development frameworks, defines sustainable development as *"development that meets the needs of the present without compromising the ability of future generations to meet their own needs"* (United Nations General Assembly, 1987, p. 43). Key to the achievement of SDGs is the sustainable implementation of programs for development at all geographical scales (international to national and city to community level) without or with less interruptions of disasters and climate-related hazards.

The negative impacts of disasters to the lives of people and the economy (i.e., human casualties, livelihoods and economic damages, among others) push back countries in terms of their development targets. And such socioeconomic repercussions brought by disasters make affected countries and localities more susceptible to future disasters which could happen during the rehabilitation process or before full recovery. Thus, disasters are a development issue that must be addressed. Disasters as a threat to development is a concern of every country and locality especially now that there is an increasing number of disasters at the global scale (EM-DAT, 2020). Many cities particularly those exposed to hazards because of their location (e.g., coastal and river cities, and cities in the slope of volcanoes and mountainous regions) are experiencing repeated disasters. And many of these disasters are linked to occurrence of more frequent and extreme climate-related hazards in the last decades.

This interdependent connection between development and disaster have long been established through scientific research in the academe and actual experiences in the development works (see Collins, 2013; Pelling, 2003). And many national and local governments, and international and regional government organizations (i.e., United Nations,

Association of Southeast Asian Nations, European Union and many other government organizations) have made concerted and coordinated efforts to prevent and reduce the risk of disasters through adoption of international frameworks. Since the adoption of the International Framework for Action for the International Decade for Natural Disaster Reduction in 1989, several international frameworks for disaster risk reduction and climate change adaption have been adopted and are still being implemented (e.g., Sendai Framework for Disaster Risk Reduction and United Nations Convention on Climate Change' Paris Agreement in 2015).

The scientific and theoretical bases of the synergy between disasters, climate change and development are well established. And much of the current literature on these topics have emphasized that the gaps between them must be addressed to achieve sustainable development as envisioned in the Sustainable Development Goals framework (Cadag, 2017). The practice or implementation of DRR-CCA without integration to the larger development agenda, and vice versa, is an example of those gaps. Lack of cooperation between stakeholders from and within the national and local level is also another concern. And finally, there remain some methodological issues on how to translate disaster and climate risk data and information into policies that would influence development programs in the cities to become more sustainable and resilient. The following sections provide insights on these challenges in the context of the Philippines, and how cities are responding to address them.

Disasters, Climate Change and Development in the Philippines

In the Philippines, climate-related hazards had caused major disasters in the last decades. In 2013, Tropical Cyclone Haiyan (local name *Typhoon Yolanda*) hit the central Philippines particularly Tacloban City in the Province of Leyte and many municipalities in the Eastern Samar Province and many adjacent provinces which killed at least 6300 people, made millions of Filipino homeless and totally devastated the local economies (National Disaster Risk Reduction and Management Council, 2014). The estimated losses of that one single event were at least US$12.9 billion. About 2.3 million people were also added to the statistics of population living below the poverty line (World Bank, 2014). And since 2014, several other strong typhoons (e.g., Tropical Cyclone Hagupit [local name *Typhoon Ruby*] often accompanied by rain-induced landslides and storm surge have occurred in the same regions [provinces and cities] making rehabilitation and recovery a difficult task especially for the local people and authorities).

Emergency database EM-DAT, the international disaster emergency database managed by Centre for Research on the Epidemiology of Disasters (CRED) of the Université Catholique de Louvain in Belgium, recorded 650 disasters associated with natural hazards in the Philippines from 1900 to 2019. At least 361 disasters associated with climate-related hazards have occurred in the last three (3) decades with a death toll of at least 32,000 people and total economic damage of 23 billion dollars (EM-DAT, 2020). Tropical Cyclone Haiyan is just one of the many disasters that have caused considerable human and economic impacts in the Philippines undermining the development efforts implemented by the government, development partners and the private sector.

To prevent or reduce the number of disasters in the country, the Philippines has enacted important laws for disaster risk reduction, climate change adaptation and sustainable development. Firstly, in 2009, the Climate Change Act (Republic Act 9729) was passed into law institutionalizing the strategies and actions to prevent climate change and the hazards associated with it. In 2010, the Disaster Risk Reduction and Management Act (Republic Act 10121) was ratified making disaster preparedness in the country more proactive and geared toward reduction of disaster risk. Finally, the medium-term and long-term development plan (i.e., Philippine Development Plan 2017–2022 and Ambisyon 2015–2040) of the Philippine Government have put "disaster resilience" at the center of its development strategies. The implementing guidelines of all these policies foster mainstreaming of disaster risk reduction and climate change adaptation in development planning.

At the local scale, these national policies are adopted by Local Government Units (LGU) through formulation of required government plans, i.e., Local Disaster Reduction and Management Plan (LDRRMP), Local Climate Change Action Plan (LCCAP), Comprehensive Land Use Plan (CLUP) and Comprehensive Development Plan (CDP). These plans are the policy instruments for the implementation of DRR-CCA and development strategies at the local level (i.e., cities and municipalities). LGUs are required to produce and update these plans regularly (e.g., every 3 to 5 years or 6 to 9 years). But City LGUs produce the plans for DRR-CCA and development not only for compliance to national government directives but also to ensure that their plans and actions are effective. City LGUs take these planning requirements seriously because they understand the negative impacts of disasters are more apparent in cities like them where population density is highest, and economic activities and physical infrastructures are concentrated. The next two (2) sections provide example of how some cities in the Philippines addressed the gaps in DRR-CCA and development planning.

Geographic Information System for the DRR-CCA Enhanced Comprehensive Land Use Plan of General Santos City

General Santos City is a port city located in the southernmost portion of Mindanao. The city is categorized as a highly urbanized city with a population of more than 656,709 (projected total population for year 2020). General Santos is threatened by several hazards including volcanic eruption, rain-induced flood, rain-induced landslide, ground shaking and liquefaction (due to earthquake), drought, and storm surge. Increased temperature for all seasons, increased rainfall during rainy season and sea-level rise are also projected for General Santos City in the mid–21st century (2036–2065). The multiple hazards and potentially hazardous climate scenario in the next 15 to 45 years make DRR-CCA and development planning a complex and challenging task for the local government authorities.

In 2014, the Department of Human Settlements and Urban Development (DHSUD), formerly known as Housing and Land Use Regulatory Board (HLURB), provided a guideline for mainstreaming DRR-CCA in Comprehensive Land Use Planning (CLUP). CLUP is a planning document prepared by LGUs to rationalize the allocation and proper use of land resources in the city (or municipality). It aims to optimize spatial organization of public and private land uses to support and promote economic and social activities in the city. All LGUs are mandated to continue to prepare, revise and update their CLUP which shall be enacted through a land use zoning ordinance. Mainstreaming of DRR-CCA in CLUP means that hazards and disaster risks are fully considered in spatial development and economic growth strategies.

Since 2014, General Santos City through its Technical Working Group (TWG), started the updating of their CLUP, and the mainstreaming of DRR-CCA to the planning process. The main challenge for the TWG was compliance to the highly technical guidance on Climate and Disaster Risk Assessment (CDRA). CDRA is a methodology to understand the potential impacts of hazards to people and their properties. CDRA requires assessment of hazards, and people's vulnerabilities and capacities which largely determine the outcomes of any disasters. CDRA goes beyond the conventional "risk assessment" as it incorporates climate-related hazards and their prospective impacts in the characteristics of hazards.

General Santos City has invested in the development of its spatial database through a Geographic Information System (GIS) database. The USAID through SURGE Project contributed by providing key personnel of General Santos City LGU training in GIS mapping and database management. And during the formulation of CLUP, and mainstreaming of DRR-CCA in the process, GIS was used to produce the required maps for land use planning (e.g., location map, building footprint map, land use map, population distribution map, etc.) and hazard and risk assessment (e.g., flood map, landslide map, storm surge map, etc.). Hazard maps were overlaid on other maps (i.e., sieve mapping) to identify areas or communities within the city that are high risk to disasters based on exposure to hazards, and vulnerabilities and capacities of exposed population, physical infrastructures and natural resources (e.g., forest, mangroves, etc.). The maps were then used by decision makers to identify policy and development options that increase resilience of the population and reduce exposure to hazards of the built-up and settlement areas.

In 2019, General Santos City has completed its DRR-CCA Enhanced Comprehensive Land Use Plan, and was approved by the DHSUD for implementation for the period 2018–2026. The vision of the DRR-enhanced CLUP is "*reflective of the desired state for an enhanced quality of life, where climate change adaptation and disaster risk reduction are of primary consideration. The city's vision also captures outcomes contributing to the targets of the SDGs.*" Some of the development indicators in the City's CLUP that mainstreams DRR-CCA in the development plans include, but are not limited, to the following:

- LGU is aware of its hazards, e.g., Flood, landslide;
- storm surge, tsunami, etc.;
- Approved Local Disaster Risk Reduction and Management (LDRRM) Plan;
- Approved Contingency Plan;
- Approved Local Climate Change Action Plan;
- 100% of barangays with approved DRR-related PPAs which includes efforts involving the communities;
- The LGU has early warning system;
- Evacuation Center Management system is in place and;
- 100% protection to Power Plants and Power substation located in hazard prone areas for possible damage

Community-Based Participatory Mapping for DRR-CCA in Legazpi City

Legazpi City is located in the eastern coast of the Province of Albay in the Bicol Region. It is a component city with a population of 212,221 (projected total population for year 2020). Component cities in the Philippines are those that remain under provincial jurisdiction, i.e., population participate in the election of provincial officials. Legazpi City is situated on the foot of Mayon Volcano, a very active stratovolcano and world-renowned for its near-perfect cone shape. The geographical location of the city makes it susceptible to many types of hydrometeorological and geophysical hazards such as volcanic hazards, tropical cyclones, earthquakes, extreme climate conditions and many secondary and associated hazards (e.g., storm surge, flooding, tsunami, etc.). The communities on the foot of the volcano have repeatedly been affected by many disasters caused by lahar especially during occurrence of tropical cyclone.

In 2006, Tropical Cyclone Durian (local name *Typhoon Reming*) greatly affected Legazpi City particularly the communities located along the river channels. The excessive precipitation brought by the tropical cyclone have caused massive lahar flow in the low-lying areas burying many communities. One of the most affected communities is the village of Padang in Legazpi City where the greatest number of deaths due to lahar was recorded. Before the Tropical Cyclone Durian disaster, Legazpi City and the entire Province of Albay are already known for their effective implementation of DRR-CCA programs. But the extremity and complexity of hazard occurrence (i.e., occurrence of multiple hazards) and gaps in terms of preparedness at the community level had contributed to the gravity of the disaster. This experience prompted the LGU of Legazpi City to revisit its strategies and priorities for DRR-CCA through formulation of LDRRMP and LCCAP with the assistance of development partners (Legazpi City LGU, 2013). One of the highlights in these plans is the strengthening of disaster preparedness at the community level through community-based participatory disaster risk reduction and management planning.

On September 19 to 22, 2017, USAID's Strengthening Urban Resilience for Growth with Equity (SURGE) Project supported the LGU of Legazpi City in developing its first participatory 3-dimensional (3-D) map and contingency plan. Located in one of the city's high-risk areas vulnerable to volcano eruption, typhoon, earthquake and tsunami, local officials, health workers and residents of Barangay Padang created a 3-D representation of their village. They identified geographic features and hazards with pushpins, colored strings and paint. Through the participatory mapping, the community integrated local spatial knowledge with data on land elevation and sea depth to produce a stand-alone, scaled and geo-referenced model.

The 3D map helped the barangay in formulating its community-level disaster risk reduction and management plan and contingency plan. The key officials and representatives of Barangay Padang presented their map to the Disaster Risk Reduction and Management Officers of Albay Province. Legazpi City is the first locality in the province that piloted participatory 3-D mapping for enhancing urban resilience at the community-level. City government delegates from fellow Cities Development Initiative (CDI) partner General Santos City also attended the workshop to apply the lessons in creating their own participatory maps. And on January 16 to 19, 2018, with the assistance of USAID through SURGE Project, the City Disaster Risk Reduction and Management Office of General Santos City replicated the process and produced their own participatory 3D map in the village of Cornel in General Santos City.

Bridging the Gaps Between DRR-CCA and Development Planning

The case studies presented above are among many best practices of USAID through SURGE Project, partner CDI cities that bridge the gaps between DRR-CCA and development planning. The case study from General Santos City shows that methodological issues (i.e., translation of disaster and climate risk information to policies that promote sustainable and resilient development) can be addressed by investing on information technology (IT) and learning new skills (i.e., GIS, mapping and database management). GIS mapping, for instance, is particularly useful in spatial analysis which is a critical aspect of decision-making, i.e., where to locate urban growth centers considering the presence of multiple hazards. Capacity development in terms of enhanced technical skills of personnel and up-to-date methods and tools is thus vital in bridging the gaps between DRR-CCA and development planning.

In the case of Legazpi City, the gaps attributed to difficulty of disaster preparedness at the local level can be addressed by utilizing more creative methodologies that invite participation of local authorities and people. The participatory 3-D map provides a bird's eye view of the village making hazards and development opportunities more apparent for the local people and decision makers. Thus, like GIS, the participatory 3-D map is a useful tool in crafting plans for DRR-CCA and local development. In addition, the participatory nature of the activity allows local and outside stakeholders (i.e., scientist, development partners and donor organizations) to engage in a dialogue to share knowledge and forge partnership. And this sharing of knowledge and partnership is important because, as noted by Wisner et al. (2012, p. 1), "*no single person can possess the knowledge and skill to map out and successfully implement DRR*" and other development agendas.

Therefore, integration of knowledge of concerned stakeholders through adoption of bottom-up and top-down approach is helpful in bridging the gaps between DRR-CCA and development planning.

This chapter exemplifies city-level actions and strategies to bridge the gaps between DRR-CCA and development planning. Based on the experiences of General Santos City and Legazpi City, the first step is recognizing the gaps that disconnect DRR-CCA and development planning. Secondly, methodologies (including methods and tools) to implement programs for DRR-CCA and development plans must be adopted to local needs and context. And finally, the strategies and action plans for DRR-CCA and development planning should be based on sharing and coproduction of knowledge among all concerned stakeholders. Local stakeholders (i.e., local authorities and people, and civil society organizations) in the cities and communities, with the support of the government and development partners, must be at the forefront of the efforts for DRR-CCA and development planning.

REFERENCES

Cadag, J.R.D. (2017). From Connections Towards Knowledge Co-Production for Disaster Risk Reduction Including Climate Change Adaptation (Chapter 18). In Kelman, I., Mercer, J., Gaillard, J.C. (eds.) *The Routledge Handbook of Disaster Risk Reduction Including Climate Change Adaptation.* Routledge: 187–198.

Collins, A.E. (2013). Linking disaster and development: further challenges and opportunities, Environmental Hazards, 12:1, 1–4, https://doi.org/10.1080/17477891.2013.779137.

EM-DAT (The Emergency Events Database) (2020). Disaster database. Université catholique de Louvain (UCL)–CRED, D. Guha-Sapir, Brussels, Belgium. Accessible at *www.emdat.be*

General Santos City LGU (2019). DRR-CCA Enhanced Comprehensive Land Use Plan (CLUP). City Government of General Santos City.

Legazpi City LGU (2019). Legazpi City Disaster Risk Reduction and Management and Climate Change Adaptation and Mitigation Plan (DRRM/CCAM) Plan. City Government of Legazpi City.

National Disaster Risk Reduction and Management Council (2013). Final Report Regarding the Effects of Tropical Cyclone Yolanda (Typhoon Haiyan). National Disaster Risk Reduction and Management Center, Camp Aguinaldo, Quezon City, Philippines.

National Disaster Risk Reduction and Management Council (2014). Situational Report No. 22 Regarding the Effects of Tropical Cyclone Hagupit (Typhoon Ruby). National Disaster Risk Reduction and Management Center, Camp Aguinaldo, Quezon City, Philippines.

Pelling, M. (2003). Natural Disaster and Development in a Globalizing World. London: Routledge, https://doi.org/10.4324/9780203402375.

United Nations General Assembly (1987). Report of the world commission on environment and development: Our common future. Oslo, Norway: United Nations General Assembly, Development and International Co-operation: Environment.

Welle, T. and Birkmann, J. (2016). The World Risk Index 2016. Bündnis Entwicklung Hilft, Berlin. https://collections.unu.edu/view/UNU:5763.

Wisner, B., Gaillard, J.C. and Kelman, I. (2012). "Challenging risk: We offer the reader a left-foot book," in B. Wisner, JC Gaillard and I. Kelman (eds.) *Handbook of Hazards and Disaster Risk Reduction*, London: Routledge, pp. 1–7.

Worldbank, 2014. Recovery and reconstructions planning in the aftermath of Typhoon Haiyan (Yolanda). The International Bank for Reconstruction and Development, Washington.

50. Trump's Defense Secretary Cites Climate Change as National Security Challenge*

Andrew Revkin

Secretary of Defense James Mattis has asserted that climate change is real, and a threat to American interests abroad and the Pentagon's assets everywhere, a position that appears at odds with the views of the president who appointed him and many in the administration in which he serves.

In unpublished written testimony provided to the Senate Armed Services Committee after his confirmation hearing in January, Mattis said it was incumbent on the U.S. military to consider how changes like open-water routes in the thawing Arctic and drought in global trouble spots can pose challenges for troops and defense planners. He also stressed this is a real-time issue, not some distant what-if.

"Climate change is impacting stability in areas of the world where our troops are operating today," Mattis said in written answers to questions posed after the public hearing by Democratic members of the committee. "It is appropriate for the Combatant Commands to incorporate drivers of instability that impact the security environment in their areas into their planning."

Mattis has long espoused the position that the armed forces, for a host of reasons, need to cut dependence on fossil fuels and explore renewable energy where it makes sense. He had also, as commander of the U.S. Joint Forces Command in 2010, signed off on the Joint Operating Environment, which lists climate change as one of the security threats the military expected to confront over the next 25 years.

But Mattis' written statements to the Senate committee are the first direct signal of his determination to recognize climate change as a member of the Trump administration charged with leading the country's armed forces.

These remarks and others in the replies to senators could be a fresh indication of divisions or uncertainty within President Donald Trump's administration over how to balance the president's desire to keep campaign pledges to kill Obama-era climate policies with the need to engage constructively with allies for whom climate has become a vital security issue.

---

*This story was originally published by ProPublica as Andrew Revkin, "Trump's Defense Secretary Cites Climate Change as National Security Challenge," https://www.propublica.org/article/trumps-defense-secretary-cites-climate-change-national-security-challenge (March 14, 2017). Reprinted with permission of the publisher.

Mattis' statements on climate change, for instance, recognize the same body of science that Scott Pruitt, the new Environmental Protection Agency administrator, seems dead-set on rejecting. In a CNBC interview last Thursday, Pruitt rejected established science pointing to carbon dioxide as the main driver of recent global warming.

Mattis' position also would appear to clash with some Trump administration budget plans, which, according to documents leaked recently to The Washington Post, include big cuts for the Commerce Department's oceanic and atmospheric research—much of it focused on tracking and understanding climate change.

Even setting aside warming driven by accumulating carbon dioxide, it's clear to a host of experts, including Dr. Will Happer, a Princeton physicist interviewed by Trump in January as a potential science adviser, that better monitoring and analysis of extreme conditions like drought is vital.

Mattis' statements could hearten world leaders who have urged the Trump administration to remain engaged on addressing global warming. German Chancellor Angela Merkel is scheduled to meet Trump on Friday.

Security questions related to rising seas and changing weather patterns in global trouble spots like the Middle East and sub-Saharan Africa are one reason that global warming has become a focus in international diplomatic forums. On March 10, the United Nations Security Council was warned of imminent risk of famine in Yemen, Somalia and South Sudan.

As well, at a Munich meeting on international security issues last month, attended by Mattis and Vice President Mike Pence, European officials pushed back on demands that they spend more on defense, saying their investments in boosting resilience to climate hazards in poor regions of the world are as valuable to maintaining security as strong military forces.

"[Y]ou need the European Union, because when you invest in development, when you invest in the fight against climate change, you also invest in our own security," Federica Mogherini, the European Union's high representative for foreign affairs and security policy, said in a panel discussion.

Concerns about the implications of global warming for national security have built within the Pentagon and national security circles for decades, including under both Bush administrations.

In September, acting on the basis of a National Intelligence Council report he commissioned, President Obama ordered more than a dozen federal agencies and offices, including the Defense Department, "to ensure that climate change-related impacts are fully considered in the development of national security doctrine, policies, and plans."

A related "action plan" was issued on Dec. 23, requiring those agencies to create a Climate and National Security Working Group within 60 days, and for relevant agencies to create "implementation plans" in that same period.

There's no sign that any of this has been done.

Whether the inaction is a function of the widespread gaps in political appointments at relevant agencies, institutional inertia or a policy directive from the Trump White House remains unclear.

Queries to press offices at the White House and half a dozen of the involved agencies—including the Environmental Protection Agency, Department of Defense, Department of Energy and Commerce Department—have not been answered. A State Department spokeswoman directed questions to the National Security Council and the

White House, writing:

"We refer you to the NSC for any additional information on the climate working group."

Mattis' statements were submitted through a common practice at confirmation hearings in which senators pose "questions for the record" seeking more detail on a nominee's stance on some issue.

The questions and answers spanned an array of issues, but five Democratic senators on the committee asked about climate change, according to a government official briefed in detail on the resulting 58-page document with the answers. The senators were Jack Reed of Rhode Island, the ranking member, Tim Kaine of Virginia, Mazie Hirono of Hawaii, Jeanne Shaheen of New Hampshire and Elizabeth Warren of Massachusetts.

Excerpts from Mattis' written comments to the committee were in material provided to ProPublica by someone involved with coordinating efforts on climate change preparedness across more than a dozen government agencies, including the Defense Department. Senate staff confirmed their authenticity.

Dustin Walker, communications director for the Senate Armed Services Committee, said responses to individual senators' follow-up questions are theirs to publish or not.

Here are two of the climate questions from Sen. Jeanne Shaheen of New Hampshire, with Mattis' replies:

SHAHEEN: "I understand that while you were commander of U.S. Joint Forces Command you signed off on a document called the Joint Operating Environment, which listed climate change as one of the security threats the military will face in the next quarter-century. Do you believe climate change is a security threat?"

MATTIS: "Climate change can be a driver of instability and the Department of Defense must pay attention to potential adverse impacts generated by this phenomenon."

SHAHEEN: "General Mattis, how should the military prepare to address this threat?"

MATTIS: "As I noted above, climate change is a challenge that requires a broader, whole-of-government response. If confirmed, I will ensure that the Department of Defense plays its appropriate role within such a response by addressing national security aspects."

In a reply to another question, Mattis said:

"I agree that the effects of a changing climate—such as increased maritime access to the Arctic, rising sea levels, desertification, among others—impact our security situation. I will ensure that the department continues to be prepared to conduct operations today and, in the future, and that we are prepared to address the effects of a changing climate on our threat assessments, resources, and readiness."

PART IV

The Future

51. Build Disaster-Proof Homes Before Storms Strike, Not Afterward*

T. REED MILLER

On Breezy Point in Queens, New York, construction will start soon on Diane Hellriegel's new house. Dubbed the #HurricaneStrong Home, it will replace a house built in 1955 by Hellriegel's grandfather that was wrecked during Superstorm Sandy in the fall of 2012.

The demonstration home was designed by private companies working with the Federal Alliance for Safe Homes, or FLASH, a nonprofit coalition that promotes action to strengthen homes and prepare for disasters. It features a solid concrete foundation that elevates the living space above floods and uses energy-efficient insulated concrete form (ICF) for the walls and floors designed to withstand wind and blown debris.

The roof deck of the demonstration home uses principles from the Fortified Home standards, a set of national guidelines designed to improve on minimum building codes and make structures more disaster-proof. They include taped plywood seams to prevent water entry, and reinforcing spray foam insulation underneath the roof to help keep wind from blowing it off and also improve energy efficiency.

Projects like the #HurricaneStrong Home demonstrate that there are many technologies we can use to make our buildings more hazard-resistant. But we are not using them as extensively as we should. Instead of designing a building to reduce potential damage from the hazards it may face over its lifetime, most construction projects focus on saving money up front. By choosing the lowest construction cost possible, homeowners, insurance agencies and taxpayers may end up paying for it many times over when natural disasters occur.

Forecasting Storms and Mitigating Damage

Although we cannot always predict far in advance when a disaster will strike, we do know that climate change will result in more frequent and intense storms than in the

*Originally published as T. Reed Miller, "Build Disaster-Proof Homes Before Storms Strike, Not Afterward," *The Conversation*, https://theconversation.com/build-disaster-proof-homes-before-storms-strike-not-afterward-61947 (August 4, 2016). Reprinted with permission of the publisher.

past. Hazard modeling has progressed considerably over the past several decades, and we can make strong predictions of roughly how often to expect disasters from coast to coast.

Researchers from a variety of disciplines are developing tools that can help us make smarter decisions about mitigating storm damage by preparing the built environment in advance. FEMA has designed free software tools that embed hazard models to help evaluate the impacts of disasters on individual buildings and the larger community. The Benefit Cost Toolkit compares the effectiveness of different mitigation strategies for a particular building and location. The Hazus-MH software maps out expected damage in a community from multiple hazards and allows comparison of "what-if" scenarios, such as "what would the economic benefit be if this community reinforced or rebuilt its vulnerable building stock?"

At the MIT Concrete Sustainability Hub, we are creating life cycle cost analysis models to include the costs and benefits of mitigation efforts alongside operational costs such as utility bills and maintenance. In our case studies we have demonstrated that investing in more hazard-resistant residential construction in certain locations is very cost-effective.

We have also developed a metric called the Break Even Mitigation Percent (BEMP) to address the cost-effectiveness of mitigation features for a particular new building in a particular location. The BEMP factors in the expected damage a building designed to code would endure over its lifetime, compared to a more resilient building design.

As an example, we compared two designs for a four-story apartment building located on the Gulf or Atlantic coasts—one constructed with nonengineered wood, the other with more resilient engineered concrete—and modeled the damage that these buildings would be expected to sustain over 50 years. For a building sited in Galveston, Texas, we estimated a BEMP of 3.4 percent, meaning that if US$340,000 was invested on top of the initial $10 million costs in order to build the stronger version, that investment would mitigate enough storm damage to the building over its lifetime to pay for itself.

It is important to note that BEMP considers costs from the perspective of society at large. That's because the original homeowners might not occupy a building 30 years later when a hurricane rolls through, so they might not directly recoup the value of investing in a resilient design—unless the mitigation features allow them to resell the house at a higher value, which can happen. But insurance agencies, taxpayers and future occupants certainly will all benefit from investing up front to make buildings more storm-resistant. Neighboring homes will also benefit from fewer building material projectiles flying off storm-resistant homes.

Injecting Mitigation into Building Codes

More hazard-resistant buildings produce broad social benefits. If a community can recover from a disaster more quickly, the disaster's negative impact on the economy and vital systems like health care and education can be reduced. Importantly, hazard resilience means lives can be saved.

But architects and designers often have a different incentive: keeping construction costs low. This is why most new construction projects just meet code requirements, instead of making extra investments to weather disasters well. Builders do not often consider reconstruction costs—the money that owners, insurance agencies and taxpayers will spend in the future to recover after the first structure fails in a storm.

To address this disconnect, the nonprofit International Code Council spearheads Building Safety Month each May to spotlight the need for modern building codes, more aggressive code enforcement and better training for building inspectors. However, the United States does not have a national building code with federal enforcement. Instead states, and sometimes municipalities, devise their own approaches. This patchwork system is inefficient and ineffective. A similar situation exists in cyclone-prone Australia.

This past May the White House hosted a Conference on Resilient Building Codes to highlight the importance of developing codes that incorporate resilience and future climate change impacts. One state that has embraced this approach is Florida, which adopted progressive statewide building codes after Hurricane Andrew in 1992. These requirements have substantially reduced insured losses in subsequent hurricanes.

Congress Underfunds Mitigation

At the federal level, though, most spending on mitigation occurs after disasters strike. Up to 15 percent of federal assistance can be allocated to long-term hazard mitigation measures after the president declares a major disaster. For instance, after a hurricane, states often use these funds to retrofit and elevate buildings, protect infrastructure and utilities, and manage stormwater.

The Federal Emergency Management Agency (FEMA) also awards pre-disaster mitigation grants (PDM), which states and communities can use to reduce risks from future events. But recent Congressional appropriations for PDM have fallen far short of what is needed. Last year FEMA requested $400 million for PDM but received only $81 million. From 2005 to 2014, appropriations averaged just $120 million each year. Compare that to the $7.2 billion spent on average on recovery assistance; PDM grants accounted for only 1.6 percent of total FEMA grants on average.

Recognizing that the current approach is not sustainable, this spring FEMA proposed a disaster deductible. The policy would require states to invest in resilience efforts before receiving public assistance funding after a disaster.

Post-Sandy Rebuilding in New York

Diane Hellreigel's home was among 100,000 damaged in New York during Superstorm Sandy. Of those, 20,000 owners applied for New York City's Build It Back program in 2013, but construction has been completed on only 1,887 units. City leaders are working to make New York more resilient against future disasters through steps that include funding coastal protection projects and modifying local building codes pertaining to flooding.

Congress earmarked over $13 billion to fund Hurricane Sandy recovery in New York City alone. That sum includes $595 million for FEMA assistance to affected individuals and families. Overall, however, just 5.3 percent of FEMA funding for Sandy went toward hazard mitigation grants.

These efforts are encouraging, but many coastal and inland communities remain vulnerable to natural disasters. To prevent the devastation from another storm, twister or quake, we need to make deep investments nationwide in mitigation now, before the next disaster strikes.

52. Extreme Weather News May Not Change Climate Change Skeptics' Minds*

Ryan Weber

The year 2018 brought particularly devastating natural disasters, including hurricanes, droughts, floods and fires—just the kinds of extreme weather events scientists predict will be exacerbated by climate change.

Amid this destruction, some people see an opportunity to finally quash climate change skepticism. After all, it seems hard to deny the realities of climate change—and object to policies fighting it—while its effects visibly wreck communities, maybe even your own.

News outlets have hesitated to connect natural disasters and climate change, though these connections are increasing, thanks to calls from experts combined with more precise data about the effects of climate change. Media voices like *The Guardian* advocate for more coverage of the weather events "when people can see and feel climate change." Harvard's Nieman Foundation dubbed 2019 "The Year of the Climate Reporter." Even conservative talk radio host Rush Limbaugh worried that media predictions about Hurricane Florence were attempts to "heighten belief in climate change."

But a recent study from Ohio State University communications scholars found that news stories connecting climate change to natural disasters actually backfire among skeptics. As someone who also studies scientific communication, I find these results fascinating. It's easy to assume that presenting factual information will automatically change people's minds, but messages can have complex, frustrating persuasive effects.

Investigating How Skeptics Hear the News

Social scientists have an unclear understanding of how climate change news affects public opinion, as not enough research has specifically explored that question. To explore the question, researchers from Ohio State recruited 1,504 volunteers. They divided them into groups who read news stories about natural disasters—fires, hurricanes or blizzards—that either emphasized or omitted the role of climate change.

---

*Originally published as Ryan Weber, "Extreme Weather News May Not Change Climate Change Skeptics' Minds," *The Conversation* https://theconversation.com/extreme-weather-news-may-not-change-climate-change-skeptics-minds-112650 (March 27, 2019). Reprinted with permission of the publisher.

Cleverly, the researchers recruited participants from geographic areas most likely to experience the disasters they read about; for instance, participants in hurricane-prone areas read the news articles about hurricanes. Further, the researchers ran the study in fall 2017, during hurricane and wildfire season, when these sorts of disasters are presumably top of mind.

After reading, participants answered 11 questions meant to measure their resistance to the article, including "Sometimes I wanted to 'argue back' against what I read" and "I found myself looking for flaws in the way information was presented."

It turned out that climate change skeptics—whether politically conservative or liberal—showed more resistance to the stories that mentioned climate change. Climate change themes also made skeptics more likely to downplay the severity of the disasters. At the same time, the same articles made people who accept climate change perceive the hazards as more severe.

The study findings suggest that reporting the relationship between climate change and hazardous weather may actually increase the skepticism of skeptics, even in the face of blatant contrary evidence. Psychologists call this the boomerang effect, because the message ultimately sends people in the opposite direction.

Who's Hearing the Message Matters

The boomerang effects seen in this latest study are less surprising than you might think. Researchers have tried a variety of strategies, including emphasizing scientific consensus around climate change and describing the negative health impacts of climate change on people near and far, only to find that skeptics often end up more entrenched after reading attempts to persuade them.

Messages can work when they use place to increase people's concern and willingness to act on climate change, but individual studies show inconsistent results. One new study gave Bay Area participants maps showing the increased flood risk in their zip code due to projected sea level rise. The maps made no difference in people's concern about the effects of climate change on future generations, developing countries or the Bay Area. But the maps did make people who accept climate change less concerned that it would personally harm them. These participants may have replaced their abstract, apocalyptic assumptions about climate change threats with the more tangible predictions, causing them to feel less vulnerable.

Another study, also involving Californians, generated slightly more success for place-based climate change news, but only among participants who were already concerned about climate change. Study participants read news articles explaining that climate change would increase droughts either globally or in California. The global message made people more likely to want policy changes, while the local messages made people more likely to say they would change their personal behavior.

Place-based appeals often have some positive effect on people's willingness to act on climate change and environmental issues.

But most studies about local messaging suggest that you cannot persuade everyone with the same message. A complex relationship of factors—including previous beliefs on climate change, political affiliation, and attachment to place and gender—can all play a role.

And psychologists offer compelling reasons why persuasive attempts sometimes backfire. Messages about the local impact of climate change might actually replace people's abstract, altruistic values with utilitarian concerns. In the case of skeptics resisting news about climate-driven disasters, the researchers from Ohio State suggest that these people are engaged in motivated reasoning, a cognitive bias where people force new and threatening information to conform to their pre-existing knowledge.

More News May Not Convince

Resistance to news about climate change disasters might be frustrating, but even the media often ignore the role of climate change in disasters, according to an analysis by the nonprofit consumer advocacy organization Public Citizen. They found only 7 percent of American news stories about hurricanes mentioned climate change in 2018. Percentages increase for stories about wildfires (27.8 percent of stories), extreme heat (34 percent of stories) and drought (35 percent of stories). But an overwhelming amount of extreme weather news coverage never mentions climate change.

Some omissions are particularly striking. Liberal research organization Media Matters found only one mention of climate change in 127 broadcast news stories during two weeks of extreme heat in 2018. Only about 4 percent of stories about Hurricane Irma and Harvey mentioned climate change, according to an academic analysis that included The Houston Chronicle and the Tampa Bay Times.

Despite these low numbers, U.S. climate change coverage related to extreme weather and disasters actually rose in 2018, according to the report from Public Citizen. This increase aligns with a trend of news slowly improving its climate reporting. For instance, U.S. print media has dropped some of the skepticism from its climate change reporting, both in terms of outright skepticism of the basic science and a subtler version that involved creating a false balance by including voices which both affirm and deny the reality of climate change.

Even if the media continues to increase and improve its climate change coverage, it might not change skeptics' minds. Of course, the media has a responsibility to report the news accurately, regardless of how some people process it. But those hoping that climate change news will convert skeptics might end up disappointed.

Given this resistance to news, other approaches, such as avoiding fear-inducing and guilt-based messaging, creating targeted messages about free-market solutions, or deploying a kind of "jiu jitsu" persuasion that aligns with pre-existing attitudes, may prove more effective at influencing skeptics. In the meantime, social scientists will continue to investigate ways to combat the stubborn boomerang effect, even as the consequences of climate change intensify all around us.

53. We Can't Save Everything from Climate Change*

Benjamin Preston *and* Johanna Nalau

Recent reports have delivered sobering messages about climate change and its consequences. They include the Intergovernmental Panel on Climate Change's Special Report on Global Warming of 1.5°C; the fourth installment of the U.S. government's National Climate Assessment; and the World Meteorological Organization's initial report on the State of the Global Climate 2018.

As these reports show, climate change is already occurring, with impacts that will become more intense for decades into the future. They also make clear that reducing greenhouse gas emissions from human activities to a level that would limit warming to 2 degrees Celsius (3.6 degrees Fahrenheit) or less above preindustrial levels will pose unprecedented challenges.

Today, however, there is a large and growing gap between what countries say they'd like to achieve and what they have committed to do. As scholars focused on climate risk management and adaptation, we believe it is time to think about managing climate change damage in terms of triage.

Hard choices already are being made about which risks society will attempt to manage. It is critically important to spend limited funds where they will have the most impact.

Triaging Climate Change

Triage is a process of prioritizing actions when the need is greater than the supply of resources. It emerged on the battlefields of World War I, and is widely used today in fields ranging from disaster medicine to ecosystem conservation and software development.

The projected global costs of adapting to climate change just in developing countries range up to US$300 billion by 2030 and $500 billion by mid-century. But according to a recent estimate by Oxfam, just $5 billion to $7 billion was invested in projects specific to climate adaptation in 2015–2016.

Triaging climate change means placing consequences into different buckets. Here, we propose three.

*Originally published as Benjamin Preston and Johanna Nalau, "We Can't Save Everything from Climate Change—Here's How To Make Choices," *The Conversation*, https://theconversation.com/we-cant-save-everything-from-climate-change-heres-how-to-make-choices-108141 (January 23, 2019). Reprinted with permission of the publisher.

The first bucket represents impacts that can be avoided or managed with minimal or no interventions. For example, assessments of how climate change will affect U.S. hydropower indicate that this sector can absorb the impacts without a need for costly interventions.

The second bucket is for impacts that are probably unavoidable despite all best efforts. Consider polar bears, which rely on sea ice as a platform to reach their prey. Efforts to reduce emissions can help sustain polar bears, but there are few ways to help them adapt. Protecting Australia's Great Barrier Reef or the Brazilian Amazon poses similar challenges.

The third bucket represents impacts for which practical and effective actions can be taken to reduce risk. For example, cities such as Phoenix, Chicago and Philadelphia have been investing for years in extreme heat warning systems and emergency response strategies to reduce risks to public health. There are a variety of options for making agriculture more resilient, from precision agriculture to biotechnology to no-till farming. And large investments in infrastructure and demand management strategies have historically helped supply water to otherwise scarce regions and reduce flood risk.

In each of these cases, the challenge is aligning what's technically feasible with society's willingness to pay.

What Triage-Based Planning Looks Like

Other experts have called for climate change triage in contexts such as managing sea level rise and flood risk and conserving ecosystems. But so far, this approach has not made inroads into adaptation policy.

How can societies enable triage-based planning? One key step is to invest in valuing assets that are at risk. Placing a value on assets exchanged in economic markets, such as agriculture, is relatively straightforward. For example, RAND and Louisiana State University have estimated the costs of coastal land loss in Louisiana owing to property loss, increased storm damage, and loss of wetland habitat that supports commercial fisheries.

Valuing non-market assets, such as cultural resources, is more challenging but not impossible. When North Carolina's Cape Hatteras lighthouse was in danger of collapsing into the sea, heroic efforts were taken to move it further inland because of its historic and cultural significance. Similarly, Congress makes judgments on behalf of the American people regarding the value of historic and cultural resources when it enacts legislation to add them to the U.S. national park system.

The next step is identifying adaptation strategies that have a reasonable chance of reducing risks. RAND's support for the Louisiana Coastal Master Plan included an analysis of $50 billion in ecosystem restoration and coastal protection projects that ranked the benefits those projects would generate in terms of avoided damages.

This approach reflects the so-called "resilience dividend"—a "bonus" that comes from investing in more climate-resilient communities. For example, a recent report from the National Institute of Building Sciences estimated that every dollar invested in federal disaster mitigation programs—enhancing building codes, subsidizing hurricane shutters or acquiring flood-prone houses—saves society $6. Nevertheless, there are limits to the level of climate change that any investment can address.

The third step is investing enough financial, social and political capital to meet the priorities that society has agreed on. In particular, this means including adaptation in the budgets of federal, state, and local government agencies and departments, and being transparent about what these organizations are investing in and why.

Much progress has been made in improving disclosure of corporate exposure to greenhouse gas reduction policies through mechanisms such as the Task Force on Climate-Related Disclosures, a private sector initiative working to help businesses identify and disclose risks to their operations from climate policy. But less attention has been given to disclosing risks to businesses from climate impacts, such as the disruption of supply chains, or those faced by public organizations, such as city governments.

Finally, governments need to put frameworks and metrics in place so that they can measure their progress. The Paris Climate Agreement calls on countries to report on their adaptation efforts. In response, tools like InformedCity in Australia are emerging that enable organizations to measure their progress toward adaptation goals. Nevertheless, many organizations—from local governments to corporate boardrooms—are not equipped to evaluate whether their efforts to adapt have been effective.

There are many opportunities to manage climate risk around the world, but not everything can be saved. Delaying triage of climate damages could leave societies making ad hoc decisions instead of focusing on protecting the things they value most.

54. Impact of Natural Disasters and Other Emergencies on Global Supply Chains*

PAUL H. JENNINGS

Public managers are increasingly concerned about the impact natural disasters and other emergencies may have on the operations of manufacturers. A disaster can affect a manufacturer to various degrees, from short-term shutdowns and employee layoffs to plant closings. This is especially true for small manufacturers that do not have robust business continuity plans in place. According to a study by the ARC Advisory Group, approximately 40 percent of businesses without a business continuity plan fail immediately because they are not prepared strategically or financially to cover the costs of extended downtime. An additional 25 percent fail within two years from lost revenues and cash flow problems. These failures, of course, have the potential to raise unemployment levels, reduce tax collections, and increase the demand and need for public services.

Public managers and local emergency professionals routinely respond to tornado destruction, fires, explosions and chemical spills that impact manufacturers in their communities. In today's economy, however, it is not enough for public managers to be cognizant of the effects of local disasters. Manufacturers are increasingly part of global supply chains in which products are made and distributed across state and national boundaries. Today's automobile, for example, has about 30,000 parts which are made and assembled across a vast tiered supply chain that spans the globe. The growth and complexity of global supply chains have increased the interdependence of firms as parts and supplies are transported from plant to plant. While supply chain interdependence can increase efficiencies and drive down costs, it also increases the risks of disruption from disasters and other emergencies that may occur, not only in a public manager's own community, but on the other side of the world.

An often-used example of global supply chain disruption is the Great East Japan earthquake in March 2011, which produced a tsunami and led to the meltdown of nuclear reactors in Fukushima. While this disaster crippled parts of the Japanese economy, it also impacted companies throughout Asia, Europe and the U.S. The disaster caused disruptions in the automotive supply chain, resulted in a shortage of small and mid-sized cars

---

*Originally published as Paul H. Jennings, "Impact of Natural Disasters and Other Emergencies on Global Supply Chains," *PA Times*, https://patimes.org/impact-natural-disasters-emergencies-global-supply-chains/ (March 4, 2016). Reprinted with permission of the publisher.

and reduced production levels in the U.S. In another example, a 2011 flood in Thailand negatively impacted the production of hard disk drives. Thailand is a major supplier of hard disk drives and is the location for many companies, notably Toshiba and Hitachi. The floods impacted the availability of needed parts, which led to increased prices for hard drives and an industry downturn. According to one report, the prices of hard disk drives made by Seagate and Western Digital tripled because of the flood.

Supply chain management is an important topic for manufacturing executives, industrial engineers and others who are working to reduce the risk of supply chain disruptions. By improving visibility across supply chains, increasing collaboration among firms and enhancing control mechanisms, manufacturers are seeking solutions to supply chain problems. Forward thinking companies are building business continuity practices into their supply chains that allow them to recover faster and avoid temporary or permanent plant shutdowns. Unfortunately, these solutions don't usually reach smaller manufacturers who don't have the time or expertise to develop risk management strategies that will reduce the impact of disruptions caused by natural disasters or other emergencies.

The public sector has an important role in helping supply chains increase resiliency. In a 2012 article addressing the impact of natural disasters on global supply chains, Linghe Ye and Masoto Abe write that governments play a fundamental role in building supply chain resilience. This includes increasing the speed and effectiveness of disaster recovery, providing timely financial support to help firms quickly restore operations and facilitating business rehabilitation and maintenance. In addition, public and private sector collaborations are exploring new mechanisms in insurance, information sharing and physical asset development that will reduce the risk of supply chain disruptions and minimize the economic impact of disasters.

On regional and state levels, public managers are taking steps to understand supply chains that affect companies in their communities. This is being done through extensive supply chain mapping, which identifies firms, products and reaches of specific industry supply chains and how various emergencies can cause disruptions in specific communities. Supply chain mapping can provide greater insight into potential emergencies before they happen and point to potential collaborations, which can avert or shorten problems.

Public managers are also developing training and technical assistance programs that facilitate business continuity planning by small and medium-size manufacturers. These initiatives will likely expand in the coming years as both the public and private sectors increase their understanding of how to better manage risk and avoid disruptions in global supply chains.

55. Alternative Facts Are the Enemy of Health Security and Resilience*

Nathan Myers

The announcement that researchers investigating the number of deaths in Puerto Rico attributable to Hurricane Maria had increased their estimate to 2,975 from an original official estimate of 64[1] again highlighted the true depth of that tragedy. Such an undercount of fatalities is unfortunately far from unprecedented. A 2008 study by Borden and Cutter[2] found that some level of undercounting should be expected, noting that some data regarding storm-related mortalities are based on the causes listed on death certificates, while others use "death estimates for hazard events that may or may not be verified."

The revision of the Hurricane Maria casualty numbers also illuminated the manner in which some political leaders try to obscure the magnitude of such data or define deaths attributable to natural disasters narrowly to paint the U.S. response in a more positive light. While the Federal Emergency Management Agency recently released an after-action report acknowledging flaws in the Hurricane Maria response,[3] the Trump administration, including the President himself, continues to insist that the U.S. did an excellent job.[4]

From the standpoint of promoting improved health security and resilience in the future, this has important implications. Research has found that many died in the hurricane's aftermath as a result of lack of electricity, medicine, water, and other resources.[5] Others died from leptospirosis, an infection sustained from drinking unsafe water.[6] Dr. Alexis Santos-Lozada, in an article for *The Conversation*,[7] wrote that the disparity between the official death count and the revised estimate may be due in part to the fact that international classifications for causes of death[8] related to natural disasters do not encompass all of these indirect factors. Reporting by Hernández, Schmidt and Achenbach noted that communication problems contributed to improper death determinations, along with physicians not being properly trained to complete death certificates and not receiving the necessary protocols from the government.[9]

Even with the best response, some of these deaths and errors in reporting may have been unavoidable. However, the fact that elected officials were so unwilling to accept such deaths as part of the official toll does not bode well for our ability to learn from these

---

*Originally published as Nathan Myers, "Alternative Facts Are the Enemy of Health Security and Resilience," *PA Times*, https://patimes.org/alternative-facts-are-the-enemy-of-health-security-and-resilience/(September 7, 2018). Reprinted with permission of the publisher and author.

issues and build resilience in the future. As Santos-Lozada writes, "[u]ndercounting deaths reduces the attention to the crisis that Puerto Ricans live day by day." An inaccurate accounting can also delay assistance from international organizations and the enactment of policies to help the most vulnerable citizens.[10]

The Blue Ribbon Study Panel for Biodefense has examined the economic and social costs of not investing adequately in resilience measures against health threats. At one of their panels, Dr. Peter Daszak, president of the EcoHealth Alliance, spoke about the value of mitigation. In a report[11] Daszak authored, he noted that the 2014–2015 Ebola outbreak resulted in over 11,000 deaths and a global economic cost of $10-$30 billion. Daszak also wrote in the paper that that the world could save between $344 billion and $360 billion over 100 years if mitigation measures are implemented.

However, investment in health mitigation in the U.S. has historically happened sporadically. There was significant, bipartisan pressure for health security spending after the 9/11 terrorist attacks and the Amerithrax letters, but since then support has largely died down between responses. The Zika public health emergency, which also significantly impacted Puerto Rico,[12] showed how slow Congress could be in its response.[13] Congress has recently showed a willingness to act quickly on providing economic assistance to help spur the economy during the COVID-19 pandemic. However, the degree to which this global emergency will affect willingness to make long-term commitments for health security and resilience remains to be seen.

Historically, lack of funding and political pressure seems to stem from disagreements over deficit spending and a focus on more immediate political priorities. The dispute over the number of deaths in Puerto Rico speaks to a more troubling trend of politicians attempting to redefine reality in order to serve their desired political narratives (for a more recent example, see Governor Brian Kemp of Georgia being forced to apologize for state health officials publishing a misleading graph regarding coronavirus trends in the state).[14] This is dangerous for a number of reasons. First, unless we reckon with the full cost of events like natural disasters and pandemics, we will not be in a position to learn from them and increase our level of resilience. One good thing that should come from understanding the true death toll from hurricanes and other public health emergencies is that the U.S. and Puerto Rican governments will invest in improved infrastructure and implement policies to provide individuals with vital necessities in the days after a disaster.

However, it should be noted that it was not until January of 2020 that over $8 billion in federal disaster recovery funds was released by the Trump administration after months of delay.[15] While Puerto Rico continues to struggle with its debt crisis, the economy was beginning to improve when the coronavirus pandemic struck. As of June 18, Puerto Rico is reported to have experienced 147 deaths from COVID-19, from a total of 6,003 cases.[16] The U.S. government should follow the lead of organizations like Healthcare Ready, and use understanding of the factors contributing to fatalities in the aftermath of a hurricane to promote both individual and community resilience. If the U.S. government has been hesitant to make investments in health security and resilience when the real numbers are known, how can we expect them to learn and make improvements if these figures are hidden?

Another troubling implication of the dispute over the number of mortalities in Puerto Rico is it speaks to a growing trend of elected officials, public figures, and ordinary citizens feeding an epidemic of misinformation and/or disinformation. A paper[17] studied how Russian hackers used social media to sow dissention among Americans by stoking the debate over vaccination on-line. This demonstrates that foreign adversaries have recognized how divided the public is over these competing public health narratives. Elected officials and others in government must be held responsible for using and communicating the most accurate, scientifically based information available.

During the Clade X pandemic exercise conducted in May 2018 by the Johns Hopkins University Center for Health Security, participants portraying cabinet and public health officials noted that during a biological attack by terrorists, one issue that would need to be addressed is countering misinformation on social media.[18] An article published on *The Hill*[19] noted that during a terrorist attack, hostile interests could weaponize misinformation to make it difficult to control the situation and protect the public. Public officials contributing to confusion regarding evidence-based information can only worsen this challenge.

There is clear evidence that the U.S. will continue to experience natural disasters and health emergencies that will be costly in terms of lives and economic resources. While we will never be able to completely eliminate these outcomes, there is work government and society at large can do to mitigate them. But the first step, as they say, is admitting we have a problem. To learn from mistakes and improve our resilience, the government and the public must be willing to admit the size of the problem and our contribution to it. Whether a weather-related emergency or public health crisis like COVID-19, we must be willing to face the facts, however difficult they might be, and share evidence-based information and sound analysis from credible, credentialed sources. To do otherwise is to play games with the lives, and deaths, of Americans and others.

Notes

1. Santiago, Leyla, Catherine Shoichet, and Jason Kravarik. 2018 August 28. "Puerto Rico's New Hurricane Maria Death Toll is 46 Times Higher than the Government's Previous Count." *CNN.* Accessed from https://www.cnn.com/2018/08/28/health/puerto-rico-gw-report-excess-deaths/index.html on June 17, 2020.

2. Borden, Kevin A., and Susan L. Cutter. 2008. "Spatial patterns of natural hazards mortality in the United States." *International journal of health geographics* 7, no. 1: 64.

3. Clark, Charles. 2018 July 13. "FEMA Acknowledges Flaws in Puerto Rico Post-Hurricane Response." *Government Executive.* Accessed from https://www.govexec.com/management/2018/07/fema-acknowledges-flaws-puerto-rico-post-hurricane-effort/149720/ on June 17, 2020.

4. Fritze, John. 2018 August 29. "Trump Describes Response to Hurricane Maria as 'Fantastic,' Days After Higher Death Count." *USA Today.* Accessed from https://www.usatoday.com/story/news/politics/2018/08/29/donald-trump-hurricane-maria-response-puerto-rico-fantastic/1123481002/ on June 17, 2020.

5. Kishore, Nishant, Domingo Marqués, Ayesha Mahmud, Mathew V. Kiang, Irmary Rodriguez, Arlan Fuller, Peggy Ebner et al. 2018. "Mortality in puerto rico after hurricane maria." *New England journal of medicine* 379, no. 2: 162–170.

6. Sutter, John, and Omaya Sosa Pascual. 2018 July 3. "Death from Bacterial Disease in Puerto Rico Spiked After Hurricane Maria." *CNN.* Accessed from https://www.cnn.com/2018/07/03/health/sutter-leptospirosis-outbreak-puerto-rico-invs/index.html on June 17, 2020.

7. Santos-Lozada, Alexis. 2018, May 31. "Why Puerto Rico's Death Toll from Hurricane Maria is So Much Higher than Officials Thought." *The Conversation.* Accessed from https://theconversation.com/why-puerto-ricos-death-toll-from-hurricane-maria-is-so-much-higher-than-officials-thought-97488 on June 17, 2020.

8. World Health Organization. 2020. "Classification of Diseases (ICD)." Accessed from https://www.who.int/classifications/icd/en/ on June 17, 2020.

9. Email, Arelis R. Hernández.

10. Email, Arelis R. Hernández.

11. Reporter covering the U.S. Southern border, Immigration, Texas and beyond.

12. Email, Bio Follow and Samantha Schmidt.

13. Email, Samantha Schmidt.

14. Reporter covering gender and family issues.

15. Email, Bio Follow and Joel Achenbach. "Study: Hurricane Maria and its Aftermath Caused a Spike in Puerto Rico Deaths, with Over 3,000 More than Normal." *The Washington Post.* Accessed from https://www.washingtonpost.com/national/study-hurricane-maria-and-its-aftermath-caused-a-spike-in-puerto-rico-deaths-with-nearly-3000-more-than-normal/2018/08/28/57d6d2d6-aa43–11e8-b1da-ff7faa680710_story.html on June 17, 2020.

10. Santos-Lozada, 2018, May 31.

11. Daszak, Peter. 2016 November. "An Economic and Policy Framework for Pandemic Control and Prevention." Scowcroft Institute of International Affairs. Accessed from https://bush.tamu.edu/scowcroft/papers/daszak/FINAL%20Daszak%20Policy%20Paper%20for%20Publication.pdf on June 17, 2020.

12. Rodríguez-Díaz, Carlos E., Adriana Garriga-López, Souhail M. Malavé-Rivera, and Ricardo L. Vargas-Molina. 2017. "Zika virus epidemic in Puerto Rico: Health justice too long delayed." *International Journal of Infectious Diseases* 65: 144–147.

13. Kodjak, Alison. 2016 September 28. "Congress Ends Spat, Agrees to Fund $1.1 Billion to Combat Zika." *NPR.* Accessed from https://www.npr.org/sections/health-shots/2016/09/28/495806979/congress-ends-spat-over-zika-funding-approves-1-1-billion on June 18, 2020.

14. Willoughby, Mariano and J. Scott Trubey. 2020, May 13. "'It's Just Cuckoo': State's Latest Data Mishap Causes Critics to Cry Foul." *Atlanta Journal-Constitution.* Accessed from https://www.ajc.com/news/state—regional-govt—politics/just-cuckoo-state-latest-data-mishap-causes-critics-cry-foul/182PpUvUX9X-EF8vO11NVGO/ on June 18, 2020.

15. Booker, Brakkton. 2020, January 15. "Months After Blowing Deadline, Trump Administration Lifts Hold on Puerto Rico Aid." *NPR.* Accessed from https://www.npr.org/2020/01/15/796658767/months-after-blowing-deadline-trump-administration-lifts-hold-on-puerto-rico-aid on June 18, 2020.

16. "United States COVID-19 Statistics." Accessed from https://covidusa.net/?state=Puerto+Rico on June 18, 2020.

17. Broniatowski, David A., et al. 2018. "Weaponized Health Communication: Twitter Bots and Vaccine Trolls Amplify the Vaccine Debate." *American Journal of Public Health, 108* (10):1378–1384.

18. Center for Health Security, Johns Hopkins Bloomberg School of Public Health. 2018, May 15. "Clade X-A Pandemic Exercise." Accessed from http://www.centerforhealthsecurity.org/our-work/events/2018_clade_x_exercise/index.html on June 18, 2020.

19. Myers, Nathan. 2018 August 24. "Terrorists Could Use Anti-vax Conspiracies to Disrupt Pandemic Emergency Response." *The Hill.* Accessed from https://thehill.com/opinion/healthcare/403512-Terrorists-could-use-anti-vax-conspiracies-to-disrupt-pandemic-emergency-response on June 18, 2020.

Appendix A

Glossary and Acronyms of Climate Change and Disaster Resilience

Joaquin Jay Gonzalez III
and Alan R. Roper

AET	Apparent equivalent temperature
ANPP	Aboveground net primary productivity
AOGCM	Atmosphere-ocean general circulation models
BT	Body temperature
CCSM	Community Climate System Model
CCSP	Climate Change Science Program
CGC	Canadian Global Coupled Model
DOY	Day of year
ENSO	El Niño-Southern Oscillation
EPA	Environmental Protection Agency
ET	Evapotranspiration
FACE	Free-Air CO2 Enrichment
GCM	General Circulation Model
GFDL	Geophysical Fluid Dynamics Laboratory
HadCM2	Hadley Centre for Climate Prediction and Research's Climate Model 2
HCN	Historical Climatology Network
HI	Harvest index
HLI	Heat load index
IBP	International Biome Project
IPCC	Intergovernmental Panel on Climate Change
IPCC AR4	Intergovernmental Panel on Climate Change 4th Assessment Report
IPCC TAR	Intergovernmental Panel on Climate Change 3rd Assessment Report
IPM	Integrated pest management
LAI	Leaf area index
LTER	Long Term Ecological Research
LWSI	Livestock weather safety index
NASA	National Aeronautics and Space Administration
NCAR	National Center for Atamospheric Research
NEON	National Ecological Observatory Network
NOAA	National Oceanic and Atmospheric Administration
NPP	Net primary productivity
NRC	National Research Council
NRCS	Natural Resources Conservation Service

NWS COOP	National Weather Service Cooperative Observer Program
PDO	Pacific Decadal Oscillation
PE	Potential evaporation
ppb	Parts per billion
ppm	Parts per million
RH	Relative humidity
RMSE	Root mean square error
RR	Respiration rate
SOM	Soil organic matter
SRAD	Solar radiation
SRES	Special Report on Emissions Scenarios
SWE	Snow water equivalent
TBCA	Total carbon allocation belowground
THI	Temperature-humidity index
UNEP	United Nations Environment Programme
USDA	United States Department of Agriculture
USGS	United States Geological Survey
USGS HCDN	United States Geological Survey Hydro-Climatic Data Network
VFI	Voluntary feed intake
VIC	Variable Infiltration Capacity
VOC	Volatile organic compound
VPD	Vapor pressure deficit
WS	Wind speed
WUE	Water use efficiency

Adaption: In human systems, the process of adjustment to actual or expected climate and its effects, in order to moderate harm or exploit beneficial opportunities. In natural systems, the process of adjustment to actual climate and its effects; human intervention may facilitate adjustment to expected climate and its effects.

Adaptive Capacity: The ability of systems, institutions, humans and other organisms to adjust to potential damage, to take advantage of opportunities, or to respond to consequences.

Aerosol: A suspension of airborne solid or liquid particles, with a typical size between a few nanometers and 10 μm that reside in the atmosphere for at least several hours.

Afforestation: Planting of new forests on lands that historically have not contained forests.

Air Pollution: Degradation of air quality with negative effects on human health, the natural or built environment, due to the introduction by natural processes or human activity in the atmosphere of substances (gases, aerosols) which have a direct (primary pollutants) or indirect (secondary pollutants) harmful effect.

Anthropocene: A new geological epoch resulting from significant human-driven changes to the structure and functioning of the Earth System, including the climate system.

Anthropogenic Emissions: Emissions of greenhouse gases (GHGs), precursors of GHGs and aerosols caused by human activities. These activities include the burning of fossil fuels, deforestation, land use and land use changes (LULUC), livestock production, fertilization, waste management, and industrial processes.

Atmosphere: The gaseous envelope surrounding the earth, divided into five layers—the troposphere which contains half of the earth's atmosphere, the stratosphere, the mesosphere, the thermosphere, and the exosphere, which is the outer limit of the atmosphere.

Biochar: Stable, carbon-rich material produced by heating biomass in an oxygen-limited environment. Biochar may be added to soils to improve soil functions and to reduce greenhouse gas emissions from biomass and soils, and for carbon sequestration.

Biofuel: A fuel derived from renewable, biological sources, including crops such as maize and sugar cane, and some forms of waste.

Black Carbon: The soot that results from the incomplete combustion of fossil fuels, biofuels, and biomass (wood, animal dung, etc.). It is the most potent climate-warming aerosol. Unlike greenhouse gases, which trap infrared radiation that is already in the Earth's atmosphere, these particles absorb all wavelengths of sunlight and then re-emit this energy as infrared radiation.

Cap and Trade: An emission trading scheme whereby businesses or countries can buy or sell allowances to emit greenhouse gases via an exchange. The volume of allowances issued adds up to the limit, or cap, imposed by the authorities.

Carbon Capture and Storage: The collection and transport of concentrated carbon dioxide gas from large emission sources, such as power plants. The gases are then injected into deep underground reservoirs. Carbon capture is sometimes referred to as geological sequestration.

Carbon Dioxide (CO2): Carbon dioxide is a gas in the Earth's atmosphere. It occurs naturally and is also a by-product of human activities such as burning fossil fuels. It is the principal greenhouse gas produced by human activity.

Carbon Dioxide Capture and Storage (CCS): A process in which a relatively pure stream of carbon dioxide (CO2) from industrial and energy-related sources is separated (captured), conditioned, compressed and transported to a storage location for long-term isolation from the atmosphere.

Carbon Dioxide Capture and Utilization (CCU): A process in which CO2 is captured and then used to produce a new product. If the CO2 is stored in a product for a climate-relevant time horizon.

Carbon Dioxide (CO2) equivalent: Six greenhouse gases are limited by the Kyoto Protocol and each has a different global warming potential. The overall warming effect of this cocktail of gases is often expressed in terms of carbon dioxide equivalent—the amount of CO2 that would cause the same amount of warming.

Carbon Footprint: The amount of carbon emitted by an individual or organization in a given period of time, or the amount of carbon emitted during the manufacture of a product.

Carbon Intensity: A unit of measure. The amount of carbon emitted by a country per unit of Gross Domestic Product.

Carbon Leakage: A term used to refer to the problem whereby industry relocates to countries where emission regimes are weaker, or non-existent.

Carbon Neutral: A process where there is no net release of CO2. For example, growing biomass takes CO2 out of the atmosphere, while burning it releases the gas again. The process would be carbon neutral if the amount taken out and the amount released were identical. A company or country can also achieve carbon neutrality by means of carbon offsetting.

Carbon Offsetting: A way of compensating for emissions of CO2 by participating in, or funding, efforts to take CO2 out of the atmosphere. Offsetting often involves paying another party, somewhere else, to save emissions equivalent to those produced by your activity.

Carbon Sequestration: The process of storing carbon dioxide. This can happen naturally, as growing trees and plants turn CO2 into biomass (wood, leaves, and so on). It can also refer to the capture and storage of CO2 produced by industry. See Carbon capture and storage.

Carbon Sink: Any process, activity or mechanism that removes carbon from the atmosphere. The biggest carbon sinks are the world's oceans and forests, which absorb large amounts of carbon dioxide from the Earth's atmosphere.

Certified Emission Reduction (CER): A greenhouse gas trading credit, under the UN Clean Development Mechanism program. A CER may be earned by participating in emission reduction programs—installing green technology, or planting forests—in developing countries. Each CER is equivalent to one ton of carbon dioxide.

CFCs: The short name for chlorofluorocarbons—a family of gases that have contributed to stratospheric ozone depletion, but which are also potent greenhouse gases. Emissions of CFCs around the developed world are being phased out due to an international control agreement, the 1989 Montreal Protocol.

Clean Coal Technology: Technology that enables coal to be burned without emitting CO2. Some systems currently being developed remove the CO2 before combustion, others remove it afterwards. Clean coal technology is unlikely to be widely available for at least a decade.

Clean Development Mechanism (CDM): A program that enables developed countries or companies to earn credits by investing in greenhouse gas emission reduction or removal projects in developing countries. These credits can be used to offset emissions and bring the country or company below its mandatory target.

Climate: Climate in a narrow sense is usually defined as the average weather, or more rigorously, as the statistical description in terms of the mean and variability of relevant quantities over a period of time ranging from months to thousands or millions of years. The classical period for averaging these variables is 30 years, as defined by the World Meteorological Organization.

Climate Change: A pattern of change affecting global or regional climate, as measured by yardsticks such as average temperature and rainfall, or an alteration in frequency of extreme weather conditions. This variation may be caused by both natural processes and human activity. Global warming is one aspect of climate change.

Climate Justice: Justice that links development and human rights to achieve a human-centered approach to addressing climate change, safeguarding the rights of the most vulnerable people and sharing the burdens and benefits of climate change and its impacts equitably and fairly.

Dangerous Climate Change: A term referring to severe climate change that will have a negative effect on societies, economies, and the environment as a whole. The phrase was introduced by the 1992 UN Framework Convention on Climate Change, which aims to prevent "dangerous" human interference with the climate system.

Decarbonization: The process by which countries, individuals or other entities aim to achieve zero fossil carbon existence. Typically refers to a reduction of the carbon emissions associated with electricity, industry and transport.

Deforestation: The permanent removal of standing forests that can lead to significant levels of carbon dioxide emissions.

Disaster: Severe alterations in the normal functioning of a community or a society due to hazardous physical events interacting with vulnerable social conditions, leading to widespread adverse human, material, economic or environmental effects that require immediate emergency response to satisfy critical human needs and that may require external support for recovery.

Drought: A period of abnormally dry weather long enough to cause a serious hydrological imbalance.

Early Warning Systems (EWS): The set of technical, financial and institutional capacities needed to generate and disseminate timely and meaningful warning information to enable individuals, communities and organizations threatened by a hazard to prepare to act promptly and appropriately to reduce the possibility of harm or loss.

Ecosystem: An ecosystem is a functional unit consisting of living organisms, their non-living environment and the interactions within and between them.

Electric Vehicle (EV): A vehicle whose propulsion is powered fully or mostly by electricity.

Emission Trading Scheme (ETS): A scheme set up to allow the trading of emissions permits between business and/or countries as part of a cap and trade approach to limiting greenhouse gas emissions. The best-developed example is the EU's trading scheme, launched in 2005.

Energy Efficiency: The ratio of output or useful energy or energy services or other useful physical outputs obtained from a system, conversion process, transmission or storage activity to the input of energy.

Flood: The overflowing of the normal confines of a stream or other body of water, or the accumulation of water over areas that are not normally submerged.

Fossil Fuels: Natural resources, such as coal, oil and natural gas, containing hydrocarbons. These fuels are formed in the Earth over millions of years and produce carbon dioxide when burnt.

G77: The main negotiating bloc for developing countries, allied with China (G77+China). The G77 comprises 130 countries, including India and Brazil, most African countries, the grouping of small island states (Aosis), the Gulf states and many others, from Afghanistan to Zimbabwe.

Geological Sequestration: The injection of carbon dioxide into underground geological formations. When CO2 is injected into declining oil fields it can help to recover more of the oil.

Glacier: A perennial mass of ice, and possibly snow, originating on the land surface by the recrystallization of snow and showing evidence of past or present flow.

Global Average Temperature: The mean surface temperature of the Earth measured from three main sources: satellites, monthly readings from a network of over 3,000 surface temperature observation stations and sea surface temperature measurements taken mainly from the fleet of merchant ships, naval ships and data buoys.

Global Dimming: An observed widespread reduction in sunlight at the surface of the Earth, which varies significantly between regions. The most likely cause of global dimming is an interaction between sunlight and microscopic aerosol particles from human activities. In some regions, such as Europe, global dimming no longer occurs, thanks to clean air regulations.

Global Energy Budget: The balance between the Earth's incoming and outgoing energy. The current global climate system must adjust to rising greenhouse gas levels and, in the very long term, the Earth must get rid of energy at the same rate at which it receives energy from the sun.

Global Mean Surface Temperature (GMST): Area-weighted global average of land surface air temperature over land and sea surface temperatures, unless otherwise specified, normally expressed relative to a specified reference period.

Global Warming: The steady rise in global average temperature in recent decades, which experts believe is largely caused by man-made greenhouse gas emissions. The long-term trend continues upwards, they suggest, even though the warmest year on record, according to the UK's Met Office, is 1998.

Global Warming Potential (GWP): A measure of a greenhouse gas's ability to absorb heat and warm the atmosphere over a given time period. It is measured relative to a similar mass of carbon dioxide, which has a GWP of 1.0. So, for example, methane has a GWP of 25 over 100 years, the metric used in the Kyoto Protocol. It is important to know the timescale, as gases are removed from the atmosphere at different rates.

Green Infrastructure: The interconnected set of natural and constructed ecological systems, green spaces and other landscape features.

Greenhouse Effect: The insulating effect of certain gases in the atmosphere, which allow solar radiation to warm the earth and then prevent some of the heat from escaping. See also Natural greenhouse effect.

Greenhouse Gases (GHGs): Natural and industrial gases that trap heat from the Earth and warm the surface. The Kyoto Protocol restricts emissions of six greenhouse gases: natural (carbon dioxide, nitrous oxide, and methane) and industrial (perfluorocarbons, hydrofluorocarbons, and sulphur hexafluoride).

Halocarbons: A collective term for the group of partially halogenated organic species, which includes the chlorofluorocarbons (CFCs), hydrochlorofluorocarbons (HCFCs), hydrofluorocarbons (HFCs), halons, methyl chloride and methyl bromide.

Heat Wave: A period of abnormally hot weather.

Heating, Ventilation, and Air Conditioning (HVAC): Heating, ventilation and air conditioning technology is used to control temperature and humidity in an indoor environment, be it in buildings or in vehicles, providing thermal comfort and healthy air quality to the occupants.

Hydrological Cycle: The cycle in which water evaporates from the oceans and the land surface, is carried over the Earth in atmospheric circulation as water vapor, condenses to form clouds, precipitates as rain or snow, which on land can be intercepted by trees and vegetation, potentially accumulates as snow or ice, provides runoff on the land surface.

Internal Displacement: Internal displacement refers to the forced movement of people within the country they live in.

IPCC: The Intergovernmental Panel on Climate Change is a scientific body established by the United Nations Environment Program and the World Meteorological Organization. It reviews and assesses the most recent scientific, technical, and socio-economic work relevant to climate change, but does not carry out its own research. The IPCC was honored with the 2007 Nobel Peace Prize.

Irreversibility: A perturbed state of a dynamical system is defined as irreversible on a given timescale, if the recovery timescale from this state due to natural processes is substantially longer than the time it takes for the system to reach this perturbed state.

Kyoto Protocol: A protocol attached to the UN Framework Convention on Climate Change, which sets legally binding commitments on greenhouse gas emissions. Industrialized countries agreed to reduce their combined emissions to 5.2 percent below 1990 levels during the five-year period 2008–2012. It was agreed by governments at a 1997 UN conference in Kyoto, Japan, but did not legally come into force until 2005. A different set of countries agreed a second commitment period in 2013 that will run until 2020.

LDCs: Least Developed Countries represent the poorest and weakest countries in the world. The current list of LDCs includes 49 countries—33 in Africa, 15 in Asia and the Pacific, and one in Latin America.

LULUCF: This refers to Land Use, Land-Use Change, and Forestry. Activities in LULUCF provide a method of offsetting emissions, either by increasing the removal of greenhouse gases from the atmosphere (i.e., by planting trees or managing forests), or by reducing emissions (i.e., by curbing deforestation and the associated burning of wood).

Major Economies Forum on Energy and Climate: A forum established in 2009 by U.S. President Barack Obama to discuss elements of the agreement that will be negotiated at Copenhagen. Its members—Australia, Brazil, Canada, China, the European Union, France, Germany, India, Indonesia, Italy, Japan, Mexico, Russia, South Africa, South Korea, the UK and the U.S.— account for 80 percent of greenhouse gas emissions. The forum is a modification of the Major Economies Meeting started by the former President George Bush, which was seen by some countries as an attempt to undermine UN negotiations.

Methane: Methane is the second most important man-made greenhouse gas. Sources include both the natural world (wetlands, termites, wildfires) and human activity (agriculture, waste dumps, leaks from coal mining).

Migration: The movement of a person or a group of persons, either across an international border, or within a State. It is a population movement, encompassing any kind of movement of people, whatever its length, composition and causes; it includes migration of refugees, displaced persons, economic migrants, and persons moving for other purposes, including family reunification.

Mitigation: Action that will reduce man-made climate change. This includes action to reduce greenhouse gas emissions or absorb greenhouse gases in the atmosphere.

Natural Greenhouse Effect: The natural level of greenhouse gases in our atmosphere, which keeps the planet about 30C warmer than it would otherwise be—essential for life as we know it. Water vapor is the most important component of the natural greenhouse effect.

Negative Emissions: Removal of greenhouse gases (GHGs) from the atmosphere by deliberate human activities, i.e., in addition to the removal that would occur via natural carbon cycle processes.

Net-Zero Emissions: Net-zero emissions are achieved when emissions of greenhouse gases to the atmosphere are balanced by anthropogenic removals.

Nitrous Oxide (N2O): One of the six greenhouse gases (GHGs) to be mitigated under the Kyoto Protocol. The main anthropogenic source of N2O is agriculture (soil and animal manure management), but important contributions also come from sewage treatment, fossil fuel combustion, and chemical industrial processes.

Ocean Acidification: The ocean absorbs approximately one-fourth of man-made CO2 from the atmosphere, which helps to reduce adverse climate change effects. However, when the CO2 dissolves in seawater, carbonic acid is formed.

1.5°C Warmer Worlds: Projected worlds in which global warming has reached and, unless otherwise indicated, been limited to 1.5°C above pre-industrial levels.

Ozone (O3): Ozone, the triatomic form of oxygen (O3), is a gaseous atmospheric constituent. In the troposphere, it is created both naturally and by photochemical reactions involving gases resulting from human activities (smog).

Paris Agreement: The Paris Agreement under the United Nations Framework Convention on Climate Change (UNFCCC) was adopted on December 2015 in Paris, France, at the 21st session of the Conference of the Parties (COP) to the UNFCCC. The agreement, adopted by 196 Parties to the UNFCCC, entered into force on 4 November 2016 and as of May 2018 had 195 Signatories and was ratified by 177 Parties.

Per-capita Emissions: The total amount of greenhouse gas emitted by a country per unit of population.

PPM (350/450): An abbreviation for parts per million, usually used as short for ppmv (parts per million by volume). The Intergovernmental Panel on Climate Change (IPCC) suggested in 2007 that the world should aim to stabilize greenhouse gas levels at 450 ppm CO2 equivalent in order to avert dangerous climate change.

Pre-industrial Levels of Carbon Dioxide: The levels of carbon dioxide in the atmosphere prior to the start of the Industrial Revolution. These levels are estimated to be about 280 parts per million (by volume). The current level is around 380ppm.

REDD: Reducing Emissions from Deforestation and forest Degradation, a concept that would provide developing countries with a financial incentive to preserve forests.

Reforestation: Planting of forests on lands that have previously contained forests but that have been converted to some other use.

Renewable Energy: Renewable energy is energy created from sources that can be replenished in a short period of time. The five renewable sources used most often are: biomass (such as wood and biogas), the movement of water, geothermal (heat from within the earth), wind, and solar.

Resilience: The capacity of social, economic and environmental systems to cope with a hazardous event or trend or disturbance, responding or reorganizing in ways that maintain their essential function, identity and structure, while also maintaining the capacity for adaptation, learning and transformation.

Sea ice: Ice found at the sea surface that has originated from the freezing of seawater. Sea ice may be discontinuous pieces (ice floes) moved on the ocean surface by wind and currents (pack ice), or a motionless sheet attached to the coast (land-fast ice). Sea ice concentration is the fraction of the ocean covered by ice.

Short-Lived Climate Forcers (SLCF): Short-lived climate forcers refers to a set of compounds that are primarily composed of those with short lifetimes in the atmosphere compared to well-mixed greenhouse gases, and are also referred to as near-term climate forcers. This set of compounds includes methane, which is also a well-mixed greenhouse gas, as well as ozone and aerosols, or their precursors, and some halogenated species that are not well-mixed greenhouse gases.

Stratosphere: The highly stratified region of the atmosphere above the troposphere extending from about 10 km (ranging from 9 km at high latitudes to 16 km in the tropics on average) to about 50 km altitude.

Sustainable Development (SD): Development that meets the needs of the present without compromising the ability of future generations to meet their own needs and balances social, economic and environmental concerns.

Technology Transfer: The process whereby technological advances are shared between different countries.

Tipping Point: A tipping point is a threshold for change, which, when reached, results in a process that is difficult to reverse. Scientists say it is urgent that policy makers halve global carbon dioxide emissions over the next 50 years or risk triggering changes that could be irreversible.

Transformational Adaptation: Adaptation that changes the fundamental attributes of a socio-ecological system in anticipation of climate change and its impacts.

Transit-Oriented Development (TOD): An approach urban development that maximizes the amount of residential, business and leisure space within walking distance of efficient public transport, so as to enhance mobility of citizens, the viability of public transport and the value of urban land in mutually supporting ways.

Troposphere: The lowest part of the atmosphere, from the surface to about 10 km in altitude at mid-latitudes (ranging from 9 km at high latitudes to 16 km in the tropics on average), where clouds and weather phenomena occur. In the troposphere, temperatures generally decrease with height.

2030 Agenda for Sustainable Development: A UN resolution in September 2015 adopting a plan of action for people, planet and prosperity in a new global development framework anchored in 17 Sustainable Development Goals (UN, 2015).

Twenty-twenty-twenty (20–20–20): This refers to a pledge by the European Union to reach three targets by 2020: (a) a 20 percent reduction in greenhouse gas emissions from 1990 levels; (b) an increase in the use of renewable energy to 20 percent of all energy consumed; and (c) a 20 percent increase in energy efficiency.

United Nations Framework Convention on Climate Change: One of a series of international agreements on global environmental issues adopted at the 1992 Earth Summit in Rio de Janeiro. The UNFCCC aims to prevent "dangerous" human interference with the climate system. It entered into force on 21 March 1994 and has been ratified by 192 countries.

Weather: The state of the atmosphere with regard to temperature, cloudiness, rainfall, wind and other meteorological conditions. It is not the same as climate which is the average weather over a much longer period.

Resources

Arctic Council (2013). "Glossary of terms," in Arctic Resilience Interim Report 2013 (Stockholm, Sweden: Stockholm Environment Institute and Stockholm Resilience Centre), viii.

Backlund, P., Janetos, A., and Schimel, D. (2008). "The effects of climate change on agriculture, land resources, water resources, and biodiversity in the United States." Synthesis and Assessment Product 4.3. Washington, D.C.: U.S. Environmental Protection Agency, Climate Change Science Program (https://www.fs.usda.gov/treesearch/pubs/32781).

IPCC (2012). Managing the Risks of Extreme Events and Disasters to Advance Climate Change Adaptation. A Special Report of Working Groups I and II of the Intergovernmental Panel on Climate Change (IPCC). , eds. C.B. Field, V. Barros, T.F. Stocker, D. Qin, D.J. Dokken, K.L. Ebi, et al. Cambridge, UK and New York, NY, USA: Cambridge University Press.

IPCC (2018), Glossary, TSU compiled version, eds. Mustapha Babiker (Sudan), Heleen De Coninck (Netherlands), Sarah Connors (UK), Renée van Diemen (Netherlands), Riyanti Djalante (Indonesia), Kristie L. Ebi (U.S.), Neville Ellis (Australia), Andreas Fischlin (Switzerland), Tania Guillén Bolaños (Germany/Nicaragua), Kiane de Kleijne (Netherlands), Valérie Masson-Delmotte (France), Richard Millar (UK), Elvira S. Poloczanska (Germany), Hans-Otto Pörtner (Germany), Andy Reisinger (New Zealand), Joeri Rogelj (Belgium/Austria), Sonia Seneviratne (Switzerland)

ISO (2018). ISO 14044:2006. Environmental management–Life cycle assessment–Requirements and guidelines. Available at: https://www.iso.org/standard/38498.html [Accessed May 31, 2018].

UNFCCC (2013). Reporting and accounting of LULUCF activities under the Kyoto Protocol. Available at: http://unfccc.int/methods/lulucf/items/4129.php.

UNISDR (2009). 2009 UNISDR Terminology on Disaster Risk Reduction. Geneva.

United States Environmental Protection Agency, (2013), Glossary of Climate Change Terms, Office of Air and Radiation/Office of Atmospheric Programs/Climate Change Division, Retrieved from https://www.epa.gov/climate-research.

Appendix B

United Nations Paris Agreement (2015)

The Parties to this Agreement,

Being Parties to the United Nations Framework Convention on Climate Change, hereinafter referred to as "the Convention,"

Pursuant to the Durban Platform for Enhanced Action established by decision l/CP.17 of the Conference of the Parties to the Convention at its seventeenth session,

In pursuit of the objective of the Convention, and being guided by its principles, including the principle of equity and common but differentiated responsibilities and respective capabilities, in the light of different national circumstances,

Recognizing the need for an effective and progressive response to the urgent threat of climate change on the basis of the best available scientific knowledge,

Also recognizing the specific needs and special circumstances of developing country Parties, especially those that are particularly vulnerable to the adverse effects of climate change, as provided for in the Convention,

Taking full account of the specific needs and special situations of the least developed countries with regard to funding and transfer of technology,

Recognizing that Parties may be affected not only by climate change, but also by the impacts of the measures taken in response to it,

Emphasizing the intrinsic relationship that climate change actions, responses and impacts have with equitable access to sustainable development and eradication of poverty,

Recognizing the fundamental priority of safeguarding food security and ending hunger, and the particular vulnerabilities of food production systems to the adverse impacts of climate change,

Taking into account the imperatives of a just transition of the workforce and the creation of decent work and quality jobs in accordance with nationally defined development priorities,

Acknowledging that climate change is a common concern of humankind, Parties should, when taking action to address climate change, respect, promote and consider their respective obligations on human rights, the right to health, the rights of indigenous peoples, local communities, migrants, children, persons with disabilities and people in vulnerable situations and the right to development, as well as gender equality, empowerment of women and intergenerational equity,

Recognizing the importance of the conservation and enhancement, as appropriate, of sinks and reservoirs of the greenhouse gases referred to in the Convention,

Noting the importance of ensuring the integrity of all ecosystems, including oceans, and the protection of biodiversity, recognized by some cultures as Mother Earth, and noting the importance for some of the concept of "climate justice," when taking action to address climate change,

Affirming the importance of education, trammg, public awareness, public participation, public access to information and cooperation at all levels on the matters addressed in this Agreement,

Recognizing the importance of the engagements of all levels of government and various actors, in accordance with respective national legislations of Parties, in addressing climate change,

247

Also recognizing that sustainable lifestyles and sustainable patterns of consumption and production, with developed country Parties taking the lead, play an important role in addressing climate change,

Have agreed as follows:

Article 1

For the purpose of this Agreement, the definitions contained in Article 1 of the Convention shall apply. In addition:

> (a) "Convention" means the United Nations Framework Convention on Climate Change, adopted in New York on 9 May 1992;
> (b) "Conference of the Parties" means the Conference of the Parties to the Convention;
> (c) "Party" means a Party to this Agreement.

Article 2

1. This Agreement, in enhancing the implementation of the Convention, including its objective, aims to strengthen the global response to the threat of climate change, in the context of sustainable development and efforts to eradicate poverty, including by:

> (a) Holding the increase in the global average temperature to well below 2°C above pre-industrial levels and pursuing efforts to limit the temperature increase to 1.5°C above pre-industrial levels, recognizing that this would significantly reduce the risks and impacts of climate change;
> (b) Increasing the ability to adapt to the adverse impacts of climate change and foster climate resilience and low greenhouse gas emissions development, in a manner that does not threaten food production; and
> (c) Making finance flows consistent with a pathway towards low greenhouse gas emissions and climate-resilient development.

2. This Agreement will be implemented to reflect equity and the principle of common but differentiated responsibilities and respective capabilities, in the light of different national circumstances.

Article 3

As nationally determined contributions to the global response to climate change, all Parties are to undertake and communicate ambitious efforts as defined in Articles 4, 7, 9, 10, 11 and 13 with the view to achieving the purpose of this Agreement as set out in Article 2. The efforts of all Parties will represent a progression over time, while recognizing the need to support developing country Parties for the effective implementation of this Agreement.

Article 4

1. In order to achieve the long-term temperature goal set out in Article 2, Parties aim to reach global peaking of greenhouse gas emissions as soon as possible, recognizing that peaking will take longer for developing country Parties, and to undertake rapid reductions thereafter in accordance with best available science, so as to achieve a balance between anthropogenic emissions by sources and removals by sinks of greenhouse gases in the second half of this century, on the basis of equity, and in the context of sustainable development and efforts to eradicate poverty.

2. Each Party shall prepare, communicate and maintain successive nationally determined contributions that it intends to achieve. Parties shall pursue domestic mitigation measures, with the aim of achieving the objectives of such contributions.

3. Each Party's successive nationally determined contribution will represent a progression beyond the Party's then current nationally determined contribution and reflect its highest possible ambition, reflecting its common but differentiated responsibilities and respective capabilities, in the light of different national circumstances.

4. Developed country Parties should continue taking the lead by undertaking economy-wide absolute emission reduction targets. Developing country Parties should continue enhancing their mitigation efforts, and are encouraged to move over time towards economy-wide emission reduction or limitation targets in the light of different national circumstances.

5. Support shall be provided to developing country Parties for the implementation of this Article, in accordance with Articles 9, 10 and 11, recognizing that enhanced support for developing country Parties will allow for higher ambition in their actions.

6. The least developed countries and small island developing States may prepare and communicate strategies, plans and actions for low greenhouse gas emissions development reflecting their special circumstances.

7. Mitigation co-benefits resulting from Parties' adaptation actions and/or economic diversification plans can contribute to mitigation outcomes under this Article.

8. In communicating their nationally determined contributions, all Parties shall provide the information necessary for clarity, transparency and understanding in accordance with decision l/CP.21 and any relevant decisions of the Conference of the Parties serving as the meeting of the Parties to this Agreement.

9. Each Party shall communicate a nationally determined contribution every five years in accordance with decision l/CP.21 and any relevant decisions of the Conference of the Parties serving as the meeting of the Parties to this Agreement and be informed by the outcomes of the global stocktake referred to in Article 14.

10. The Conference of the Parties serving as the meeting of the Parties to this Agreement shall consider common time frames for nationally determined contributions at its first session.

11. A Party may at any time adjust its existing nationally determined contribution with a view to enhancing its level of ambition, in accordance with guidance adopted by the Conference of the Parties serving as the meeting of the Parties to this Agreement.

12. Nationally determined contributions communicated by Parties shall be recorded in a public registry maintained by the secretariat.

13. Parties shall account for their nationally determined contributions. In accounting for anthropogenic emissions and removals corresponding to their nationally determined contributions, Parties shall promote environmental integrity, transparency, accuracy, completeness, comparability and consistency, and ensure the avoidance of double counting, in accordance with guidance adopted by the Conference of the Parties serving as the meeting of the Parties to this Agreement.

14. In the context of their nationally determined contributions, when recognizing and implementing mitigation actions with respect to anthropogenic emissions and removals, Parties should take into account, as appropriate, existing methods and guidance under the Convention, in the light of the provisions of paragraph 13 of this Article.

15. Parties shall take into consideration in the implementation of this Agreement the concerns of Parties with economies most affected by the impacts of response measures, particularly developing country Parties.

16. Parties, including regional economic integration organizations and their member States, that have reached an agreement to act jointly under paragraph 2 of this Article shall notify the secretariat of the terms of that agreement, including the emission level allocated to each Party within the relevant time period, when they communicate their nationally determined contributions. The secretariat shall in turn inform the Parties and signatories to the Convention of the terms of that agreement.

17. Each party to such an agreement shall be responsible for its emission level as set out in the agreement referred to in paragraph 16 of this Article in accordance with paragraphs 13 and 14 of this Article and Articles 13 and 15.

18. If Parties acting jointly do so in the framework of, and together with, a regional economic integration organization which is itself a Party to this Agreement, each member State of that regional economic integration organization individually, and together with the regional economic integration organization, shall be responsible for its emission level as set out in the agreement communicated under paragraph 16 of this Article in accordance with paragraphs 13 and 14 of this Article and Articles 13 and 15.

19. All Parties should strive to formulate and communicate long-term low greenhouse gas emission development strategies, mindful of Article 2 taking into account their common but differentiated responsibilities and respective capabilities, in the light of different national circumstances.

Article 5

1. Parties should take action to conserve and enhance, as appropriate, sinks and reservoirs of greenhouse gases as referred to in Article 4, paragraph 1 (d), of the Convention, including forests.

2. Parties are encouraged to take action to implement and support, including through results-based payments, the existing framework as set out in related guidance and decisions already agreed under the Convention for: policy approaches and positive incentives for activities relating to reducing emissions from deforestation and forest degradation, and the role of conservation, sustainable management of forests and enhancement of forest carbon stocks in developing countries; and alternative policy approaches, such as joint mitigation and adaptation approaches for the integral and sustainable management of forests, while reaffirming the importance of incentivizing, as appropriate, non-carbon benefits associated with such approaches.

Article 6

1. Parties recognize that some Parties choose to pursue voluntary cooperation in the implementation of their nationally determined contributions to allow for higher ambition in their mitigation and adaptation actions and to promote sustainable development and environmental integrity.

2. Parties shall, where engaging on a voluntary basis in cooperative approaches that involve the use of internationally transferred mitigation outcomes towards nationally determined contributions, promote sustainable development and ensure environmental integrity and transparency, including in governance, and shall apply robust accounting to ensure, inter alia, the avoidance of double counting, consistent with guidance adopted by the Conference of the Parties serving as the meeting of the Parties to this Agreement.

3. The use of internationally transferred mitigation outcomes to achieve nationally determined contributions under this Agreement shall be voluntary and authorized by participating Parties.

4. A mechanism to contribute to the mitigation of greenhouse gas emissions and support sustainable development is hereby established under the authority and guidance of the Conference of the Parties serving as the meeting of the Parties to this Agreement for use by Parties on a voluntary basis. It shall be supervised by a body designated by the Conference of the Parties serving as the meeting of the Parties to this Agreement, and shall aim:

(a) To promote the mitigation of greenhouse gas emissions while fostering sustainable development;

(b) To incentivize and facilitate participation in the mitigation of greenhouse gas emissions by public and private entities authorized by a Party;

(c) To contribute to the reduction of emission levels in the host Party, which will benefit from mitigation activities resulting in emission reductions that can also be used by another Party to fulfill its nationally determined contribution; and

(d) To deliver an overall mitigation in global emissions.

5. Emission reductions resulting from the mechanism referred to in paragraph 4 of this Article shall not be used to demonstrate achievement of the host Party's nationally determined contribution if used by another Party to demonstrate achievement of its nationally determined contribution.

6. The Conference of the Parties serving as the meeting of the Parties to this Agreement shall ensure that a share of the proceeds from activities under the mechanism referred to in paragraph 4 of this Article is used to cover administrative expenses as well as to assist developing country Parties that are particularly vulnerable to the adverse effects of climate change to meet the costs of adaptation.

7. The Conference of the Parties serving as the meeting of the Parties to this Agreement shall adopt rules, modalities and procedures for the mechanism referred to in paragraph 4 of this Article at its first session.

8. Parties recognize the importance of integrated, holistic and balanced non-market approaches being available to Parties to assist in the implementation of their nationally determined contributions, in the context of sustainable development and poverty eradication, in a coordinated and effective manner, including through, inter alia, mitigation, adaptation, finance, technology transfer and capacity building, as appropriate. These approaches shall aim to:

(a) Promote mitigation and adaptation ambition;

(b) Enhance public and private sector participation in the implementation of nationally determined contributions; and

(c) Enable opportunities for coordination across instruments and relevant institutional' arrangements.

9. A framework for non-market approaches to sustainable development is hereby defined to promote the non-market approaches referred to in paragraph 8 of this Article.

Article 7

1. Parties hereby establish the global goal on adaptation of enhancing adaptive capacity, strengthening resilience and reducing vulnerability to climate change, with a view to contributing to sustainable development and ensuring an adequate adaptation response in the context of the temperature goal referred to in Article 2.

2. Parties recognize that adaptation is a global challenge faced by all with local, subnational, national, regional and international dimensions, and that it is a key component of and makes a contribution to the long-term global response to climate change to protect people, livelihoods and ecosystems, taking into account the urgent and immediate needs of those developing country Parties that are particularly vulnerable to the adverse effects of climate change.

3. The adaptation efforts of developing country Parties shall be recognized, in accordance with the modalities to be adopted by the Conference of the Parties serving as the meeting of the Parties to this Agreement at its first session.

4. Parties recognize that the current need for adaptation is significant and that greater levels of mitigation can reduce the need for additional adaptation efforts, and that greater adaptation needs can involve greater adaptation costs.

5. Parties acknowledge that adaptation action should follow a country-driven, gender-

responsive, participatory and fully transparent approach, taking into consideration vulnerable groups, communities and ecosystems, and should be based on and guided by the best available science and, as appropriate, traditional knowledge, knowledge of indigenous peoples and local knowledge systems, with a view to integrating adaptation into relevant socioeconomic and environmental policies and actions, where appropriate.

6. Parties recognize the importance of support for and international cooperation on adaptation efforts and the importance of taking into account the needs of developing country Parties, especially those that are particularly vulnerable .to the adverse effects of di mate change.

7. Parties should strengthen their cooperation on enhancing action on adaptation, taking into account the Cancun Adaptation Framework, including with regard to:

(a) Sharing information, good practices, experiences and lessons learned, including, as appropriate, as these relate to science, planning, policies and implementation in relation to adaptation actions;

(b) Strengthening institutional arrangements, including those under the Convention that serve this Agreement, to support the synthesis of relevant information and knowledge, and the provision of technical support and guidance to Parties;

(c) Strengthening scientific knowledge on climate, including research, systematic observation of the climate system and early warning systems, in a manner that informs climate services and supports decision-making;

(d) Assisting developing country Parties in identifying effective adaptation practices, adaptation needs, priorities, support provided and received for adaptation actions and efforts, and challenges and gaps, in a manner consistent with encouraging good practices; and

(e) Improving the effectiveness and durability of adaptation actions.

8. United Nations specialized organizations and agencies are encouraged to support the efforts of Parties to implement the actions referred to in paragraph 7 of this Article, taking into account the provisions of paragraph 5 of this Article.

9. Each Party shall, as appropriate, engage in adaptation planning processes and the implementation of actions, including the development or enhancement of relevant plans, policies and/or contributions, which may include:

(a) The implementation of adaptation actions, undertakings and/or efforts;

(b) The process to formulate and implement national adaptation plans;

(c) The assessment of climate change impacts and vulnerability, with a view to formulating nationally determined prioritized actions, taking into account vulnerable people, places and ecosystems;

(d) Monitoring and evaluating and learning from adaptation plans, policies, programmes and actions; and

(e) Building the resilience of socioeconomic and ecological systems, including through economic diversification and sustainable management of natural resources.

10. Each Party should, as appropriate, submit and update periodically an adaptation communication, which may include its priorities, implementation and support needs, plans and actions, without creating any additional burden for developing country Parties.

11. The adaptation communication referred to in paragraph 10 of this Article shall be, as appropriate, submitted and updated periodically, as a component of or in conjunction with other communications or documents, including a national adaptation plan, a nationally determined contribution as referred to in Article 4, paragraph 2, and/or a national communication.

12. The adaptation communications referred to in paragraph 10 of this Article shall be recorded in a public registry maintained by the secretariat.

13. Continuous and enhanced international support shall be provided to developing

country Parties for the implementation of paragraphs 7, 9, 10 and 11 of this Article, in accordance with the provisions of Articles 9, 10 and 11.

14. The global stocktake referred to in Article 14 shall, inter alia:

(a) Recognize adaptation efforts of developing country Parties;

(b) Enhance the implementation of adaptation action taking into account the adaptation communication referred to in paragraph 10 of this Article;

(c) Review the adequacy and effectiveness of adaptation and support provided for adaptation; and

(e) Review the overall progress made in achieving the global goal on adaptation referred to in paragraph 1 of this Article.

Article 8

1. Parties recognize the importance of averting, minimizing and addressing loss and damage associated with the adverse effects of climate change, including extreme weather events and slow onset events, and the role of sustainable development in reducing the risk of loss and damage.

2. The Warsaw International Mechanism for Loss and Damage associated with Climate Change Impacts shall be subject to the authority and guidance of the Conference of the Parties serving as the meeting of the Parties to this Agreement and may be enhanced and strengthened, as determined by the Conference of the Parties serving as the meeting of the Parties to this Agreement.

3. Parties should enhance understanding, action and support, including through the Warsaw International Mechanism, as · appropriate, on a cooperative and facilitative basis with respect to loss and damage associated with the adverse effects of climate change.

4. Accordingly, areas of cooperation and facilitation to enhance understanding, action and support may include:

(a) Early warning systems;

(b) Emergency preparedness;

(c) Slow onset events;

(d) Events that may involve irreversible and permanent loss and damage;

(e) Comprehensive risk assessment and management;

(f) Risk insurance facilities, climate risk pooling and other insurance solutions;

(g) Non-economic losses; and

(h) Resilience of communities, livelihoods and ecosystems.

5. The Warsaw International Mechanism shall collaborate with existing bodies and expert groups under the Agreement, as well as relevant organizations and expert bodies outside the Agreement.

Article 9

1. Developed country Parties shall provide financial resources to assist developing country Parties with respect to both mitigation and adaptation in continuation of their existing obligations under the Convention.

2. Other Parties are encouraged to provide or continue to provide such support voluntarily.

3. As part of a global effort, developed country Parties should continue to take the lead in mobilizing climate finance from a wide variety of sources, instruments and channels, noting the significant role of public funds, through a variety of actions, including supporting country-driven strategies, and taking into account the needs and priorities of developing country

Parties. Such mobilization of climate finance should represent a progression beyond previous efforts.

    4. The provision of scaled-up financial resources should aim to achieve a balance between adaptation and mitigation, taking into account country-driven strategies, and the priorities and needs of developing country Parties, especially those that are particularly vulnerable to the adverse effects of climate change and have significant capacity constraints, such as the least developed countries and small island developing States, considering the need for public and grant-based resources for adaptation.

    5. Developed country Parties shall biennially communicate indicative quantitative and qualitative information related to paragraphs 1 and 3 of this Article, as applicable, including, as available, projected levels of public financial resources to be provided to developing country Parties. Other Parties providing resources are encouraged to communicate biennially such information on a voluntary basis.

    6. The global stocktake referred to in Article 14 shall take into account the relevant information provided by developed country Parties and/or Agreement bodies on efforts related to climate finance.

    7. Developed country Parties shall provide transparent and consistent information on support for developing country Parties provided and mobilized through public interventions biennially in accordance with the modalities, procedures and guidelines to be adopted by the Conference of the Parties serving as the meeting of the Parties to this Agreement, at its first session, as stipulated in Article 13, paragraph 13. Other Parties are encouraged to do so.

    8. The Financial Mechanism of the Convention, including its operating entities, shall serve as the financial mechanism of this Agreement.

    9. The institutions serving this Agreement, including the operating entities of the Financial Mechanism of the Convention, shall aim to ensure efficient access to financial resources through simplified approval procedures and enhanced readiness support for developing country Parties, in particular for the least developed countries and small island developing States, in the context of their national climate strategies and plans.

Article 10

    1. Parties share a long-term vision on the importance of fully realizing technology development and transfer in order to improve resilience to climate change and to reduce greenhouse gas emissions.

    2. Parties, noting the importance of technology for the implementation of mitigation and adaptation actions under this Agreement and recognizing existing technology deployment and dissemination efforts, shall strengthen cooperative action on technology development and transfer.

    3. The Technology Mechanism established under the Convention shall serve this Agreement.

    4. A technology framework is hereby established to provide overarching guidance to the work of the Technology Mechanism in promoting and facilitating enhanced action on technology development and transfer in order to support the implementation of this Agreement, in pursuit of the long-term vision referred to in paragraph 1 of this Article.

    5. Accelerating, encouraging and enabling innovation is critical for an effective, long-term global response to climate change and promoting economic growth and sustainable development. Such effort shall be, as appropriate, supported, including by the Technology Mechanism and, through financial means, by the Financial Mechanism of the Convention, for collaborative approaches to research and development, and facilitating access to technology, in particular for early stages of the technology cycle, to developing country Parties.

    6. Support, including financial support, shall be provided to developing country Parties for the implementation of this Article, including for strengthening cooperative action on

technology development and transfer at different stages of the technology cycle, with a view to achieving a balance between support for mitigation and adaptation. The global stocktake referred to in Article 14 shall take into account available information on efforts related to support on technology development and transfer for developing country Parties.

Article 11

1. Capacity-building under this Agreement should enhance the capacity and ability of developing country Parties, in particular countries with the least capacity, such as the least developed countries, and those that are particularly vulnerable to the adverse effects of climate change, such as small island developing States, to take effective climate change action, including, inter alia, to implement adaptation and mitigation actions, and should facilitate technology development, dissemination and deployment, access to climate finance, relevant aspects of education, training and public awareness, and the transparent, timely and accurate communication of information.

2. Capacity-building should be country-driven, based on and responsive to national needs, and foster country ownership of Parties, in particular, for developing country Parties, including at the national, subnational and local levels. Capacity-building should be guided by lessons learned, including those from capacity-building activities under the Convention, and should be an effective, iterative process that is participatory, cross-cutting and gender-responsive.

3. All Parties should cooperate to enhance the capacity of developing country Parties to implement this Agreement. Developed country Parties should enhance support for capacity-building actions in developing country Parties.

4. All Parties enhancing the capacity of developing country Parties to implement this Agreement, including through regional, bilateral and multilateral approaches, shall regularly communicate on these actions or measures on capacity building. Developing country Parties should regularly communicate progress made on implementing capacity-building plans, policies, actions or measures to implement this Agreement.

5. Capacity-building activities shall be enhanced through appropriate institutional arrangements to support the implementation of this Agreement, including the appropriate institutional arrangements established under the Convention that serve this Agreement. The Conference of the Parties serving as the meeting of the Parties to this Agreement shall, at its first session, consider and adopt a decision on the initial institutional arrangements for capacity-building.

Article 12

Parties shall cooperate in taking measures, as appropriate, to enhance climate change education, training, public awareness, public participation and public access to information, recognizing the importance of these steps with respect to enhancing actions under this Agreement.

Article 13

1. In order to build mutual trust and confidence and to promote effective implementation, an enhanced transparency framework for action and support, with built-in flexibility which takes into account Parties' different capacities and builds upon collective experience is hereby established.

2. The transparency framework shall provide flexibility in the implementation of the provisions of this Article to those developing country Parties that need it in the light of their capacities. The modalities, procedures and guidelines referred to in paragraph 13 of this Article shall reflect such flexibility.

3. The transparency framework shall build on and enhance the transparency arrangements under the Convention, recognizing the special circumstances of the least developed countries and small island developing States, and be implemented in a facilitative, non-intrusive, non-punitive manner, respectful of national sovereignty, and avoid placing undue burden on Parties.

4. The transparency arrangements under the Convention, including national communications, biennial reports and biennial update reports, international assessment and review and international consultation and analysis, shall form part of the experience drawn upon for the development of the modalities, procedures and guidelines under paragraph 13 of this Article.

5. The purpose of the framework for transparency of action is to provide a clear understanding of climate change action in the light of the objective of the Convention as set out in its Article 2, including clarity and tracking of progress towards achieving Parties' individual nationally determined contributions under Article 4, and Parties' adaptation actions under Article 7, including good practices , priorities, needs and gaps, to inform the global stocktake under Article 14.

6. The purpose of the framework for transparency of support is to provide clarity on support provided and received by relevant individual Parties in the context of climate change actions under Articles 4, 7, 9, 10 and 11, and, to the extent possible, to provide a full overview of aggregate financial support provided, to inform the global stocktake under Article 14.

7. Each Party shall regularly provide the following information:

(a) A national inventory report of anthropogenic emissions by sources and removals by sinks of greenhouse gases, prepared using good practice methodologies accepted by the Intergovernmental Panel on Climate Change and agreed upon by the Conference of the Parties serving as the meeting of the Parties to this Agreement; and
(b) Information necessary to track progress made in implementing and achieving its nationally determined contribution under Article 4.

8. Each Party should also provide information related to climate change impacts and adaptation under Article 7, as appropriate.

9. Developed country Parties shall, and other Parties that provide support should, provide information on financial, technology transfer and capacity-building support provided to developing country Parties under Articles 9, 10 and 11.

10. Developing country Parties should provide information on financial, technology transfer and capacity-building support needed and received under Articles 9, 10 and 11.

11. Information submitted by each Party under paragraphs 7 and 9 of this Article shall undergo a technical expert review, in accordance with decision 1/CP.21. For those developing country Parties that need it in the light of their capacities, the review process shall include assistance in identifying capacity-building needs. In addition, each Party shall participate in a facilitative, multilateral consideration of progress with respect to efforts under Article 9, and its respective implementation and achievement of its nationally determined contribution.

12. The technical expert review under this paragraph shall consist of a consideration of the Party's support provided, as relevant, and its implementation and achievement of its nationally determined contribution. The review shall also identify areas of improvement for the Party, and include a review of the consistency of the information with the modalities, procedures and guidelines referred to in paragraph 13 of this Article, taking into account the flexibility accorded to the Party under paragraph 2 of this Article. The review shall pay particular attention to the respective national capabilities and circumstances of developing country Parties.

13. The Conference of the Parties serving as the meeting of the Parties to this Agreement shall, at its first session, building on experience from the arrangements related to transparency under the Convention, and elaborating on the provisions in this Article, adopt common modalities, procedures and guidelines, as appropriate, for the transparency of action and support.

14. Support shall be provided to developing countries for the implementation of this Article.

15. Support shall also be provided for the building of transparency-related capacity of developing country Parties on a continuous basis.

Article 14

1. The Conference of the Parties serving as the meeting of the Parties to this Agreement shall periodically take stock of the implementation of this Agreement to assess the collective progress towards achieving the purpose of this Agreement and its long-term goals (referred to as the "global stocktake"). It shall do so in a comprehensive and facilitative manner, considering mitigation, adaptation and the means of implementation and support, and in the light of equity and the best available science.

2. The Conference of the Parties serving as the meeting of the Parties to this Agreement shall undertake its first global stocktake in 2023 and every five years thereafter unless otherwise decided by the Conference of the Parties serving as the meeting of the Parties to this Agreement.

3. The outcome of the global stocktake shall inform Parties in updating and enhancing, in a nationally determined manner, their actions and support in accordance with the relevant provisions of this Agreement, as well as in enhancing international cooperation for climate action.

Article 15

1. A mechanism to facilitate implementation of and promote compliance with the provisions of this Agreement is hereby established.

2. The mechanism referred to in paragraph 1 of this Article shall consist of a committee that shall be expert-based and facilitative in nature and function in a manner that is transparent, non-adversarial and non-punitive. The committee shall pay particular attention to the respective national capabilities and circumstances of Parties.

3. The committee shall operate under the modalities and procedures adopted by the Conference of the Parties serving as the meeting of the Parties to this Agreement at its first session and report annually to the Conference of the Parties serving as the meeting of the Parties to this Agreement.

Article 16

1. The Conference of the Parties, the supreme body of the Convention, shall serve as the meeting of the Parties to this Agreement.

2. Parties to the Convention that are not Parties to this Agreement may participate as observers in the proceedings of any session of the Conference of the Parties serving as the meeting of the Parties to this Agreement. When the Conference of the Parties serves as the meeting of the Parties to this Agreement, decisions under this Agreement shall be taken only by those that are Parties to this Agreement.

3. When the Conference of the Parties serves as the meeting of the Parties to this Agreement, any member of the Bureau of the Conference of the Parties representing a Party to the Convention but, at that time, not a Party to this Agreement, shall be replaced by an additional member to be elected by and from amongst the Parties to this Agreement.

4. The Conference of the Parties serving as the meeting of the Parties to this Agreement shall keep under regular review the implementation of this Agreement and shall make, within

its mandate, the decisions necessary to promote its effective implementation. It shall perform the functions assigned to it by this Agreement and shall:

(a) Establish such subsidiary bodies as deemed necessary for the implementation of this Agreement; and

(b) Exercise suchother functions as may be required for the implementation of this Agreement.

5. The rules of procedure of the Conference of the Parties and the financial procedures applied under the Convention shall be applied mutatis mutandis under this Agreement, except as may be otherwise decided by consensus by the Conference of the Parties serving as the meeting of the Parties to this Agreement.

6. The first session of the Conference of the Parties serving as the meeting of the Parties to this Agreement shall be convened by the secretariat in conjunction with the first session of the Conference of the Parties that is scheduled after the date of entry into force of this Agreement. Subsequent ordinary sessions of the Conference of the Parties serving as the meeting of the Parties to this Agreement shall be held in conjunction with ordinary sessions of the Conference of the Parties, unless otherwise decided by the Conference of the Parties serving as the meeting of the Parties to this Agreement.

7. Extraordinary sessions of the Conference of the Parties serving as the meeting of the Parties to this Agreement shall be held at such other times as may be deemed necessary by the Conference of the Parties serving as the meeting of the Parties to this Agreement or at the written request of any Party, provided that, within six months of the request being communicated to the Parties by the secretariat, it is supported by at least one third of the Parties.

8. The United Nations and its specialized agencies and the International Atomic Energy Agency, as well as any State member thereof or observers thereto not party to the Convention, may be represented at sessions of the Conference of the Parties serving as the meeting of the Parties to this Agreement as observers. Anybody or agency, whether national or international, governmental or non-governmental, which is qualified in matters covered by this Agreement and which has informed the secretariat of its wish to be represented at a session of the Conference of the Parties serving as the meeting of the Parties to this Agreement as an observer, may be so admitted unless at least one third of the Parties present object. The admission and participation of observers shall be subject to the rules of procedure referred to in paragraph 5 of this Article.

Article 17

1. The secretariat established by Article 8 of the Convention shall serve as the secretariat of this Agreement.

2. Article 8, paragraph 2, of the Convention on the functions of the secretariat, and Article 8, paragraph 3, of the Convention, on the arrangements made for the functioning of the secretariat, shall apply mutatis mutandis to this Agreement. The secretariat shall, in addition, exercise the functions assigned to it under this Agreement and by the Conference of the Parties serving as the meeting of the Parties to this Agreement.

Article 18

1. The Subsidiary Body for Scientific and Technological Advice and the Subsidiary Body for Implementation established by Articles 9 and 10 of the Convention shall serve, respectively, as the Subsidiary Body for Scientific and Technological Advice and the Subsidiary Body for Implementation of this Agreement. The provisions of the Convention relating to the functioning of these two bodies shall apply mutatis mutandis to this Agreement. Sessions of

the meetings of the Subsidiary Body for Scientific and Technological Advice and the Subsidiary Body for Implementation of this Agreement shall be held in conjunction with the meetings of, respectively, the Subsidiary Body for Scientific and Technological Advice and the Subsidiary Body for Implementation of the Convention.

    2. Parties to the Convention that are not Parties to this Agreement may participate as observers in the proceedings of any session of the subsidiary bodies. When the subsidiary bodies serve as the subsidiary bodies of this Agreement, decisions under this Agreement shall be taken only by those that are Parties to this Agreement.

    3. When the subsidiary bodies established by Articles 9 and 10 of the Convention exercise their functions with regard to matters concerning this Agreement, any member of the bureaux of those subsidiary bodies representing a Party to the Convention but, at that time, not a Party to this Agreement, shall be replaced by an additional member to be elected by and from amongst the Parties to this Agreement.

Article 19

    1. Subsidiary bodies or other institutional arrangements established by or under the Convention, other than those referred to in this Agreement, shall serve this Agreement upon a decision of the Conference of the Parties serving as the meeting of the Parties to this Agreement. The Conference of the Parties serving as the meeting of the Parties to this Agreement shall specify the functions to be exercised by such subsidiary bodies or arrangements.

    2. The Conference of the Parties serving as the meeting of the Parties to this Agreement may provide further guidance to such subsidiary bodies and institutional arrangements.

Article 20

    1. This Agreement shall be open for signature and subject to ratification, acceptance or approval by States and regional economic integration organizations that are Parties to the Convention. It shall be open for signature at the United Nations Headquarters in New York from 22 April 2016 to 21 April 2017. Thereafter, this Agreement shall be open for accession from the day following the date on which it is closed for signature. Instruments of ratification, acceptance, approval or accession shall be deposited with the Depositary.

    2. Any regional economic integration organization that becomes a Party to this Agreement without any of its member States being a Party shall be bound by all the obligations under this Agreement. In the case of regional economic integration organizations with one or more member States that are Parties to this Agreement, the organization and its member States shall decide on their respective responsibilities for the performance of their obligations under this Agreement. In such cases, the organization and the member States shall not be entitled to exercise rights under this Agreement concurrently.

    3. In their instruments of ratification, acceptance, approval or accession, regional economic integration organizations shall declare the extent of their competence with respect to the matters governed by this Agreement. These organizations shall also inform the Depositary, who shall in turn inform the Parties, of any substantial modification in the extent of their competence.

Article 21

    1. This Agreement shall enter into force on the thirtieth day after the date on which at least 55 Parties to the Convention accounting in total for at least an estimated 55 per cent of the total global greenhouse gas emissions have deposited their instruments of ratification, acceptance, approval or accession.

2. Solely for the limited purpose of paragraph 1 of this Article, "total global greenhouse gas emissions" means the most up-to-date amount communicated on or before the date of adoption of this Agreement by the Parties to the Convention.

3. For each State or regional economic integration organization that ratifies, accepts or approves this Agreement or accedes thereto after the conditions set out in paragraph 1 of this Article for entry into force have been fulfilled, this Agreement shall enter into force on the thirtieth day after the date of deposit by such State or regional economic integration organization of its instrument of ratification, acceptance, approval or accession .

4. For the purposes of paragraph 1 of this Article, any instrument deposited by a regional economic integration organization shall not be counted as additional to those deposited by its member States.

Article 22

The provisions of Article 15 of the Convention on the adoption of amendments to the Convention shall apply mutatis mutandis to this Agreement.

Article 23

1. The provisions of Article 16 of the Convention on the adoption and amendment of annexes to the Convention shall apply mutatis mutandis to this Agreement.

2. Annexes to this Agreement shall form an integral part thereof and, unless otherwise expressly provided for, a reference to this Agreement constitutes at the same time a reference to any annexes thereto. Such annexes shall be restricted to lists, forms and any other material of a descriptive nature that is of a scientific, technical, procedural, or administrative character.

Article 24

The provisions of Article 14 of the Convention on settlement of disputes shall apply mutatis mutandis to this Agreement.

Article 25

1. Each Party shall have one vote, except as provided for in paragraph 2 of this Article.

2. Regional economic integration organizations, in matters within their competence, shall exercise their right to vote with a number of votes equal to the number of their member States that are Parties to this Agreement. Such an organization shall not exercise its right to vote if any of its member States exercises its right, and vice versa.

Article 26

The Secretary-General of the United Nations shall be the Depositary of this Agreement.

Article 27

No reservations may be made to this Agreement.

Article 28

1. At any time after three years from the date on which this Agreement has entered into force for a Party, that Party may withdraw from this Agreement by giving written notification to the Depositary.

2. Any such withdrawal shall take effect upon expiry of one year from the date of receipt by the Depositary of the notification of withdrawal, or on such later date as may be specified in the notification of withdrawal.

3. Any Party that withdraws from the Convention shall be considered as also having withdrawn from this Agreement.

Article 29

The original of this Agreement, of which the Arabic, Chinese, English, French, Russian and Spanish texts are equally authentic, shall be deposited with the Secretary-General of the United Nations.

DONE at Paris this twelfth day of December two thousand and fifteen.

IN WITNESS WHEREOF, the undersigned, being duly authorized to that effect, have signed this Agreement.

Appendix C

FEMA Climate Change Adaptation Policy Statement (2011-OPPA-01)*

FEDERAL EMERGENCY MANAGEMENT AGENCY

I. Purpose

The purpose of this policy statement is to establish an Agency-wide directive to integrate climate change adaptation planning and actions into Agency programs, policies, and operations.

II. Scope

This directive applies to all Agency activities and is intended to guide FEMA personnel responsible for the oversight and implementation of organizational plans, policies, and procedures.

III. Background

While the scope, severity, and pace of future climate change impacts are difficult to predict, it is clear that potential changes could affect our Agency's ability to fulfill its mission. The challenges posed by climate change, such as more intense storms, frequent heavy precipitation, heat waves, drought, extreme flooding, and higher sea levels could significantly alter the types and magnitudes of hazards faced by communities and the emergency management professionals serving them. Some specific areas where climate change could influence our capabilities and the need for our services are:

- Impacts on mitigation, preparedness, response, and recovery operations: as coastal regions become increasingly populated and developed, more frequent or severe storms may increase the requirements for emergency services and response and recovery capacity.
- Resiliency of critical infrastructure and various emergency assets: continuity of operations, delivery of services, and emergency response efforts may be challenged and made increasingly complex by damages or disruptions to the interconnected energy and infrastructure networks.
- Climate change could trigger indirect impacts that increase mission risks: intensifying droughts, heat waves, and periods of heavy precipitation could create human and economic suffering that may lead to internal displacement, cross-border migration, and the spread of life-threatening diseases.

---

*Public document originally published as Federal Emergency Management Agency, FEMA Climate Change Adaptation Policy Statement, https://www.fema.gov/media-library-data/20130726–1919–25045–6267/signed_climate_change_policy_statement.pdf.

The need to address risks associated with future disaster-related events, including those that may be linked to climate change, is inherent to FEMA's long-term vision of promoting physical and economic loss reduction and life saving measures. Working within existing statutes and authorities, FEMA will strive to be consistent in the Agency's incorporation of climate change adaptation actions and activities into on-going plans, policies, and procedures.

This policy statement identifies seven initial actions we will take to help integrate climate change adaptation considerations into our programs and operations. These actions also align with our vision of a Whole Community approach to emergency management, as it is expected that extensive collaboration with the public, all levels of government, the private sector, non-governmental organizations, and community organizations will be required.

IV. Policy and Procedures

A.In addition to the actions taken pursuant to Executive Order 13514, Federal Leadership in Environmental, Energy, and Economic Performance, with respect to federal facilities, FEMA will undertake the below high-level actions to integrate climate change adaptation considerations into the Agency's programs, policies, and operations. These actions directly support the White House Council for Environmental Quality's (CEQ) Implementing Instructions for Federal Agency Climate Change Adaptation Planning and are designed to enhance our climate change awareness, further evaluate the effects climate change may have on FEMA programs and operations, and identify potential areas for future exploration.

1. To enhance climate research, monitoring, and adaptation capabilities, FEMA will continue to establish partnerships with other agencies and organizations that possess climate science and climate change adaptation expertise. FEMA will continue to develop and maintain partnerships that enable the Agency to monitor the projected effects of climate change, and communicate climate science data and research needs related to emergency management and disaster resilience. FEMA will also collaborate with other Federal agencies, State, Local, Tribal and Territorial (SLTT) partners, intergovernmental organizations, nongovernmental organizations, the private sector, academia, and the international community to share lessons learned and develop best practices regarding climate adaptation.

2. FEMA will continue to study the impacts of climate change on the National Flood Insurance Program (NFIP) and incorporate climate change considerations in the NFIP reform effort. An initial 2-year study concluded that climate change is likely to have significant impacts on the NFIP; Special Flood Hazard Areas are projected to increase significantly across the nation, with impacts mounting over time as the number of policyholders are projected to double by 2100. In order to ensure the program serves the public most effectively, FEMA will continue efforts to understand the potential impacts of climate change on the NFIP and identify areas where future climate conditions can be included as part of the larger reform effort.

3. FEMA will evaluate how climate change considerations can be incorporated into grant investment strategies with specific focus on infrastructure and evaluation methodologies or tools such as benefit/cost analysis. FEMA will evaluate methods for addressing future climate conditions through its grant programs to SLTT entities. FEMA will also study how to introduce long-term climate change risks into the benefit/cost analysis methods that guide the awarding of grants.

4. FEMA will seek to understand how climate change will impact local communities and engage them in addressing those impacts. FEMA will proactively engage and partner with SLTT communities to gain a greater understanding of their climate change adaptation challenges and activities, and look for ways FEMA can take action to support them in those efforts.

5. FEMA will promote building standards and practices, both within FEMA programs and in general, that consider the future impacts of climate change. FEMA currently promotes programmatic guidance and standards for use by SLTT partners to mitigate hazards through regulation of building and infrastructure construction. The current standards and guidance,

based on today's climate, may not anticipate the risks structures will face as the climate changes. Therefore, it is important to review guidance and standards to determine the feasibility of incorporating future climate change considerations and encourage the integration of adaptation measures into local planning and development practices.

6. Through partnerships with the climate science community, FEMA will evaluate the potential impact climate change may have on existing risk data and the corresponding implications for Threat Hazard Identification Risk Assessment (THIRA) development and operational planning. Changes in the climate will affect the accuracy and practice of using historical records to predict the magnitude, location, and frequency of future hazards-with significant challenges for important analytic processes and decisions. In response, FEMA will continue to work with the climate science and risk analysis community to evaluate the impacts of climate change on the viability of existing risk data.

7. FEMA will continue to pursue a flexible, scalable, well equipped, and well-trained workforce that is educated about the potential impacts of climate change. Changes in the frequency and magnitude of severe weather events could potentially strain FEMA resources. FEMA will continue to assess and address its staffing and equipment needs to create a more flexible workforce by increasing employee readiness, cross-training staff, and increasing the pool of employees who are qualified and trained to respond to disasters or other events.

V. Responsibilities

Roles, responsibilities, and timelines for completing each of the above actions will be set forth in the follow-on FEMA Climate Change Adaptation Implementation Plan.

VI. Definitions

Climate Change: According to the Intergovernmental Panel on Climate Change (IPCC), climate change refers to "a statistically significant variation in either the mean state of the climate or in its variability, persisting for an extended period (typically decades or longer). Climate change may be due to natural internal processes or external forcings, or to persistent anthropogenic changes in the composition of the atmosphere or in land use."

Climate Change Adaptation: The IPCC defines climate change adaptation as "the adjustment in natural or human systems in response to actual or expected climatic stimuli or their effects, which moderates harm or exploits beneficial opportunities."

VII. Authorities

The Homeland Security Act of 2002, as amended (6 U.S.C. 101 et seq.), the Robert T. Stafford Disaster Relief and Emergency Assistance Act, as amended (42 U.S.C. 5121 et seq.), the President's Executive Order 13514 of October 2009, the 2010 Climate Change Adaptation Report drafted by ICCATF, and the Instructions for Implementing Climate Change Adaptation Planning issued by the CEQ.

VIII. Responsible Office

The Office of Policy and Program Analysis is responsible for the coordination and oversight of all aspects of this directive.

IX. Supersession

None
Approved and signed:
W. Craig Fugate, Administrator, 1/23/12
David J. Kaufman, Director, OPPA, 11/1/11

About the Contributors

Melissa **Agnes** is an adviser on crisis management and the author of *Crisis Ready: Building an Invincible Brand in an Uncertain World*.

Sergio **Andal**, Jr., is the Chief of Party of USAID-ICMA's Strengthening Urban Resilience for Growth with Equity (SURGE) Project.

Niles **Anderegg** is an ICMA research and content development associate.

Shahzeen **Attari** is an associate professor of public and environmental affairs at Indiana University.

Hiba **Baroud** is an assistant professor of civil and environmental engineering at Vanderbilt University.

Anna Maria **Barry-Jester** reports for *Kaiser Health News*.

Jake Rom D. **Cadag** is a DRR-Resilience Specialist with USAID-ICMA's Strengthening Urban Resilience for Growth with Equity (SURGE) Project and a senior lecturer of geography at the University of the Philippines.

City of San Rafael is in Marin County, Northern California.

Alder K. **Delloro** is the managing partner of Delloro & Saulog Law Offices and a senior lecturer at the University of the Philippines' National College of Public Administration and Governance.

Melissa **Diede** is a franchise owner and inspector of Pillar To Post Home Inspectors in Napa, California.

Julie-Ann Ross **Deus** is a Junior Project Officer with USAID-ICMA's Strengthening Urban Resilience for Growth with Equity (SURGE) Project.

Katherine Levine **Einstein** is an assistant professor of political science at Boston University.

Environmental Protection Agency is a U.S. federal government agency that protects people and the environment from significant health risks, sponsors and conducts research, and develops and enforces environmental regulations.

Nicole **Errett** is a lecturer in environmental and occupational health at the University of Washington.

Federal Emergency Management Agency is a U.S. federal government agency that supports citizens and emergency personnel to build, sustain, and improve the nation's capability to prepare for, protect against, respond to, recover from, and mitigate all hazards.

Gabriel **Filippelli** is a professor of earth sciences and director of the Center for Urban Health, IUPUI.

Conor K. **Gately** is a postdoctoral associate at Boston University.

David **Glick** is an assistant professor of political science at Boston University.

Joaquin Jay **Gonzalez** III is Mayor George Christopher Professor of Public Administration at the Edward S. Ageno School of Business of Golden Gate University and Technical Adviser of USAID-ICMA's Strengthening Urban Resilience for Growth with Equity (SURGE) Project.

Patrick **Howell** is a program manager for community resilience at the Institute for Building Technology and Safety, and chairman of the Equitable Climate Resilience for U.S. Local Governments Advisory Panel.

Astrid J. **Hsu** is a research associate at the Scripps Institution of Oceanography at the University of California, San Diego.

Lucy **Hutyra** is an associate professor of earth and environment at Boston University.

International City/County Management Association is an association representing professionals in local government management.

Paul H. **Jennings** serves as executive director for the Center for Industrial Services (CIS), an agency of the University of Tennessee Institute for Public Service.

Sadhu Aufochs **Johnston** is a city manager in Vancouver, British Columbia, Canada, and was formerly chief environmental officer in Chicago, Illinois.

Joe **Kantenbacher** is a research associate in environmental science at Indiana University.

Roger L. **Kemp** is Distinguished Adjunct Professor at Golden Gate University and has worked as a city manager in the largest council-manager governments in California, New Jersey, and Connecticut.

Nicole **Lance** is the CEO of Lance Strategies and managing partner of EXB Team that serves those who serve by providing training, coaching, facilitation, and strategic planning services.

David L. **Levy** is a professor of management and director of the Center for Sustainable Enterprise and Regional Competitiveness at the University of Massachusetts Boston.

Minch **Lewis** is an adjunct professor at Syracuse University's Maxwell School.

Janice **Lloyd** reports for *Kaiser Health News*.

Anne **Lusk** is a research scientist at Harvard University.

T. Reed **Miller** is a researcher in environmental engineering and technology policy at the Massachusetts Institute of Technology.

C.H. "Burt" **Mills**, Jr., is the county judge of Aransas County, Texas.

Deidra **Miniard** is a Ph.D. student in environmental science at Indiana University.

Gabby V. **Moraleda** is the executive director of the Pilipino Senior Resource Center in San Francisco, California.

Melynda **Moran** is an EMPA graduate of Golden Gate University and works for the Department of Homeland Security.

Nathan **Myers** is an associate professor of political science at Indiana State University.

Johanna **Nalau** is a research fellow in climate adaptation at Griffith University.

National Aeronautics and Space Administration is an independent agency of the United States Federal Government responsible for the civilian space program, as well as aeronautics and space research.

National Oceanic and Atmospheric Administration is an American scientific agency within the United States Department of Commerce that focuses on the conditions of the oceans, major waterways, and the atmosphere.

Joseph D. **Ortiz** is a professor and assistant chair of geology and Kent State University.

Benjamin **Paley** is a board member of the South Florida Chapter of American Society for Public Administration.

Maxwell **Palmer** is an assistant professor of political science at Boston University.

Benjamin **Preston** is a senior policy researcher and program director of infrastructure resilience and environmental policy at the Pardee RAND Graduate School.

Kate **Ramsayer** is with NASA's Goddard Space Flight Center in Greenbelt, Maryland.

Peter Lyn **René** is a certified mediator and political consultant in Houston.

Andrew **Revkin** is a senior reporter at ProPublica covering climate and related issues.

Carmen Heredia **Rodriguez** reports for *Kaiser Health News*.

Alan R. **Roper**, Ed.D., is Distinguished Adjunct Professor of Public Administration at Golden Gate University, and Teaching and Learning Specialist Manager for the University of California, Los Angeles (UCLA).

Cynthia **Rosenzweig** is a senior research scientist for NASA.

Evelyn **Sagun** is a Component Lead with USAID-ICMA's Strengthening Urban Resilience for Growth with Equity (SURGE) Project.

Arielle **Samuelson** is with the Jet Propulsion Laboratory in Pasadena, California.

Talia **Shea** works for Tesla's Energy division as a permit coordinator in San Francisco, California, has a BA in environmental studies from UC Santa Cruz, and an EMPA from Golden Gate University.

William **Solecki** is a professor of geography at Hunter College.

Lisa **Song** reports on the environment, energy, and climate change for ProPublica.

United Nations Environment Programme is responsible for coordinating the UN's environmental activities and assisting developing countries in implementing environmentally sound policies and practices.

U.S. Department of Agriculture is the U.S. federal executive department responsible for developing and executing federal laws related to farming, forestry, rural economic development, and food.

U.S. Geological Survey is a scientific agency of the United States government.

U.S. Global Change Research Program is a federal program mandated by Congress to coordinate Federal research and investments in understanding the forces shaping the global environment, both human and natural, and their impacts on society.

Maria Fe **Villamejor-Mendoza** is a professor and former dean of the University of the Philippines' National College of Public Administration and Governance.

Ryan **Weber** is an associate professor of English at the University of Alabama in Huntsville.

William R. **Whitson** is a retired city manager of Hapeville, Georgia; East Ridge, Tennessee; and Cairo, Georgia, among others, with over 25 years in the profession.

Index